Martin Mak, Xixia Wang and Ivy Liu

Cambridge IGCSE®
Mandarin as a Foreign Language

Coursebook

CAMBRIDGE
UNIVERSITY PRESS

University Printing House, Cambridge CB2 8BS, United Kingdom

One Liberty Plaza, 20th Floor, New York, NY 10006, USA

477 Williamstown Road, Port Melbourne, VIC 3207, Australia

314–321, 3rd Floor, Plot 3, Splendor Forum, Jasola District Centre, New Delhi – 110025, India

79 Anson Road, #06–04/06, Singapore 079906

Cambridge University Press is part of the University of Cambridge.

It furthers the University's mission by disseminating knowledge in the pursuit of education, learning and research at the highest international levels of excellence.

Information on this title: www.cambridge.org
© Cambridge University Press 2017

This publication is in copyright. Subject to statutory exception and to the provisions of relevant collective licensing agreements, no reproduction of any part may take place without the written permission of Cambridge University Press.

First published 2017

20 19 18 17 16 15 14 13 12 11 10 9 8 7 6 5 4

Printed in Spain by GraphyCems

A catalogue record for this publication is available from the British Library

ISBN 978-1-316-62984-0 Coursebook with Audio CDs (2)
ISBN 978-1-316-62986-4 Cambridge Elevate edition (2 years)
ISBN 978-1-316-62985-7 Digital edition

Additional resources for this publication at www.cambridge.org/

Cambridge University Press has no responsibility for the persistence or accuracy of URLs for external or third-party internet websites referred to in this publication, and does not guarantee that any content on such websites is, or will remain, accurate or appropriate. Information regarding prices, travel timetables, and other factual information given in this work is correct at the time of first printing but Cambridge University Press does not guarantee the accuracy of such information thereafter.

NOTICE TO TEACHERS IN THE UK

It is illegal to reproduce any part of this work in material form (including photocopying and electronic storage) except under the following circumstances:

(i) where you are abiding by a licence granted to your school or institution by the Copyright Licensing Agency;

(ii) where no such licence exists, or where you wish to exceed the terms of a licence, and you have gained the written permission of Cambridge University Press;

(iii) where you are allowed to reproduce without permission under the provisions of Chapter 3 of the Copyright, Designs and Patents Act 1988, which covers, for example, the reproduction of short passages within certain types of educational anthology and reproduction for the purposes of setting examination questions.

® IGCSE is the registered trademark of Cambridge International Examinations.
Example answers and all questions were written by the authors.

Contents

Introduction		v
Acknowledgements		vi
How to use this book		vii

Unit A Everyday activities
rì cháng huó dòng
日常活动

1	Greetings and introductions	
	wèn hòu yǔ jiè shào	
	问候与介绍	2
2	Family and pets	
	jiā tíng hé chǒng wù	
	家庭和宠物	11
3	Everyday life	
	wǒ de měi yì tiān	
	我的每一天	20
4	Hobbies	
	ài hào	
	爱好	29
5	Eating and drinking	
	yǐn shí	
	饮食	40

Unit B Personal and social life
gè rén yǔ shè huì
个人与社会

6	Health and fitness	
	jiàn kāng yǔ yùn dòng	
	健康与运动	54
7	Home life	
	jiā jū shēng huó	
	家居生活	65
8	Clothes	
	yī fu	
	衣服	75
9	Shopping	
	mǎi dōng xi	
	买东西	85
10	Living environment	
	jū zhù huán jìng	
	居住环境	95

11	School routine	
	xué xiào shēng huó	
	学校生活	105
12	School facilities	
	xué xiào shè shī	
	学校设施	115

Unit C The world around us
zhōu yóu shì jiè
周游世界

13	Weather and climate	
	tiān qì yǔ qì hòu	
	天气与气候	126
14	Transportation	
	jiāo tōng gōng jù	
	交通工具	135
15	Holidays: Travel experiences	
	lǚ yóu jīng lì	
	旅游经历	144
16	Holidays: Planning a trip	
	lǚ yóu jì huà	
	旅游计划	154
17	Public services and customs	
	gōnggòng fú wù yǔ hǎi guān	
	公共服务与海关	163

Unit D The world of work
gōng zuò yǔ zhí yè guī huà
工作与职业规划

18	Work experience	
	gōng zuò jīng yàn	
	工作经验	176
19	Applying for a job	
	shēn qǐng gōng zuò	
	申请工作	184
20	Future education and career plans	
	wèi lái xué yè hé zhí yè guī huà	
	未来学业和职业规划	191

Unit E International world
guó jì shì yě
国际视野

21 Interviewing Chinese celebrities
cǎi fǎng míng rén
采访名人 200

22 Technology and social media
kē jì yǔ shè jiāo méi tǐ
科技与社交媒体 208

23 Chinese festivals
Zhōng guó jié rì
中国节日 215

24 Learning Chinese as a foreign language
xué Zhōng wén
学中文 224

25 Saving the planet
jiù jiù dì qiú
救救地球 233

Introduction

Martin Mak, Xixia Wang, Ivy Liu

Why was this book written?

We have written this book to provide material to cover the Cambridge IGCSE Mandarin Chinese as a Foreign Language syllabus (0547). In addition to this, the book will help you to develop your communication skills in Mandarin; materials have been written based on real-life contexts, and real-life materials have been chosen in order to give you a taste of culture along with language.

How is the book organised?

The book has 25 chapters, grouped under the five topic areas in the 0547 syllabus: Everyday Activities, Personal and Social Life, The World Around Us, The World of Work and International World. Each topic area has 3–7 sub-topics, each of which constitutes a chapter, and you will find material to cover listening, reading, speaking and writing under each sub-topic.

This book has been written for beginners. Therefore, from Chapter 1 to 5, pinyin and English meanings for rubrics are provided. However, they are gradually reduced in the later chapters and there will be no pinyin and English meanings for the rubrics to enable you to reach the appropriate standards needed at IGCSE level.

How should you use this book?

You will need to take an active role in your learning. Following the sequence of our activities will reinforce your language learning and expand your Mandarin vocabulary to help you become a more fluent reader. We introduce sentence structures in each chapter to help you improve your writing. It is important that you complete all the exercises as they will help you develop your communication skills in Chinese.

We have also written a Workbook, which contains further activities to help you to develop and consolidate what you learn in this Coursebook.

Acknowledgements

The authors and publishers acknowledge the following sources of copyright material and are grateful for the permissions granted. While every effort has been made, it has not always been possible to identify the sources of all the material used, or to trace all copyright holders. If any omissions are brought to our notice, we will be happy to include the appropriate acknowledgements on reprinting.

Cover Pansaa/Getty Images; Chapter Opener 1 Multi-bits/Getty Images; Caspar Benson/Getty Images; paresh3d/Getty Images; Larry Bray/Getty Images; kool99/Getty Images; Gilmanshin/Getty Images; Rob Lewine/Getty Images; Chapter Opener 2 Todd Pearson/Getty Images; Inti St Clair/Getty Images; Sam Diephuis/Getty Images; Mary Grace Long/Getty Images; Inti St Clair/Getty Images; Chapter Opener 3 Cheryl Chan/Getty Images; Amwell/Getty Images; Chapter Opener 4 Maria Jauregui Ponte/Getty Images; Michael S. Yamashita/Getty Images; Lane Oatey/Getty Images; K-King Photography Media Co. Ltd/Getty Images; Grant Faint/Getty Images; Cole Burston/Toronto Star/Getty Images; Sovfoto/UIG/Getty Images; Hero Images/Getty Images; wonry/Getty Images; Pat Behnke/Alamy Stock Photo; Christian Kober/Getty Images; Chapter Opener 5 Jasper James/Getty Images; image supplied by authors; Nikolay Pozdeev/Getty Images; monticelllo/Getty Images; Johner Images/Getty Images; Steve Wisbauer/Getty Images; milanfoto/Getty Images; Judd Pilossof/Getty Images; Atw Photography/Getty Images; Carlos Gawronski/Getty Images; Joakim Leroy/Getty Images; kyoshino/Getty Images; images supplied by authors; Chapter Opener 6 James Ross/Getty Images; Sino Images/Getty Images; S.P.O/Getty Images; Jill Watcher/Getty Images; Robert E Daemmrich/Getty Images; Tassii/Getty Images; Chapter Opener 7 Alberto Manuel Urosa Toledano/Getty Images; images supplied by authors; Chapter Opener 8 Michael Möller / EyeEm/Getty Images; Ikonica/Getty Images; image supplied by authors; Chapter Opener 9 Sean Malyon/Getty Images; images supplied by authors; Paschelle/Getty Images; Devonyu/Getty Images; glasslanguage/Getty Images; ViewStock/Getty Images; Chapter Opener 10 Michael H/Getty Images; Hans Neleman/Getty Images; RosaIreneBetancourt 6/Alamy Stock Photo; Ed Jones/AFP/Getty Images; Michael Coyne/Getty Images; Matthew Ecker/Alamy Stock Photo; Craig Auckland/Getty Images; Stefano Oppo/Getty Images; Ernest Lee / EyeEm/Getty Images; images supplied by authors; Nelson Ching/Bloomberg/Getty Images; Chapter Opener 11 NYstudio/Getty Images; Great Art Productions/Getty Images; Hero Images/Getty Images; Pulati/VCG/Getty Images; Chapter Opener 12 Uko_Jesita/Getty Images; ColorBlind Images/Getty Images; thelinke/Getty Images; Image Source/Getty Images; Spaces Images/Getty Images; Werner OTTO/ullstein bild/Getty Images; image supplied by authors; ViewStock/Getty Images; Chapter Opener 13 lakemans/Getty Images; Naoki Mutai/Getty Images; Samuel D. Barricklow/Getty Images; Damocless/Getty Images; Yiu Yu Hoi/Getty Images; Tom Merton/Getty Images; Chapter Opener 14 Cultura RM Exclusive/Philip Lee Harvey/Getty Images; urbancow/Getty Images; Gary Conner/Getty Images; TAMVISUT/Getty Images; William Ju/Getty Images; image supplied by authors; Zhang Peng/LightRocket/Getty Images; Chapter Opener 15 Topic Images Inc/Getty Images; Glenn Sundeen - TigerPal/Getty Images; SteveAllenPhoto/Getty Images; Tom Bonaventure/Getty Images; inigoarza/Getty Images; Marcel Lam/Getty Images; Juan Camilo Bernal Photographer/Getty Images; superjoseph/Getty Images; Pawel Libera/Getty Images; Chapter Opener 16 Jamie Grill/Getty Images; inigoarza/Getty Images; Juan Camilo Bernal Photographer/Getty Images (repeats x 2); Glenn Sundeen - TigerPal/Getty Images; Christian Kober/Getty Images (repeats x 4); Sebastiaan Kroes/Getty Images; DEA/W.Buss/DeAgostini/Getty Images; Caiaimage/Robert Daly/Getty Images; Kimberley Coole/Getty Images (repeats x 1) Michael Coyne/Getty Images; Chapter Opener 17 Joanna Czerniawski / EyeEm/Getty Images; RM World/Alamy Stock Photo; image supplied by authors; Chapter Opener 18 Peter Durant/Getty Images; sturti/Getty Images; Klaus Vedfelt/Getty Images; Chapter Opener 19 Jamie Grill/Getty Images; Inti St Clair/Getty Images; XiXinXing/Getty Images; Chapter Opener 20 Nick Daly/Getty Images; Barry Winiker/Getty Images; Chapter Opener 21 Mihajlo Maricic/Getty Images; Ragnar Singsaas/Getty Images; Lisa Blumenfeld/Getty Images; Bertrand Rindoff Petroff/Getty Images; Walter McBridge/Getty Images; Archive Photos/Stringer/Getty Photos; Chapter Opener 22 pixelnest/Getty Images; Simon Dawson/Bloomberg/Getty Images; Chapter Opener 23 Pan Hong/Getty Images; Lucas Schifres/Getty Images; Chapter Opener 24 Ferdi Merkx, E-in-Motion/Getty Images; Grant Faint/Getty Images; XiXinXing/Getty Images; kitchakron/Getty Images; Xinhua/Getty Images; Chapter Opener 25 Julija Svetlova / EyeEm/Getty Images; baona/Getty Images; Atlaspix/Shutterstock (repeats x2); Cividin/Shutterstock; Rawpixel.com/Shutterstock; Andrey_Popov/Shutterstock; ValeStock/Shutterstock; IxMaster/Shutterstock; pio3/Shutterstock; LanKS/Shutterstock; Dr Neil Overy/Science Photo Library/Getty Images (repeats x 1); LdF/Getty Images (repeats x 1); kabVisio/Getty Images; Nixx Photography/Shutterstock; Karin Hildebrand Lau/Shutterstock; Prasit Chansareekorn/Getty Images; Christian Kober/Getty Images; Chris Tobin/Getty Images; Yongyuan Dai/Getty Images; UrbanEye/Getty Images; Aigars Reinholds/Shutterstock; Fotocrisis/Shutterstock; Travel Ink/Getty Images; Science Photo Library/Getty Images; Umberto Shtanzman/Shutterstock; Woods Wheatcroft/Getty Images; Benchaporn Maiwat/Shutterstock; China Photos/Getty Images.

How to use this book

Learning objectives 学习目标

This unit will concentrate on talking about self, family and pets. In particular, you will:
- Introduce yourself with more personal information
- Introduce your family members
- Talk about friends
- Talk about pets
- Understand and complete conversations with more question words, e.g. 几, 有没有, 是不是

In addition, you are going to learn:
- The measure words: 个, 口, 岁, 只
- The difference between 二 and 两
- Declarative sentences (2): 我有一个哥哥
- Use of 的

本单元，你会：
- 继续学习自我介绍
- 介绍家庭成员
- 介绍你的朋友
- 说说你的宠物
- 使用更多的疑问词，例如"几"、"有没有"、"是不是"，来理解和完成交流

你还会学到：
- 量词：个、口、岁、只
- "二"和"两"的区别
- 陈述句（2）："有"的用法
- "的"的用法

Learning objectives
– set the scene of each chapter, help with navigation through the book and give a reminder of what is important about each topic.

Before starting activities
– simple tasks to help you revise and build on prior knowledge.

一　温故知新
1 'Before starting' activity

说一说你学校有什么科目。

> 我们学校有英语、数学、美术课，我最喜欢汉语课。

> 我们学校有＿＿＿、＿＿＿、＿＿＿课，我最喜欢＿＿＿。

yán shēn huó dòng
延伸活动
AIM HIGHER

Where can we put the time phrases? Try to translate this sentence into Chinese:

'I sleep for ten hours every day.'

Aim higher
– to challenge yourself a little bit more.

小贴士
TOP TIP

Try to put the vocabulary items into different categories such as 'languages' and 'science subjects'. It will help you remember them, e.g. 'languages' include 法语, 英语, 汉语.

Top tip
– quick suggestions to help you further improve your language.

wén huà
文化　文化
CULTURE

Zhōng guó rén de xìng míng
中国人的姓名 Chinese Names

When Chinese people introduce themselves, they give their family name first, followed by their given name.

For example, 王小云's family name is 王 and her first name is 小云. In English, however, she would be called 'Xiaoyun Wang'.

Culture
– interesting facts about Chinese culture.

> **jù xíng**
> **句型**
> **LANGUAGE**
>
> Declarative sentences (2), e.g. 我有一个哥哥。
>
> 有 is a verb to indicate what the subject has. This subject can be a person, a place or an object. To negate the sentence, we add 没.
>
> e.g.
> a 我有一个哥哥。I have one elder brother.
> b 我没有兄弟姐妹。I do not have brothers or sisters.

Language
– all the sentence structures you need to know.

Vocabulary
– Chinese characters, pinyin and English meanings are provided for the most important words in each topic.

> **cí yǔ**
> **词语**
> **VOCABULARY**
>
> | | | | |
> |---|---|---|---|
> | 1 | 家庭 | jiā tíng | family |
> | 2 | 家 | jiā | family, home |
> | 3 | 爸爸 | bà ba | dad |
> | 4 | 妈妈 | mā ma | mum |
> | 5 | 哥哥 | gē ge | elder brother |
> | 6 | 姐姐 | jiě jie | elder sister |
> | 7 | 弟弟 | dì di | younger brother |
> | 8 | 妹妹 | mèi mei | younger sister |
> | 9 | 有 | yǒu | to have |
> | 10 | 几 | jǐ | how many |
> | 11 | 口 | kǒu | measure word for family members |

> **bǔ chōng cí yǔ**
> **补充词语**
> **SUPPLEMENTARY VOCABULARY**
>
> 成员　chéng yuán　member

Supplementary vocabulary
– extra vocabulary and idioms help you gain a native flair.

> **yǔ fǎ**
> **语法**
> **GRAMMAR**
>
> 吗 is a 'yes-or-no' question indicator. When asking a 'yes-or-no' question, you just need to add 吗 at the end of the sentence.
>
> e.g. 你是中国人吗？
>
> 吗 sentences can also be replaced by 是不是 or 有没有 patterns.
>
> e.g. 你是不是中国人？ Are you Chinese?

Grammar
– clear grammatical rules are given with examples.

Exam-style question
– to help you consolidate what you have learnt in the unit.

> **考试练习题**
> **Exam-style question**
>
> **听力**
> 🔊 **Listening**
>
> 对一个在中国的新闻记者陈一心的采访
> An interview with a news reporter in China
>
> 请先阅读一下问题。
> Read the questions first.
>
> 请听采访，用中文或拼音回答问题。
> Listen to the interview, and answer the questions in Chinese. You may write your answers in Chinese characters or pinyin.
> CD 02, Track 24
>
> 1 陈一心为什么想做记者？
> _____
>
> 2 陈一心的爸妈觉得他应该找一份怎么样的工作？
> _____
>
> 3 为什么陈一心以前来中国读书？
> a _____
> b _____
>
> 4 陈一心在中国有什么有趣的事情？
> _____

> **自我评估**
> **Self-Assessment**
>
> ☐ I know the basic vocabulary for houses, furniture and household appliances
>
> ☐ I can describe a house and its rooms by using the sentence structure Place + Localiser 有 + Object
>
> ☐ I can use localisers to describe the location of something using the two sentence structures Subject 在 + Localiser and A 在 B（的）+ Localiser
>
> ☐ Use of measure words 朵，棵，张，台，部
>
> ☐ Use of reduplication of verbs, e.g. 看看，听听

Self-assessment
– to check your understanding at the end of each chapter.

Cambridge IGCSE Mandarin as a Foreign Language

rì cháng huó dòng
A 日常活动 Everyday activities

问候与介绍
1 Greetings and introductions

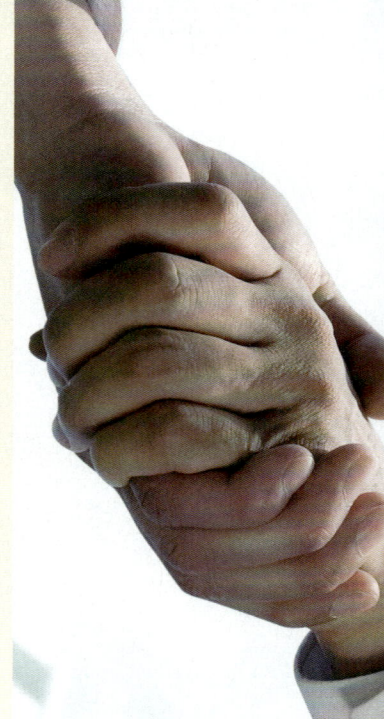

Learning objectives

This unit will concentrate on greetings and introductions. In particular, you will:

- Use the basic numbers
- Use greeting phrases when meeting friends
- Talk about countries and continents
- Understand the difference between Chinese names and English names
- Ask questions using question words including 吗, 什么, 哪, 哪儿

In addition, you are going to learn:

- The pronouns
- The plural 们
- Declarative sentences (1): 我是中国人。我很好。

学习目标

本单元，你会：

- 使用基本数字
- 明白打招呼的基本用语
- 了解国家和洲的名字
- 了解中英文名字的分别
- 使用疑问词，例如"吗"、"什么"、"哪"、"哪儿"

你还会学到：

- 代词
- 复数：们
- 陈述句（1）："我是中国人。""我很好。"

Cambridge IGCSE Mandarin as a Foreign Language

yī wēn gù zhī xīn
一、温故知新

1 'Before starting' activities

cí yǔ
词语
VOCABULARY

| 新 | xīn | new |

bǔ chōng cí yǔ
补充词语
SUPPLEMENTARY VOCABULARY

wēn gù zhī xīn
温故知新 is an old saying from Confucius. It means that you will learn something new from revision.

yī qǐng cóng xià miàn shù zì zhōng quān chū nǐ tīng dào de
一、请从下面数字中圈出你听到的
wǔ gè shù zì, měi gè shù zì dú yí biàn
五个数字，每个数字读一遍。

1   🔊 Circle the FIVE numbers you hear from the numbers below. You will hear each number once.
   CD 01, Track 02

| 20 | 45 | 53 | 14 | 77 | 41 |
| 11 | 10 | 43 | 10 | 34 | 40 |

cí yǔ
词语
VOCABULARY

| 从 | cóng | from |

yǔ fǎ
语法
GRAMMAR

shù zì de dú fǎ
数字的读法 Numbers

For numbers from 11 to 19, we say 十 (10) 一 (1), 十 (10) 二 (2), …… 十 (10) 九 (9). For numbers from 20–99, we say 二 (2) 十 (10), 三 (3) 十 (10), …… 九 (9) 十 (10) 九 (9), etc.

èr dā pèi shù zì hé hàn zì
二、搭配数字和汉字。

2   Match the numbers with the characters.

1	450	A	三百
2	300	B	四百五十
3	1 100	C	一百零七
4	17 000	D	一千一百
5	107	E	一百七十
6	170	F	一万七千

cí yǔ
词语
VOCABULARY

1	零	líng	zero
2	百	bǎi	hundred
3	千	qiān	thousand
4	万	wàn	ten thousand
5	幺	yāo	same as 一 but pronounced as 'yāo' in counting to avoid confusion with 七

sān dú chū xià miàn de cí yǔ
三、读出下面的词语。

3   Read aloud the following words.

wǒ 我 I	wǒ men 我们 we
nǐ 你 you	nǐ men 你们 (more than one person)
tā 他 he	tā men 他们 they (including everyone)
tā 她 she	tā men 她们 they (females)
tā 它 it	tā men 它们 they (not for human)
nín 您 you (respectful)	

Unit A 1 Everyday activities: Greetings and introductions

yǔ fǎ
语法
GRAMMAR

1 All the words in the table are called 代词 (dài cí) 'pronouns'.

   Note that we usually do not say 您们 (nín men).

2 Use of 们 (men)

   们 (men) is used to make personal nouns plural. As well as the plural pronouns, there are also some nouns that can be used with 们, e.g.

Singular	Plural
老师 (lǎo shī) teacher	老师们 teachers
同学 (tóng xué) student	同学们 students

sì shuō chū xià miàn guó jiā de míng zì
四、说出下面国家的名字。

4 Say the names of the following countries.

1
2
3
4
5

cí yǔ
词语
VOCABULARY

1	说	shuō	to say
2	国家	guó jiā	country
3	中国	Zhōng guó	China
4	英国	Yīng guó	UK
5	美国	Měi guó	USA
6	德国	Dé guó	Germany
7	法国	Fǎ guó	France
8	日本	Rì běn	Japan
9	印度	Yìn dù	India
10	新加坡	Xīn jiā pō	Singapore
11	马来西亚	Mǎ lái xī yà	Malaysia

èr shuō huà yī
二 说话（一）

2 Speaking (1)

kàn shì jiè dì tú shuō chū xià miàn zhè xiē guó jiā zài
看世界地图，说出下面这些国家在
nǎr
哪儿？

Look at the map. Where are these countries?

e.g.

Měi guó zài nǎr
Q：美国在哪儿？

Měi guó zài Měi zhōu
A：美国在美洲。

Zhōng guó zài nǎr
Q：中国在哪儿？

Zhōng guó zài
A：中国在_____。

Yīng guó zài nǎr
Q：英国在哪儿？

A：_____。

Cambridge IGCSE Mandarin as a Foreign Language

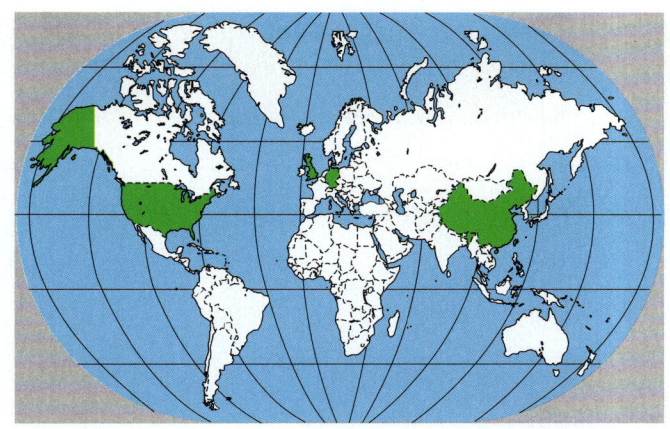

词语 VOCABULARY

1	世界	shì jiè	world
2	地图	dì tú	map
3	这些	zhè xiē	these
4	在	zài	to be located at
5	哪儿 / 哪里	nǎr/nǎ li	where
6	洲	zhōu	continent
7	亚洲	Yà zhōu	Asia
8	欧洲	Ōu zhōu	Europe
9	非洲	Fēi zhōu	Africa
10	美洲	Měi zhōu	America

三 阅读（一）
3 Reading (1)

选择合适的句子填空，完成打招呼的对话。

Choose the appropriate phrases to complete the dialogues.

A 我很好，谢谢。
B 认识你我很高兴。
C 没关系
D 再见
E 谢谢

小明 (Xiao Ming): 你好吗?

美美 (May): _____1_____

大卫 (David): _____2_____

丽丽 (Lily): 不用谢。

刘思天 (Lucy): 你好，_____3_____。

小红 (Xiao Hong): 认识你我也很高兴。

小明 (Xiao Ming): 对不起

美美 (May): _____4_____

丽丽 (Lily): 再见。

大卫 (David): _____5_____

Unit A 1 Everyday activities: Greetings and introductions

词语 VOCABULARY

1	打招呼	dǎ zhāo hu	greeting
2	填空	tián kòng	to fill in the gap; 空 empty space
3	好	hǎo	good
4	吗	ma	yes or no question word
5	你好	nǐ hǎo	hello
6	你好吗	nǐ hǎo ma	how are you?
7	再见	zài jiàn	goodbye; 再 again
8	谢谢	xiè xie	thank you
9	很	hěn	very
10	认识	rèn shí	to know
11	高兴	gāo xìng	happy
12	对不起	duì bù qǐ	sorry
13	不用谢	bú yòng xiè	you're welcome; 不用 to not need
14	没关系	méi guān xi	it doesn't matter

四 阅读（二）
4 Reading (2)

姓： 王
名： 小云
年龄： 15 岁
国籍： 中国
城市： 北京

词语 VOCABULARY

1	姓	xìng	surname
2	名字	míng zi	name
3	年龄	nián líng	age
4	国籍	guó jí	nationality
5	城市	chéng shì	city
6	北京	Běi jīng	Beijing

一、你是王小云。请在空白处填空回答问题。

1 You are Wang Xiaoyun. Fill in the blanks to answer the questions.

问：你姓什么？
答：我姓_____1_____。
问：你叫什么名字？
答：我叫_____2_____。
问：你多大？
答：我_____3_____岁。
问：你是哪国人？
答：我是_____4_____人。
问：你住在哪儿？
答：我住在_____5_____。

词语 VOCABULARY

1	空白处	kòng bái chù	gap/blank
2	问	wèn	to ask
3	叫	jiào	to be called
4	什么	shén me	what
5	多大	duō dà	how old
6	岁	suì	years old

Cambridge IGCSE Mandarin as a Foreign Language

cí yǔ 词语 VOCABULARY

7	是	shì	to be (am, is, are)
8	哪	nǎ	which
9	国	guó	country
10	人	rén	person, people
11	住	zhù	to live

cí yǔ 词语 VOCABULARY

| 同学 | tóng xué | classmate |

hǎo cí hǎo jù 好词好句 USEFUL EXPRESSIONS

- nǐ xìng shén me
  你姓什么?
- nǐ jiào shén me míng zì
  你叫什么名字?
- nǐ duō dà
  你多大?
- nǐ shì nǎ guó rén
  你是哪国人?
- nǐ zhù zài nǎr
  你住在哪儿?

èr qǐng gēn jù shàng miàn de biǎo gé tián kòng
二、请根据上面的表格填空。

2 According to the information above, fill in the gaps and complete the self-introduction for Wang Xiaoyun.

你好，我姓 __1__，我叫 __2__。
我 __3__ 岁。我是 __4__ 人。
我住在 __5__。

wén huà 文化 CULTURE

Zhōng guó rén de xìng míng
中国人的姓名 Chinese Names

When Chinese people introduce themselves, they give their family name first, followed by their given name.

For example, 王小云's family name is 王 and her first name is 小云. In English, however, she would be called 'Xiaoyun Wang'.

wǔ shuō huà èr
五 说话（二）
5 Speaking (2)

cǎi fǎng hé tián biǎo
采访和填表。

Interview two of your classmates and record the information in the table below.

	姓	名	年龄	国籍	城市
同学 1					
同学 2					

liù tīng lì
六 听力
6 🔊 Listening

wǔ gè xué sheng zài tán tā men de guó jí tīng lù yīn
五个学生在谈他们的国籍。听录音，
xuǎn zé wéi yī zhèng què de dá àn jiāng zì mǔ tián rù fāng
选择唯一正确的答案，将字母填入方
gé zhōng
格中。

Five students are talking about their nationalities. Listen to the recording, choose the only correct answer and put the letter in the box. **CD 01, Track 03**

A	英国人	B	印度人
C	中国人	D	日本人
E	马来西亚人		

例: Chén hǎi 陈海	1 Wáng míng 王明	2 Tián zhōng 田中	3 Mǎ lì 马丽	4 Lǐ shān 李山
E				

Unit A 1 Everyday activities: Greetings and introductions

cí yǔ
词语
VOCABULARY

1	学生	xué sheng	student; 学 to learn
2	句子	jù zi	sentence
3	遍	biàn	time
4	回答	huí dá	to answer
5	录音	lù yīn	recording

七 阅读（三）
7 Reading (3)

一、四个学生在介绍他们自己。

1 Four students are introducing themselves.

1. 你好。我叫陈小花。我十五岁。我是中国人。我住在北京。

2. 你好吗？我姓李，叫李明。我十六岁。我是中国人。我住在上海。

3. 早上好！我叫马可。我十四岁。我是美国人。我住在香港。

4. 你们好。我叫田中。我十三岁。我是日本人。我住在东京。

二、根据上面的介绍，回答问题。

2 According to the introductions above, answer the questions.

1 陈小花多大？
2 马可是哪国人？
3 谁住在北京？
4 李明住在哪儿？

cí yǔ
词语
VOCABULARY

1	介绍	jiè shào	to introduce
2	自己	zì jǐ	self
3	早上好	zǎo shàng hǎo	good morning; 早 morning, early
4	谁	shuí	who

bǔ chōng cí yǔ
补充词语
SUPPLEMENTARY VOCABULARY

1	上海	Shàng hǎi	Shanghai; 海 sea, ocean
2	香港	Xiāng gǎng	Hong Kong
3	东京	Dōng jīng	Tokyo

wén huà
文化
CULTURE

Zhōng guó rén de xìng hé míng
中国人的姓和名
Chinese Surnames and Given Names

There are more than 500 commonly used surnames in China. Some of the most common are:

Huáng Lǐ Lín Liú Mǎ Wáng Zhào Wú Zhāng
黄、李、林、刘、马、王、赵、吴、张、
Tián Jīn
田、金。

When using a professional title to address someone, their surname should be put before the title. For example, 王老师, 张同学 etc.

Cambridge IGCSE Mandarin as a Foreign Language

八 说话（三）
8 Speaking (3)

两人一组，做角色扮演。
Work in pairs and complete the role play.

情景：你在中国，和中国人说话。
Scenario: You are in China and talking to a Chinese person for the first time.

A 中国人
Chinese person

B 你自己
Yourself

A1: 你好吗？

B1: _____

A2: 你叫什么名字？

B2: _____

A3: 你是哪国人？

B3: _____

A4: 你住在哪儿？

B4: _____

A5: 你喜欢中国吗？

B5: _____

词语 VOCABULARY

喜欢　　xǐ huān　　to like

九 写作
9 Writing

一、汉字的笔画。

1. Strokes of characters.

   Chinese characters are constructed by strokes. The basic strokes are as follows:

一	Horizontal stroke	丨	Vertical stroke
丿	Down stroke to the left	丶	Dot
㇏	Down stroke to the right	㇀	Upward stroke
亅	Vertical stroke with a hook	㇕	Horizontal stroke with a vertical turn

写出下面汉字的第一笔是什么？
What are the first strokes of the following characters?

例子：你 → 丿

1 五　2 六　3 中　4 我

Unit A 1 Everyday activities: Greetings and introductions

> **xiǎo tiē shì**
> **小贴士**
> TOP TIP
>
> Chinese characters are made out of simple single strokes, all of which are variations of only eight basic ones. It is very important to learn to recognise them, since counting the number of strokes in a character is often the easiest way to find it in an index.

jù xíng
句型
LANGUAGE

Declarative sentences (1)

There are different structures of declarative sentences depending on what kind of verbs are used.

1. Subject + 是 + Object
   e.g. 我是中国人。I am Chinese.

2. Subject + 很 (hěn) + Stative Verb

   In Chinese, an adjective often acts as a stative verb. These stative verbs are usually used to indicate statuses rather than actions. e.g. 好, 忙, 高兴. When using a stative verb, 是 should NOT be used in a sentence. Rather, we usually use 很 before stative verbs, although 很 does not necessarily mean 'very'.

   e.g. 我很高兴。I'm happy.

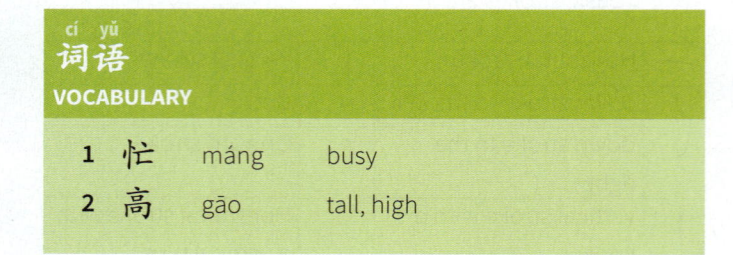

èr yòng kuò hào lǐ de cí yǔ fān yì jù zi
二、用括号里的词语翻译句子。

2 Translate the sentences into Chinese, using the key words provided in the brackets.

1 We are busy. _____ （忙）

2 She is tall. _____ （高）

3 He is happy. _____ （高兴）

4 She is fine. _____ （好）

cí yǔ
词语
VOCABULARY

| 1 | 忙 | máng | busy |
| 2 | 高 | gāo | tall, high |

zì wǒ píng gū
自我评估
Self-Assessment

☐ I can use the basic numbers

☐ I can use greeting phrases when meeting friends

☐ I can talk about countries and continents

☐ I can ask questions using question words including 吗, 什么, 哪, 哪儿

☐ Pronouns 你, 我, 他

☐ Plural 们

☐ Declarative sentences, e.g. 我是中国人。我很好。

Cambridge IGCSE Mandarin as a Foreign Language

jiā tíng hé chǒng wù
家庭和宠物
2 Family and pets

Learning objectives

This unit will concentrate on talking about self, family and pets. In particular, you will:

- Introduce yourself with more personal information
- Introduce your family members
- Talk about friends
- Talk about pets
- Understand and complete conversations with more question words, e.g. 几，有没有，是不是

In addition, you are going to learn:

- The measure words: 个，口，岁，只
- The difference between 二 and 两
- Declarative sentences (2):
  我有一个哥哥
- Use of 的

学习目标

本单元，你会：

- 继续学习自我介绍
- 介绍家庭成员
- 介绍你的朋友
- 说说你的宠物
- 使用更多的疑问词，例如"几"、"有没有"、"是不是"，来理解和完成交流

你还会学到：

- 量词：个、口、岁、只
- "二"和"两"的区别
- 陈述句（2）："有"的用法
- "的"的用法

Unit A 2 Everyday activities: Family and pets

一 温故知新
1 'Before starting' activities

一、读一读、写一写。
1 Read the questions and write down your answers.

1 请写出五个家庭成员的词语。
Write down five words for family members.

_____

2 请写出你家有几口人,他们是谁?
Write down how many people there are in your family and who they are.

我家有_____口人,他们是_____、
_____、_____……。

词语 VOCABULARY

1	家庭	jiā tíng	family
2	家	jiā	family, home
3	爸爸	bà ba	dad
4	妈妈	mā ma	mum
5	哥哥	gē ge	elder brother
6	姐姐	jiě jie	elder sister
7	弟弟	dì di	younger brother
8	妹妹	mèi mei	younger sister
9	有	yǒu	to have
10	几	jǐ	how many
11	口	kǒu	measure word for family members

补充词语 SUPPLEMENTARY VOCABULARY

成员	chéng yuán	member

语法 GRAMMAR

吗 is a 'yes-or-no' question indicator. When asking a 'yes-or-no' question, you just need to add 吗 at the end of the sentence.

e.g. 你是中国人吗?

吗 sentences can also be replaced by 是不是 or 有没有 patterns.

e.g. 你是不是中国人? Are you Chinese?

二、填表,完成句子。
2 Complete the sentences in the table. Then read the sentences aloud or work in pairs to practise them as dialogues.

吗 question	是不是 or 有没有 pattern	Yes	No
这是 Mary 吗?	这是不是 Mary?	这是 Mary.	这不是 Mary.
那是姐姐吗?	那___1___姐姐?	那___2___姐姐。	那___3___姐姐。
你有哥哥吗?	你有没有哥哥?	我有哥哥。	我没有哥哥。
你有宠物吗?	你___4___宠物?	我___5___宠物。	___6___宠物。

词语 VOCABULARY

1	这	zhè	this
2	那	nà	that
3	没有	méi yǒu	not to have; same as 没
4	宠物	chǒng wù	pet

Cambridge IGCSE Mandarin as a Foreign Language

小贴士 (xiǎo tiē shì) TOP TIP

1. When answering a 吗 question, repeat the verb for a YES answer. If you want to answer NO, use 不 or 没 before the verb.
2. A 吗 question can be replaced by a 是不是 or 有没有 pattern. When using these patterns, 吗 SHOULD NOT be used in the sentence.

语法 (yǔ fǎ) GRAMMAR

量词 liàng cí 'measure words' should be used:

- after numbers, e.g. 一个哥哥 one elder brother, 三个姐姐 three elder sisters
- after 这 / 那, e.g. 这只宠物 this pet, 那个人 that person
- after 几 / 哪, e.g. 几个妹妹 how many younger sisters, 哪个学生 which student

The 'must-know' measure words from this lesson:

1. 个 The most frequently used measure word; can be used to describe people or things in general.
2. 口 Only used for talking about how many family members in total, e.g. 我家有三口人. Note that we do not say 我有三口姐姐.
3. 只 Used for animals
4. 岁 Used for talking about age

三、在空白处填量词。(sān, zài kòng bái chù tián liàng cí)

3 Fill in the gaps with the correct measure words.

1. 一＿＿＿姐姐
2. 哪＿＿＿老师
3. 那＿＿＿人
4. 这＿＿＿狗
5. 几＿＿＿猫
6. 我家有八＿＿＿人。
7. 我十六＿＿＿
8. 十＿＿＿朋友
9. 我叫李小天，今年十五＿＿＿。我家有六＿＿＿人：爸爸、妈妈、三＿＿＿哥哥和我。我有一＿＿＿宠物，是一＿＿＿可爱的鸟。

词语 (cí yǔ) VOCABULARY

1	个	gè	measure word for persons
2	只	zhī	measure word for animals
3	动物	dòng wù	animal
4	朋友	péng yǒu	friend
5	狗	gǒu	dog
6	猫	māo	cat
7	今年	jīn nián	this year
8	和	hé	and
9	可爱	kě ài	cute, lovely
10	鸟	niǎo	bird

语法 (yǔ fǎ) GRAMMAR

区别"二"和"两" (qū bié èr hé liǎng)
Difference between 二 and 两

Both 二 and 两 mean 'two' in English. In Chinese, we use 二 in counting or saying a number by itself, such as 十二、二十、五十二, while 两 is used when you talk about an amount and is usually used with a measure word, e.g. 两只小猫、两个人、两岁、两个老师.

四、请用"两"或者"二"填空。(sì, qǐng yòng liǎng huò zhě èr tián kòng)

4 Use 两 or 二 to fill in the gaps.

1. 我有＿＿＿只小狗。
2. 妹妹今年十＿＿＿岁。
3. 弟弟今年＿＿＿岁。

Unit A 2 Everyday activities: Family and pets

二 <ruby>听力<rt>tīng lì</rt></ruby>（<ruby>一<rt>yī</rt></ruby>）
2 🔊 Listening (1)

<ruby>你将听到几个中文句子，每个句子读两遍。在唯一正确的括号内打勾(✓)回答问题。<rt>nǐ jiāng tīng dào jǐ gè Zhōng wén jù zi, měi gè jù zi dú liǎng biàn. zài wéi yī zhèng què de kuò hào nèi dǎ gōu huí dá wèn tí.</rt></ruby>

You will hear some short phrases in Chinese. You will hear each phrase twice. Answer each question by ticking one bracket only. **CD 1, Track 04**

1 <ruby>她家有几口人？<rt>tā jiā yǒu jǐ kǒu rén</rt></ruby>
  ( ) A 五口人 ( ) B 六口人
  ( ) C 四口人 ( ) D 十口人

2 <ruby>她有几个兄弟姐妹？<rt>tā yǒu jǐ gè xiōng dì jiě mèi</rt></ruby>
  ( ) A 四个 ( ) B 两个
  ( ) C 三个 ( ) D 一个

3 <ruby>她有什么宠物？<rt>tā yǒu shén me chǒng wù</rt></ruby>
  ( ) A 狗 ( ) B 猫
  ( ) C 马 ( ) D 鸟

<ruby>词语<rt>cí yǔ</rt></ruby> VOCABULARY

1	兄弟姐妹	xiōng dì jiě mèi	brothers and sisters
2	马	mǎ	horse

<ruby>句型<rt>jù xíng</rt></ruby> LANGUAGE

Declarative sentences (2), e.g. **我有一个哥哥。**

有 is a verb to indicate what the subject has. This subject can be a person, a place or an object. To negate the sentence, we add **没**.

e.g.
a 我有一个哥哥。 I have one elder brother.
b 我没有兄弟姐妹。 I do not have brothers or sisters.

三 <ruby>阅读<rt>yuè dú</rt></ruby>（<ruby>一<rt>yī</rt></ruby>）
3 📖 Reading (1)

<ruby>张文和陈月谈她的家庭。请用下列的句子完成对话。<rt>Zhāng wén hé Chén yuè tán tā de jiā tíng. qǐng yòng xià liè de jù zi wán chéng duì huà.</rt></ruby>

Zhang Wen is talking about her family photo with Chen Yue. Use the following sentences to complete the dialogue.

陈月　　张文

A <ruby>他们是我爷爷、奶奶、爸爸、妈妈、哥哥、妹妹和我。<rt>tā men shì wǒ yé ye, nǎi nai, bà ba, mā ma, gē ge, mèi mei hé wǒ</rt></ruby>

B <ruby>我家有七口人。<rt>wǒ jiā yǒu qī kǒu rén</rt></ruby>

C <ruby>这是我的猫。<rt>zhè shì wǒ de māo</rt></ruby>

D <ruby>那不是我姐姐，那是我妹妹。<rt>nà bú shì wǒ jiě jie, nà shì wǒ mèi mei</rt></ruby>

E <ruby>我有一个哥哥，一个妹妹。<rt>wǒ yǒu yí gè gē ge, yí gè mèi mei</rt></ruby>

F <ruby>我没有弟弟。<rt>wǒ méi yǒu dì di</rt></ruby>

Cambridge IGCSE Mandarin as a Foreign Language

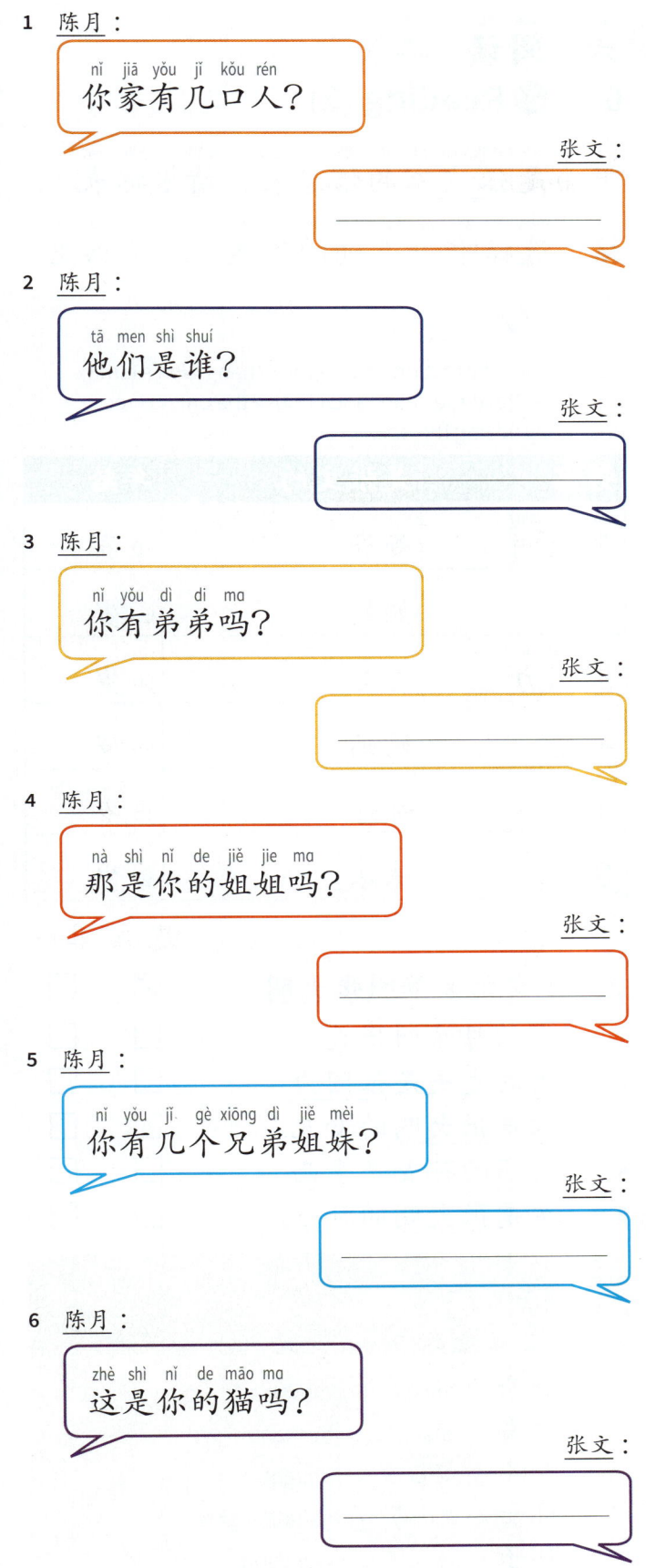

词语
VOCABULARY

1. 爷爷 — yé ye — grandpa
2. 奶奶 — nǎi nai — grandma
3. 的 — de — particle of possession

语法
GRAMMAR

Use of 的

Pronouns/nouns	Meaning	Possessive	Meaning
我	I	我的	my, mine
你	You	你的	your, yours
他	He	他的	his
她	She	她的	her/hers
我们	We	我们的	our/ours

的 shows possession, the structure is
(pro)noun + 的 + noun

e.g.

a 这是我的猫。This is my cat.
b 这只猫是我的。This cat is mine.

However, 的 can often be omitted where the two nouns have a close relationship. For example, 我爸爸 = my father, 我姐姐 = my elder sister, 我妈妈 = my mum.

小贴士
TOP TIP

When reading Chinese, read the characters very carefully and watch out for 的 to ensure you do not muddle 'I/my', 'she/her' and 'they/their'.

Unit A 2 Everyday activities: Family and pets

四 说话（一）
4 Speaking (1)

两人一组，读阅读（一）中的对话。

Work in pairs to act out the dialogue in Reading (1).

五 写作（一）
5 Writing (1)

陈月写了一段话，介绍张文一家。根据阅读（一）的图，填空。

Chen Yue is writing a paragraph to introduce Zhang Wen's family.

Look at the picture in Reading (1) and fill in the gaps.

张文家有＿＿1＿＿口人。他们是爷爷、奶奶、＿＿2＿＿、＿＿3＿＿、一个＿＿4＿＿、一个＿＿5＿＿和张文。张文＿＿6＿＿弟弟，也＿＿7＿＿姐姐。他们有很多宠物：一只＿＿8＿＿和一只＿＿9＿＿。

词语 VOCABULARY

1	也	yě	also
2	金鱼	jīn yú	goldfish
3	兔子	tù zi	rabbit
4	很多	hěn duō	many

六 阅读（二）
6 Reading (2)

下面是张文家的信息表。请根据表格，选择唯一正确的答案，在方格里打勾（✓）。

Below is an information chart about Zhang Wen's family members. Read the chart, and choose the only correct answer by ticking the box.

姓名	是张文的……	年龄
张大明 Zhāng dà míng	爷爷	70 岁
李西 Lǐ xī	奶奶	65 岁
张国力 Zhāng guó lì	爸爸	50 岁
吴英 Wú yīng	妈妈	48 岁
张天 Zhāng tiān	哥哥	15 岁
张红 Zhāng hóng	妹妹	10 岁

　　　　　　　　　　　　　　　　是 Yes　非 No

例：张文的爷爷叫张大明。　　　✓　□

1　张文的母亲叫张天。　　　　□　□
2　吴英的丈夫是张国力。　　　□　□
3　张红是张大明的女儿。　　　□　□
4　张大明的孙女是李西。　　　□　□
5　张文是张大明的孙子。　　　□　□

词语 VOCABULARY

1	母亲	mǔ qīn	mother
2	丈夫	zhàng fu	husband
3	女儿	nǚ ér	daughter
4	孙女	sūn nǚ	granddaughter
5	孙子	sūn zi	grandson

Cambridge IGCSE Mandarin as a Foreign Language

wén huà 文化
CULTURE

jiā tíng chéngyuán de chēng hu
家庭成员的称呼
Addressing Family Members

In Chinese, the titles of family members are different between the father's side and the mother's side.

e.g.

In English	Father's side	Mother's side
Grandfather	爷爷 (yé ye)	外公 (wài gōng) / 姥爷 (lǎo yé)
Grandmother	奶奶 (nǎi nai)	外婆 (wài pó) / 姥姥 (lǎo lao)
Uncle	叔叔 (shū shu)	舅舅 (jiù jiu)
Aunt	姑姑 (gū gu)	阿姨 (ā yí)
Cousin	堂哥 / 堂弟 / 堂姐 / 堂妹 (táng)	表哥 / 表弟 / 表姐 / 表妹 (biǎo)

Note: 外公 and 外婆 are usually used in southern China while 姥爷 and 姥姥 are used more often in northern China.

xiǎo tiē shì
小贴士
TOP TIP

Before listening, it will be very helpful if you spend some time reading the instructions and going through the questions quickly and anticipate what you are going to hear. It helps familiarise yourself with the context.

qī   tīng lì   èr
七 听力（二）
7 Listening (2)

tīng   shuō tā de jiā tíng   qǐng yòng Zhōng wén huò pīn yīn
听 May 说她的家庭。请用中文或拼音
tián kòng
填空。

You will hear May talking about her family. Write your answers in Chinese characters or pinyin to fill in the gaps.
CD 01, Track 05

____1____！我叫 May。我家有____2____口人。爸爸、妈妈、一个____3____、一个哥哥和我。我们有一只宠物，是一只____4____。我的爸爸很____5____这只猫。我爸爸是____6____。我妈妈是美国人。我的哥哥____7____岁，我十三岁。我弟弟八岁。我们都在香港出生。但是我们现在都住在____8____。

cí yǔ
词语
VOCABULARY

1	出生	chū shēng	to be born
2	但是	dàn shì	but
3	现在	xiàn zài	now

bā   yuè dú   sān
八 阅读（三）
8 Reading (3)

yì jiā sān kǒu rén zài jiǎng tā men de jiā tíng   qǐng yuè dú
一家三口人在讲他们的家庭。请阅读
xià miàn de wén zì   huí dá wèn tí
下面的文字，回答问题。

A family of three are talking about their family. Read the text below and answer the questions. **CD 01, Track 06**

Unit A 2 Everyday activities: Family and pets

我叫马可。今年四十五岁。
我是英国人。我妻子是中国人，她叫刘文。我出生在伦敦。我的父亲、母亲、两个哥哥都住在伦敦，但是我、我的妻子和一个儿子住在香港。

我叫刘文。今年四十岁。
我是中国人，出生在马来西亚。我丈夫是英国人。我们有一个儿子。他叫大卫(David)。我们也养一只宠物猫。我们都住在香港。

我叫大卫。我是中英混血儿。我今年十岁。我的爸爸是英国人，妈妈是中国人。我们住在香港。我没有兄弟姐妹，但是我有很多朋友。

1 马可 多大?
2 马可在 哪儿 出生?
3 刘文是 哪 国人?
4 大卫家有 几 口人? 他们是 谁?
5 大卫的妈妈叫 什么名字? 她多大?
6 大卫家有 什么宠物?

> **xiǎo tiē shì**
> **小 贴 士**
> **TOP TIP**
>
> It is very important to identify the question words, as this helps you extract the information from the text.

九　说话（二）
9　Speaking (2)

liǎng rén yì zǔ　zuò jué sè bàn yǎn
两人一组，做角色扮演。

Work in pairs and act out the role play.

　　Zhōng guó tóng xué
A 中国同学

　　Měi guó liú xué shēng
B 美国留学生

qíng jǐng　yí gè Měi guó liú xué shēng hé Zhōng guó tóng xué tán tā
情景：一个美国留学生和中国同学谈他
men de jiā tíng
们的家庭。

Scenario: An American exchange student and a Chinese classmate are talking about their families.

> **xiǎo tiē shì**
> **小 贴 士**
> **TOP TIP**
>
> Read the scenario very carefully, so that you know in what setting you are going to act out the role play and who you are going to speak to during the activity. For example, in this role play, you are an overseas student from the USA. All your answers should be related to the student rather than yourself.

词语 cí yǔ
VOCABULARY

1	讲	jiǎng	to talk about
2	妻子	qī zi	wife
3	父亲	fù qīn	father
4	都	dōu	all
5	儿子	ér zi	son
6	养	yǎng	to raise

补充词语 bǔ chōng cí yǔ
SUPPLEMENTARY VOCABULARY

| 1 | 伦敦 | Lúndūn | London |
| 2 | 混血儿 | hùn xuè ér | mixed race |

Cambridge IGCSE Mandarin as a Foreign Language

	nǐ jiào shén me míng zi	
A1	你叫什么名字?	B1 _____

	nǐ shì měi guó rén ma	
A2	你是美国人吗?	B2 _____

	nǐ duō dà	
A3	你多大?	B3 _____

	nǐ jiā yǒu jǐ kǒu rén　tā men shì shuí	
A4	你家有几口人? 他们是谁?	B4 _____

	nǐ yǒu chǒng wù ma	
A5	你有宠物吗?	B5 _____

cí yǔ
词语
VOCABULARY

| 留学生 | liú xué shēng | exchange student, overseas student |

cí yǔ
词语
VOCABULARY

| 1 | 意思 | yì si | meaning |
| 2 | 汉字 | hàn zì | character |

bǔ chōng cí yǔ
补充词语
SUPPLEMENTARY VOCABULARY

| 偏旁部首 | piān páng bù shǒu | radical |

xiǎo tiē shì
小贴士
TOP TIP

Radicals are components of Chinese characters. They give you clues to the meaning of a character.

shí　　xiě zuò　　èr
十　写作（二）
10 Writing (2)

piān páng bù shǒu　　　　jiāng xià miàn de hàn zì àn bù shǒu fēn
偏旁部首 (1)：将下面的汉字按部首分
lèi　tián rù biǎo gé
类，填入表格。

Radicals (1): Sort the following characters by radicals.

| 你 | 们 | 认 | 识 | 很 | 没 | 吗 | 国 | 叫 | 她 |

	piān páng bù shǒu 偏旁部首 Radicals	yì si 意思 Meanings	hàn zì 汉字 Characters
1	亻	human	例：们, _____
2	彳	double human	_____
3	口	mouth	_____ , _____
4	囗	enclosure	_____
5	女	female	_____
6	讠	speech	_____
7	氵	water	_____

zì wǒ píng gū
自我评估
Self-Assessment

☐ I can understand words for self, family, friends and pets
☐ I can introduce family members
☐ I can identify the question words from sentences in both spoken and written language
☐ Measure words 个, 口, 岁, 只
☐ Difference between 二 and 两
☐ Declarative sentences (2): use of 有
☐ Use of 的

Unit A 2 Everyday activities: Family and pets

wǒ de měi yì tiān
我的每一天
3 Everyday life

Learning objectives

This unit will concentrate on learning vocabulary about everyday life. You will:

- Talk about times, days of the week, months, dates

- Read about someone's daily routine

- Talk about your own daily routine

- Learn to use 正 / 在 / 正在

- Use basic time expressions, e.g. 的时候，以前，以后

- Continue to learn some more question words to do with time, e.g. 几点，什么时候

In addition, you are going to learn:

- Declarative sentences (3): 今天星期二

- Word order

学习目标

本单元，你会：

- 谈论时间、星期、月份和日期

- 阅读介绍关于人们日常生活的文字

- 介绍自己的日常生活

- "正 / 在 / 正在"的用法

- 使用时间词，例如"的时候"，"以前"，"以后"

- 继续学习更多的疑问词，例如"几点"，"什么时候"

你还会学到：

- 陈述句（3）：今天星期二

- 词序

Cambridge IGCSE Mandarin as a Foreign Language

一 温故知新
1 'Before starting' activities

一、把中文和英文搭配起来。

1 Match the Chinese with the English.

例：星期一（ A ）

1 星期二（ ） 2 今天（ ） 3 昨天（ ）
4 星期五（ ） 5 明天（ ） 6 星期天（ ）
7 星期几（ ） 8 今年（ ） 9 明年（ ）
10 去年（ ）

A Monday   B Friday   C Tuesday
D Sunday   E Today   F This year
G Last year   H Next year   I Yesterday
J Tomorrow   K What day of the week is it?

词语 VOCABULARY

| 星期 | xīng qī | week |

二、写出下面的时间。

2 Write the time in Chinese.

1 8:00 AM   2 6:15 PM   3 7:30 AM
4 11:20 AM   5 3:45 PM

词语 VOCABULARY

1	点	diǎn	o'clock
2	分	fēn	minute
3	半	bàn	half
4	刻	kè	quarter
5	上午	shàng wǔ	morning, AM
6	下午	xià wǔ	afternoon, PM
7	时间	shí jiān	time

三、用方格里的词替换划线的词，练习对话。

3 Replace the underlined words with the words in the boxes and practise the dialogues.

| 昨天 | 明天 |

Q1: 今天星期几？
A1: 今天星期二。

| 五点一刻 | 八点半 |

Q2: 现在几点？
A2: 现在三点半。

句型 LANGUAGE

Declarative sentences (3)

When talking about date and time, we can say the sentences without using a verb.

e.g. 今天星期二。 Today is Tuesday.

In English, 'is' should be used in the sentence. However, in Chinese, 是 can be omitted from the sentence.

练习: Now, translate these sentences into Chinese.
1 It's Monday tomorrow.
2 It's 5:00 now.

四、把词语重新排列组成句子。

4 Put the words into the right order to make sentences.

1 早上 / 九点 / 上课 / 我 / 和 / 弟弟
2 晚上 / 做作业 / 我 / 七点半
3 我 / 放学 / 每天 / 五点 / 下午
4 我们 / 吃饭 / 七点半 / 每天
5 妈妈 / 两点 / 听音乐 / 下午 / 昨天

Unit A 3 Everyday activities: Everyday life

cí yǔ 词语 VOCABULARY

1	上学	shàng xué	to go to school
2	下学	xià xué	to finish school
3	下课	xià kè	to finish class; 课 class
4	上课	shàng kè	to attend class
5	早上	zǎo shang	morning
6	晚上	wǎn shang	evening
7	做	zuò	to do
8	作业	zuò yè	homework; 作 to work (see 工作)
9	放学	fàng xué	to leave school
10	每天	měi tiān	every day
11	吃饭	chī fàn	to have a meal; 吃 to eat
12	听音乐	tīng yīn yuè	to listen to music

jù xíng 句型 LANGUAGE

In Chinese, the sentence order is as follows:

Subject + Time phrase + Verb + Object   or
Time phrase + Subject + Verb + Object

Note that time phrases should come BEFORE verbs. If you want to emphasise the time, you can put it at the beginning of the sentence.

e.g.

a 我八点上学。 I go to school at 8:00.

b 三点半我下课／放学。 I finish my classes at 3:30.

When more than one time phrase occurs in a sentence, the order is from the general to the relatively detailed,

e.g. 昨天晚上七点半 7:30 yesterday evening.

èr tīng lì yī 二 听力（一）
2 🔊 Listening (1)

wǔ gè xué shēng zài jiǎng tā men de shēng rì　qǐng tīng xià miàn
五个学生在讲他们的生日。请听下面

de jù zi　xuǎn zé zhèng què de zì mǔ tián kòng
的句子，选择正确的字母填空。

Five students are talking about their birthdays. Listen and choose the correct letter for each student. **CD 01, Track 07**

Lǐ léi 李雷	Wángdōng 1 王东	Lǐ dà shān 2 李大山	Mǎ péngpeng 3 马朋朋	Fāng xuě 4 方雪
例：A				

A **3rd October, 1995**
B 10th March, 2001
C 18th August, 1999
D 4th May, 2003
E 5th October, 1987

cí yǔ 词语 VOCABULARY

1	生日	shēng rì	birthday
2	年	nián	year
3	月	yuè	month
4	日	rì	day, date

Cambridge IGCSE Mandarin as a Foreign Language

文化 CULTURE

中国的日历 Calendars in Chinese

When talking about months from January to December, we just add the numbers 1 to 12 before 月. For example, 一月 is January, 二月 is February, 三月 is March and 十二月 is December. When giving an exact date, the day comes after the month. For example, 7th June is 六月七日 in Chinese.

When including the year (年) in a date, the year should come first. For example, 二零一二年八月五日 is 5th August, 2012. The picture is an extract from a calendar which shows the dates in both the solar calendar and the lunar calendar.

三 阅读（一）
3 Reading (1)

下面是吴海每天的生活。读下面的表格，回答问题。

Read Wu Hai's daily routine below and answer the following questions.

早上	7:10	起床、穿衣服
	7:20	刷牙、洗脸
	7:30	吃早饭
	8:10	上学
中午	12:00	吃午饭
下午	3:15	放学
	4:00	休息

晚上	7:00	吃晚饭
	8:00	做作业
	10:00	洗澡
	10:30	睡觉

1 吴海每天几点起床？
2 吴海每天几点睡觉？
3 现在是早上七点半，吴海正在做什么？
4 现在是中午十二点，吴海正在做什么？
5 现在是晚上八点，吴海正在做什么？

词语 VOCABULARY

1	生活	shēng huó	life
2	中午	zhōng wǔ	noon
3	起床	qǐ chuáng	to get up
4	穿	chuān	to wear
5	衣服	yī fu	clothes
6	洗脸	xǐ liǎn	to wash face
7	早饭	zǎo fàn	breakfast
8	午饭	wǔ fàn	lunch
9	休息	xiū xi	to rest, rest
10	晚饭	wǎn fàn	dinner
11	睡觉	shuì jiào	to sleep, to go to bed
12	几点	jǐ diǎn	what time
13	洗澡	xǐ zǎo	to have a bath
14	正在	zhèng zài	in the process of

补充词语 SUPPLEMENTARY VOCABULARY

| 刷牙 | shuā yá | to brush teeth |

Unit A 3 Everyday activities: Everyday life

句型 jù xíng
LANGUAGE

Subject + 正 / 正在 / 在 + Verb indicates that an action is in progress, i.e. someone is doing something.
Note that 正在 can also be used as simply 在 or 正.
e.g.
a 爷爷正在休息。Grandpa is having a rest.
b 弟弟在吃早饭。Little brother is having breakfast.

四 说话 (一) sì shuō huà yī
4 Speaking (1)

liǎng rén yì zǔ, zuò jiǎo sè bàn yǎn
两人一组，做角色扮演。

Work in pairs and complete the role play.

Zhōng guó péng yǒu   nǐ zì jǐ
A 中国朋友   B 你自己

qíng jǐng: nǐ hé nǐ de Zhōng guó péng yǒu zài tán nǐ de shēng huó
情景：你和你的中国朋友在谈你的生活。

Scenario: You are talking about your life with your Chinese friend.

nǐ de shēng rì shì shén me shí hòu
A1: 你的生日是什么时候？
B1: _____

nǐ měi tiān jǐ diǎn qǐ chuáng
A2: 你每天几点起床？
B2: _____

nǐ měi tiān jǐ diǎn shàng xué
A3: 你每天几点上学？
B3: _____

nǐ shén me shí hòu bú shàng xué
A4: 你什么时候不上学？
B4: _____

nǐ xīng qī wǔ wǎn shàng zuò shén me
A5: 你星期五晚上做什么？
B5: _____

好词好句 hǎo cí hǎo jù
USEFUL EXPRESSIONS

wǒ de shēng rì shì wǔ yuè shí liù rì
· 我的生日是五月十六日。

wǒ xīng qī liù hé xīng qī tiān bú shàng xué
· 我星期六和星期天不上学。

wǒ xīng qī wǔ wǎn shàng kàn diàn shì
· 我星期五晚上看电视。

词语 cí yǔ
VOCABULARY

什么时候   shén me shí hòu   when

语法 yǔ fǎ
GRAMMAR

1 几点 and 什么时候 are both question words related to time.

几点 is to ask 'What time is it?'
e.g. Q: 你几点起床？ What time do you get up?
A: 我五点起床。 I get up at five o'clock.

2 什么时候 is to ask 'When is it?'
e.g. Q: 你什么时候起床？ When do you get up?
A: 我五点起床。I get up at five o'clock.
Q: 你什么时候听音乐？ When do you listen to music?
A: 我晚上听音乐。I listen to music in the evening.

From the examples above you can see that when using 什么时候, the answers can be both specific and more general.

Cambridge IGCSE Mandarin as a Foreign Language

五 阅读（二）
5 Reading (2)

三个朋友在谈星期六，请读一读，然后回答问题。

Three friends are talking about their plans this Saturday. Read the texts and answer the following questions.

选择正确的答案。

Choose 'true' or 'false' for each statement.

		对	错
1	王英星期六生日。	☐	☐
2	高文星期六下午打羽毛球。	☐	☐
3	吴明星期六上午和下午都在家。	☐	☐

词语 VOCABULARY

1	去	qù	to go
2	生日会	shēng rì huì	birthday party
3	一起	yì qǐ	together
4	打	dǎ	to play
5	羽毛球	yǔ máo qiú	badminton; 球 ball
6	学校	xué xiào	school
7	演出	yǎn chū	performance
8	对	duì	correct
9	错	cuò	wrong

王英：
星期六是我朋友的十六岁生日。我去他的生日会。

高文：
我星期六上午在家做作业，下午我和妈妈一起打羽毛球。

吴明：
星期六上午我在家休息，下午我和妹妹一起去学校看演出。

句型 LANGUAGE

1 在 + Place is used to say that something is located at a place.
   e.g. 在家 at home

2 去 + Place is used when talking about going somewhere.
   e.g. 去学校 go to school

3 和……一起 means 'together with'. Note that it is different from English, as we should put 和 + someone (with someone) before 一起 at all times.
   e.g. 我和姐姐一起上学。 I go to school with my elder sister.

Unit A 3 Everyday activities: Everyday life

六 听力（二）
6 🔊 Listening (2)

<u>小英</u>在讲她的一个星期天。请先阅读一下问题。

Xiaoying is talking about what she did last Sunday. Read the questions first.

一、请听下面的一段话，在唯一正确的括号里打勾（✓）回答问题。

1 Listen to the passage and answer each question by ticking one bracket only. **CD 01, Track 08**

1 小英上午九点做什么？
( ) A 看报纸　　　( ) B 看书
( ) C 做作业

2 小英中午十二点做什么？
( ) A 吃午饭　　　( ) B 看书
( ) C 看报纸

3 午饭以后，小英和谁一起打网球？
( ) A 妈妈　　　　( ) B 朋友
( ) C 弟弟

4 每个星期天晚上，小英不做什么？
( ) A 去朋友的生日派对
( ) B 在家听音乐
( ) C 打网球

二、听录音，填空。

2 Listen to the recording and fill in the gaps.

每个星期天上午九点，我在家＿1＿。我做作业的时候，妈妈＿2＿和看报纸。中午十二点我和＿3＿去吃午饭。午饭以后，我和弟弟一起打网球。晚上，我有时候去朋友的生日派对，有时候在家＿4＿。十点半以前，我睡觉。

词语 VOCABULARY

1	……的时候	…… de shí hòu	when…
2	看	kàn	to read, to look at, to watch
3	书	shū	book
4	报纸	bào zhǐ	newspaper
5	以后	yǐ hòu	after
6	网球	wǎng qiú	tennis
7	有时候	yǒu shí hòu	sometimes
8	派对	pài duì	party
9	以前	yǐ qián	before
10	篮球	lán qiú	basketball

语法 GRAMMAR

1 **Use of 的时候, 以前 and 以后**
When talking about 'when', 'before' and 'after' in Chinese, you should say the first event, followed by 的时候 (when), 以前 (before) or 以后 (after) and then the other event.
e.g.
a 弟弟两岁的时候，喜欢听音乐。
When my younger brother was two years old, he liked listening to music.
b 下课以后，我去打篮球。After class, I go to play basketball.
c 睡觉以前，我看书。Before going to bed, I read books.

2 **Use of 有时候**
When talking about 'sometimes', you can use this phrase.
e.g.
星期天下午，有时候我去打羽毛球，有时候我去打网球。On Sunday afternoon, sometimes I play badminton and sometimes I play tennis.

Cambridge IGCSE Mandarin as a Foreign Language

七 说话（二）
7 Speaking (2)

小演讲：谈谈你的星期天。

Topic conversation: Talk about your Sundays. Use the text of Listening (2) for reference.

八 听力（三）
8 Listening (3)

下面是对中学生黄丽丽的采访。请先阅读一下问题。

This is an interview with Huang Lili, a secondary school student. Read the questions first. **CD 01, Track 09**

请听采访，用中文或拼音回答问题。

Listen to the interview, and answer the questions in Chinese. You may write in characters or pinyin.

1 黄丽丽的生日是几月几号？
2 黄丽丽上几年级？
3 她每天几点睡觉？
4 她在哪儿做作业？
5 不上学的时候，她和家人做什么？

词语 VOCABULARY

1	年级	nián jí	grade/year in a school
2	快乐	kuài lè	happy
3	乒乓球	pīng pāng qiú	table tennis
4	中学	zhōng xué	secondary school

补充词语 SUPPLEMENTARY VOCABULARY

采访 cǎi fǎng interview

小贴士 TOP TIP

There are usually three steps to answering questions that contain question words:

Step 1: Spot the question word.
Step 2: Return to the text to find a sentence with similar words.
Step 3: Write down the answer. Double check if your answer is relevant to the question.

九 写作
9 Writing

偏旁部首 (2)：将下面的汉字按部首分类，填入表格。

Radicals (2): Sort the following characters by radicals.

爸 家 狗 介 孙 都 籍 爷 那 猫 金

	偏旁部首 Radicals	意思 Meanings	汉字 Characters
1	宀	home	家
2	父	father	____ , ____
3	犭	animal	____ , ____
4	人	human	____
5	子	son, child	____
6	阝	city	____ , ____
7	竹	bamboo	____

Unit A 3 Everyday activities: Everyday life

zì wǒ píng gū
自我评估
Self-Assessment

- ☐ I can talk about times, days of the week, months and dates
- ☐ I can read about someone's daily routine and talk about my own
- ☐ Use of 正 / 在 / 正在
- ☐ I understand how to use time expressions accurately, e.g. 的时候, 以前, 以后
- ☐ I understand how to ask and answer questions with 几点 and 什么时候
- ☐ Use of declarative sentences such as 今天星期几

ài hào
爱好
4 Hobbies

Learning objectives

This unit will concentrate on learning vocabulary about hobbies. You will:

- Listen to conversations about leisure activities and sports

- Read about leisure activities and sports

- Talk about the leisure activities you do and sports you play

- Write your opinions of hobbies by using complements of degree

In addition, you are going to learn:

- The difference between 不 and 没

- The use of the sentence structure 一边……一边……

- How to describe duration

学习目标

本单元，你会：

- 听关于休闲活动和运动的对话

- 阅读关于休闲活动和运动的文字

- 讨论你做的休闲活动和运动

- 用程度补语写你对爱好的看法

你还会学到：

- "不"和"没"的分别

- 句型"一边……一边……"的用法

- 怎样描述"多长时间"

Unit A 4 Everyday activities: Hobbies

一、 温故知新
1 'Before starting' activities

一、将中文和英文搭配起来。

1 Match the Chinese with the English.

1 唱歌 (chàng gē)   A Playing games
2 跳舞;跳 to jump (tiào wǔ)   B Singing
3 玩游戏 (wán yóu xì)   C Dancing
4 滑冰 (huá bīng)   D Reading newspapers
5 看报 (kàn bào)   E Skating

二、找出下面哪些是动词 (verb), 哪些是宾语 (object), 它们又可以组成什么动宾结构短语 (verb+object activities)。请分类填表。

2 Find the verbs and objects in the box; then match them to form verb+object activities and fill in the table.

玩	冰	睡
看	游	觉
报	滑	戏
唱	歌	冰

Verb	Object	Activity
e.g. 玩	游戏	玩游戏

三、完成下面的问卷调查。

3 Complete this survey on hobbies.

问卷调查 (wèn juàn diào chá)

年龄 (nián líng): _____   国籍 (guó jí): _____

圈出你的答案 (quān chū nǐ de dá àn)。 Circle your answers.

性别 (xìng bié): 男 (nán)   女 (nǚ)

1 你有什么爱好? (nǐ yǒu shén me ài hào)
  A 唱歌 (chàng gē)   B 看电影 (kàn diàn yǐng)
  C 看电视 (kàn diàn shì) D 听音乐 (tīng yīn lè)
  E 逛街 (guàng jiē)   F 上网 (shàngwǎng)

2 你会跳舞吗? (nǐ huì tiào wǔ ma)
  A 会 (huì)   B 不会 (bú huì)

3 你会不会拉小提琴? (nǐ huì bú huì lá xiǎo tí qín)
  A 会 (huì)   B 不会 (bú huì)

4 你每天做作业做多长时间? (nǐ měi tiān zuò zuò yè zuò duō cháng shí jiān)
  A 半个小时 (bàn gè xiǎo shí)
  B 二十分钟 (èr shí fēn zhōng)
  C 两个小时 (liǎng gè xiǎo shí)

5 你每天做多长时间的运动? (nǐ měi tiān zuò duō cháng shí jiān de yùn dòng)
  A 一个小时 (yí gè xiǎo shí)
  B 十五分钟 (shí wǔ fēn zhōng)
  C 一刻钟 (yí kè zhōng)

Cambridge IGCSE Mandarin as a Foreign Language

词语 cí yǔ
VOCABULARY

1	男	nán	male
2	女	nǚ	female
3	爱好	ài hào	hobbies
4	会	huì	can, to have the ability to do something
5	电影	diàn yǐng	film, movie; 看电影 to watch a film/movie
6	电视	diàn shì	TV; 看电视 to watch TV
7	逛街	guàng jiē	to go shopping; 逛 to stroll
8	上网	shàng wǎng	to go online
9	运动	yùn dòng	sport
10	多长时间	duō cháng shí jiān	how long a time
11	小时	xiǎo shí	hour
12	分钟	fēn zhōng	minute; 钟 clock

句型 jù xíng
LANGUAGE

There are two ways of asking and answering 多长时间 questions:

1. Subject + Activity + repeat the Verb in the activity + 多长时间?

2. Subject + Verb in the activity + 多长时间 + 的 + Object in the activity?

These both mean *how long does it take (to do the activity)*? When answering the questions, you should replace the 多长时间 with phrases of duration, e.g. 两年 *liǎng nián* two years, 五天 *wǔ tiān* five days, 一个小时 *yí gè xiǎo shí* one hour.

The tables below show you how the sentences work.

练习: Follow the examples and complete the rest of the sentences according to the English meanings.

Subject	Activity	Repeat the verb in the activity	多长时间 / phrases of duration	English
你	做运动	做	多长时间?	How long do you do sport?
我	睡觉	睡	八个小时。	I sleep for eight hours.
				How long do you go online?
				I read a book for half an hour.

Subject	Verb in the activity	多长时间	的	Object in the activity	English
你	做	多长时间	的	运动?	How long do you do sport?
你	睡	八个小时	的	觉。	I sleep for eight hours.
					How long do you go online?
					I read a book for two hours.

延伸活动 yán shēn huó dòng
AIM HIGHER

Where can we put the time phrases? Try to translate this sentence into Chinese:

'I sleep for ten hours every day.'

wén huà 文化 / CULTURE

Zhōng guó chuán tǒng ài hào
中国传统爱好
Traditional Hobbies in China

Zhōng guó rén yǒu hěn duō chuán tǒng ài hào. Yǒu de rén xǐ huan xiě shū fǎ, yǒu de rén xǐ huan dǎ tài jí quán. Měi tiān zǎo shang, lǎo rén xǐ huan yì biān tīng jīng jù, yì biān xià xiàng qí.

中国人有很多传统爱好。有的人喜欢写书法，有的人喜欢打太极拳。每天早上，老人喜欢一边听京剧，一边下象棋。

---

cí yǔ 词语 / VOCABULARY

1	照片	zhào piàn	photo
2	一边…… 一边……	yì biān…… yì biān……	while…
3	写	xiě	to write
4	书法	shū fǎ	calligraphy
5	放风筝	fàng fēng zhēng	kite-flying; 放 to release

bǔ chōng cí yǔ 补充词语 / SUPPLEMENTARY VOCABULARY

1	传统	chuán tǒng	traditional, tradition
2	有的人	yǒu de rén	some people
3	老人	lǎo rén	old people

---

sì qǐng kàn xià miàn de zhào piàn, jiāng Zhōng wén cí yǔ hé tú piàn dā pèi qǐ lái.

四、请看下面的照片，将中文词语和图片搭配起来。

4 Look at the pictures and match them with the Chinese phrases.

1 (　) 2 (　)
3 (　) 4 (　)
5 (　)

	tīng jīng jù		xiě shū fǎ		xià xiàng qí
A	听京剧	B	写书法	C	下象棋
	fàng fēng zhēng		dǎ tài jí quán		
D	放风筝	E	打太极拳		

---

jù xíng 句型 / LANGUAGE

一边……一边……

The sentence structure 一边……一边…… is used to describe two actions taking place at the same time. Both actions are being carried out by the same person/parties and the subject should be used before 一边……一边…….

练习：Read the example sentences below and complete the sentences according to the English.

马力	一边	唱歌,	一边	跳舞。	Mali is singing while dancing.
我	一边	1	一边	做作业。	I am listening to music while doing my homework.

CAMBRIDGE IGCSE Mandarin as a Foreign Language

我爷爷喜欢	爷爷	一边	2	一边	3	My grandfather likes listening to Beijing Opera while writing calligraphy.
4						My younger brother is watching a movie while browsing online.

	例： Xiǎo wáng 小王	Zhāng yīng 1 张英	Dà péng 2 大朋	Lǐ nà 3 李那	Wú wén 4 吴文
爱好	钓鱼				
什么时候做	五岁的时候				
做了多长时间了	五年				

二 听力（一）
2 🔊 Listening (1)

wǔ gè xué shēng zài tán tā men de ài hào   qǐng tīng xià miàn
五个学生在谈他们的爱好。请听下面
de lù yīn   tián xiě biǎo gé
的录音，填写表格。

Five students are talking about their hobbies. Listen to the recording and fill in the table. **CD 01, Track 10**

词语 cí yǔ
VOCABULARY

1	学	xué	to learn, to study
2	钓鱼	diào yú	to fish
3	了	le	particle to show completion of an action
4	游泳	yóu yǒng	swimming
5	保龄球	bǎo líng qiú	bowling
6	滑雪	huá xuě	skiing
7	排球	pái qiú	volleyball

❗ xiǎo tiē shì
小贴士
TOP TIP

什么时候 vs 多长时间

When answering 什么时候 and 多长时间 questions, remember that 什么时候 is asking for an exact time (e.g. 三点, 明天, 去年), whereas 多长时间 is asking for the duration in time (e.g. 三个小时).

三 阅读（一）
3 📖 Reading (1)

yuè dú yǐ xià de wén zì   xuǎn zé zhèng què de dá àn
阅读以下的文字，选择正确的答案，
huí dá wèn tí
回答问题。

Read the following text and choose the correct answers.

33

Unit A 4 Everyday activities: Hobbies

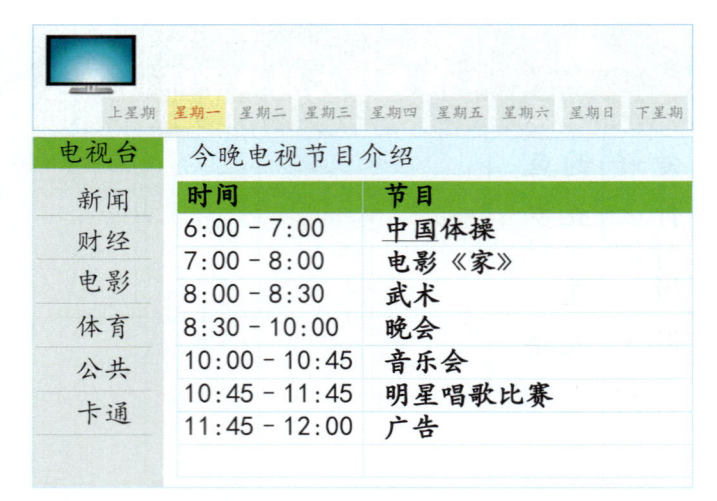

电视台	今晚电视节目介绍	
新闻	时间	节目
财经	6:00 - 7:00	中国体操
电影	7:00 - 8:00	电影《家》
体育	8:00 - 8:30	武术
公共	8:30 - 10:00	晚会
卡通	10:00 - 10:45	音乐会
	10:45 - 11:45	明星唱歌比赛
	11:45 - 12:00	广告

上星期 星期一 星期二 星期三 星期四 星期五 星期六 星期日 下星期

cí yǔ 词语 VOCABULARY

1 节目 jié mù programme
2 体操 tǐ cāo gymnastics
3 武术 wǔ shù martial art
4 晚会 wǎn huì gala
5 音乐会 yīn yuè huì concert
6 比赛 bǐ sài competition
7 广告 guǎng gào advertisement
8 表演 biǎo yǎn performance

1 什么时候有音乐会?
　☐ A 八点半　　　☐ B 十点五十分
　☐ C 十一点　　　☐ D 十点十分

2 几点有明星唱歌?
　☐ A 十点半　　　☐ B 十一点
　☐ C 十二点　　　☐ D 十点

3 武术表演了多长时间?
　☐ A 一个小时　　☐ B 半个小时
　☐ C 四十五分钟　☐ D 两个小时

4 音乐会表演了多长时间?
　☐ A 一个小时　　☐ B 半个小时
　☐ C 四十五分钟　☐ D 两个小时

四 说话（一）
4 Speaking (1)

shì hé nǐ de tóng xué liǎng rén yì zǔ wán chéng duì huà
试和你的同学两人一组，完成对话。

Work in pairs to ask and answer the questions.

nǐ de ài hào shì shén me
A1: 你的爱好是什么?　　　　B1: _____

nǐ shén me shí hòu zuò zhè gè huó dòng
A2: 你什么时候做这个活动?　B2: _____

nǐ hé shuí yì qǐ zuò zhè gè huó dòng
A3: 你和谁一起做这个活动?　B3: _____

nǐ xǐ huān zuò shén me yùn dòng
A4: 你喜欢做什么运动?　　　B4: _____

nǐ zuò yùn dòng zuò duō cháng shí jiān
A5: 你做运动做多长时间?　　B5: _____

cí yǔ 词语 VOCABULARY

活动　huó dòng　activity

五 阅读（二）
5 Reading (2)

yuè dú yǐ xià de wén zì tián kòng
阅读以下的文字，填空。

Read the following and fill in the gaps. **CD 01, Track 11**

Cambridge IGCSE Mandarin as a Foreign Language

王文文

我叫王文文，我是中国人。我今年十五岁。我家有三口人，爸爸、妈妈和我。

从小到大，我有很多爱好。五岁的时候，我喜欢画画儿。但是，我画画儿画得不好。八岁的时候，我喜欢弹钢琴。因为妈妈会弹钢琴，她弹得非常好。但是，昨天和今天我没有时间弹钢琴。现在，我的爱好是跑步和弹吉他。我喜欢跑步，因为跑步是非常好的运动。我常常和爸爸一起跑步。

我每天晚上弹一个小时的吉他。我的妈妈总是说："你弹吉他弹得非常好！"

1 王文文画画儿_____得不好。(line 6)

2 王文文的妈妈弹钢琴_____得非常好。(line 8)

3 王文文_____得非常好。(lines 13–14)

4 王文文每天晚上弹_____的吉他。(lines 13–14)

句型 jù xíng
LANGUAGE

得 + complement of degree

When describing how an action is performed, we should use the following sentence structures:

1 Object of the activity + Verb of the activity + 得 + Adj./adv.

2 Activity + Verb of the activity + 得 + Adj./adv.

The table below shows you how the sentences work.

练习：Follow the examples and complete the rest of the sentences according to the English meanings.

Subject	Option 1: Activity / Option 2: Object of the activity	Verb of the activity	得	Adj./adv.	English
他	唱歌	唱	得	好。	He's good at singing.
他	足球	踢	得	不好。	He's not good at playing football.
1 我					I am not good at painting.
2					She's very good at dancing.

词语 cí yǔ
VOCABULARY

1	画	huà	to draw, to paint
2	画儿	huàr	painting
3	因为	yīn wèi	because
4	非常	fēi cháng	very
5	跑步	pǎo bù	to run; 跑 to run
6	总是	zǒng shì	always
7	常常	cháng cháng	often; 常 often
8	足球	zú qiú	football (soccer)

Unit A 4 Everyday activities: Hobbies

补充词语 / SUPPLEMENTARY VOCABULARY

1	从小到大	cóng xiǎo dào dà	since childhood
2	吉他	jí tā	guitar
3	弹	tán	to play (a musical instrument)
4	钢琴	gāng qín	piano

好词好句 / USEFUL EXPRESSIONS

1 我喜欢看小说，因为我觉得看小说很有意思。
（wǒ xǐ huān kàn xiǎo shuō, yīn wèi wǒ jué de kàn xiǎo shuō hěn yǒu yì si）

2 我每天看一个小时的小说。
（wǒ měi tiān kàn yí gè xiǎo shí de xiǎo shuō）

六 说话（二）
6 Speaking (2)

填空。然后两人一组练习，准备小演讲。
(tián kòng. rán hòu liǎng rén yì zǔ liàn xí, zhǔn bèi xiǎo yǎn jiǎng.)

Fill in the gaps. Practise the script in pairs before presenting it to the class.

你好，我叫_____，今年_____岁。今天我讲的是"我的爱好"。
(nǐ hǎo, wǒ jiào _____, jīn nián _____ suì. jīn tiān wǒ jiǎng de shì "wǒ de ài hào".)

我的爱好是_____（什么？）和_____（什么？）。我_____（什么时候？）_____（爱好）。我喜欢_____（什么？），因为我觉得_____（opinions）。我会_____（什么活动？）。
(wǒ de ài hào shì _____ hé _____. wǒ _____ _____. wǒ xǐ huān _____, yīn wéi wǒ jué de _____. wǒ huì _____.)

我_____得很好。
(wǒ _____ de hěn hǎo.)

我不喜欢_____（什么活动？），因为我觉得_____（opinions）。
(wǒ bù xǐ huān _____, yīn wéi wǒ jué de _____.)

我每天看_____（多长时间？）电视/书/电影。
(wǒ měi tiān kàn _____ diàn shì / shū / diàn yǐng.)

词语 / VOCABULARY

1	滑旱冰	huá hàn bīng	roller-skating
2	觉得	jué de	to think, to feel
3	小说	xiǎo shuō	novel
4	有意思	yǒu yì si	interesting
5	没（有）意思	méi (yǒu) yì si	not interesting
6	好玩儿	hǎo wánr	fun; 玩儿 to play, to have fun

句型 / LANGUAGE

觉得 + comments is for expressing your opinion about something, e.g.

a 我觉得打桌球很好玩儿。I think playing snooker is fun.

b 哥哥觉得这个生日派对没意思。My older brother thinks this birthday party is not interesting.

You can use the following words with 觉得 to describe your opinions.

有意思 interesting	没意思 not interesting
好玩儿 fun	不好玩儿 not fun

Cambridge IGCSE Mandarin as a Foreign Language

cí yǔ 词语 VOCABULARY

| 桌球 | zhuō qiú | snooker; also called | 台球 tái qiú |

yǔ fǎ 语法 GRAMMAR

不 vs 没

不 and 没 both mean 'no' or 'not' in English. However, we use them in different situations.

1 不 is to negate something that does not take place and will not take place, e.g.
   a 我不喜欢运动。 I do not like sports.
   b 我不是中国人。 I am not Chinese.
   c 明天我不上学。 I am not going to school tomorrow.

2 没 is to negate something that did not happen before, e.g.
   昨天我没上学。 I did not go to school yesterday.

Also, the negation of 有 SHOULD ALWAYS be 没, meaning 'not to have'; sometimes 有 can be omitted. e.g. 没有 not to have, 没（有）意思 not interesting, 没（有）弟弟 have no younger brothers.

xiǎo tiē shì 小贴士 TOP TIP

When starting a presentation, it is a good idea to engage the audience by briefly introducing yourself and what your topic is about. When introducing the topic, you can start with 今天我讲的是……

qī tīng lì (èr) 七 听力（二）
7 🔊 Listening (2)

Zhāng měi yīng shì wǎng qiú míng xīng. Qǐng tīng cǎi fǎng, xuǎn zé
张美英是网球明星。请听采访，选择
zhèng què de dá àn huí dá wèn tí
正确的答案回答问题。

Zhang Meiying is a star tennis player. Listen to the interview and choose the correct answer to each question. **CD 01, Track 12**

1 张美英打网球打了多长时间了？
  ( ) A 二年 ( ) B 十二年
  ( ) C 二十年

2 张美英十岁的时候，和姐姐一起看了一个_____，认识了网球。
  ( ) A 展览 ( ) B 运动会
  ( ) C 音乐会

3 不打网球的时候，张美英有什么爱好？
  ( ) A 滑冰 ( ) B 滑雪
  ( ) C 滑板

4 张美英喜欢和女儿一起做什么？
  ( ) A 看小人书和连环画
  ( ) B 看杂志和唱歌
  ( ) C 看展览

5 张美英的女儿多大？
  ( ) A 三岁 ( ) B 两岁
  ( ) C 六岁

cí yǔ 词语 VOCABULARY

1	明星	míng xīng	super star
2	展览	zhǎn lǎn	exhibition
3	运动会	yùn dòng huì	sports day
4	滑板	huá bǎn	skateboard

Unit A 4 Everyday activities: Hobbies

词语 cí yǔ VOCABULARY

5	杂志	zá zhì	magazine
6	小人书	xiǎo rén shū	comic book
7	连环画	lián huán huà	= 小人书
8	不客气	bú kè qi	You're welcome; 客气 polite

文化 wén huà CULTURE

中国有很多很受欢迎的小人书，比如《老夫子》、《三毛流浪记》等等。这些书也可以叫连环画或者漫画。

There are many popular comics (xiao ren shu) in China, for example, *Old Scholar*, *Winter Of Three Hairs*. These books can also be called lian huan hua or man hua.

八 写作 bā xiě zuò
8 Writing

一、偏旁部首 (3)：将下面的汉字按部首分类，填入表格。

1. Radicals (3): Sort the following characters by radicals.

昨 点 踢 穿 打 睡 看

	偏旁部首 piān páng bù shǒu Radicals	意思 yì si Meanings	汉字 hàn zì Characters
1	日	sun	_____
2	灬	fire	_____
3	穴	cave	_____
4	足	foot	_____
5	扌	hand	_____
6	目	eyes	_____ , _____

二、你第一次写信给你的笔友李明，谈谈你的爱好。根据括号里的提示填空。

2. You are writing a letter to Li Ming, your pen pal, for the first time and talk about your hobbies. Fill in the gaps as instructed by the questions or English words in the brackets.

亲爱的李明：

　　你好吗？我叫林美美。今年_____ 1
岁（你多大？）。我住在_____。（你住在 2
哪儿？）我有各种各样的爱好。 3

　　我喜欢运动。我_____（什么时 4
候？）做运动。我喜欢的运动是_____， 5
_____和_____（什么运动？）。我每 6
天运动_____（多长时间？）。我觉得 7
_____（什么运动？）很好玩儿，但是 8
（什么运动？）_____没意思。 9

　　我也喜欢听音乐。_____（classical 10
music）和_____（pop songs）我都喜欢。 11
我喜欢一边_____（listen to music），一边 12
_____（do homework）。 13

你有什么爱好？期待你的回信。 14
祝 15
好！ 16

　　　　　　　　　　　林美美 17
　　　　　　　　　　　三月一日 18

Cambridge IGCSE Mandarin as a Foreign Language

cí yǔ
词语
VOCABULARY

1	写信	xiě xìn	to write a letter; 信 letter	
2	笔友	bǐ yǒu	pen pal	
3	亲爱的	qīn ài de	dear	
4	古典音乐	gǔ diǎn yīn yuè	classical music	
5	流行歌曲	liú xíng gē qǔ	pop songs	
6	爬山	pá shān	to climb a mountain; 山 mountain, hill	
7	回信	huí xìn	to reply	
8	祝（好）	zhù (hǎo)	wish you well	
9	踢足球	tī zú qiú	to play football; 踢 to kick	

bǔ chōng cí yǔ
补充词语
SUPPLEMENTARY VOCABULARY

各种各样　　gè zhǒng gè yàng　　different kinds

yán shēn huó dòng
延伸活动
AIM HIGHER

qǐng nǐ bāng Lǐ míng xiě yì fēng huí xìn gěi Lín měi měi
请你帮李明写一封回信给林美美。
Help Li Ming write a letter in reply to Lin Meimei.

xiǎo tiē shì
小贴士
TOP TIP

Letter format is very important. Use the letter above as an example to complete the reply letter.

zì wǒ píng gū
自我评估
Self-Assessment

- ☐ I can understand vocabulary about hobbies
- ☐ I can listen to conversations about leisure activities and sports
- ☐ I can read about leisure activities and sports
- ☐ I can talk about leisure activities and sports
- ☐ I can write to express my opinions of various hobbies by using complements of degree
- ☐ Difference between 不 and 没
- ☐ Use of sentence structure 一边……一边……
- ☐ Expression of duration

Unit A 4 Everyday activities: Hobbies

yǐn shí
饮食
5 Eating and drinking

Learning objectives

This unit will concentrate on food and drink vocabulary. You will:

- Read menus and order food in a Chinese restaurant

- Listen to conversations in a restaurant

- Ask and answer 怎么样 questions and give your opinions

- Write a food review

In addition, you are going to learn:

- The measure words 包, 盒, 盘, 碗, 块, 杯 and 瓶

- The position phrases 在……这儿/那儿

- Particles 吧, 呢, 了

- Questions with options using ……还是……

学习目标

本单元, 你会：

- 阅读餐馆里的菜单和点菜

- 听餐馆里的对话

- 用"怎么样"提问和回答、表达你的看法

- 写食评

你还会学到：

- 量词：包、盒、盘、碗、块、杯、瓶

- "在……这儿/那儿"的用法

- 语气助词：吧、呢、了

- 选择疑问句：……还是……

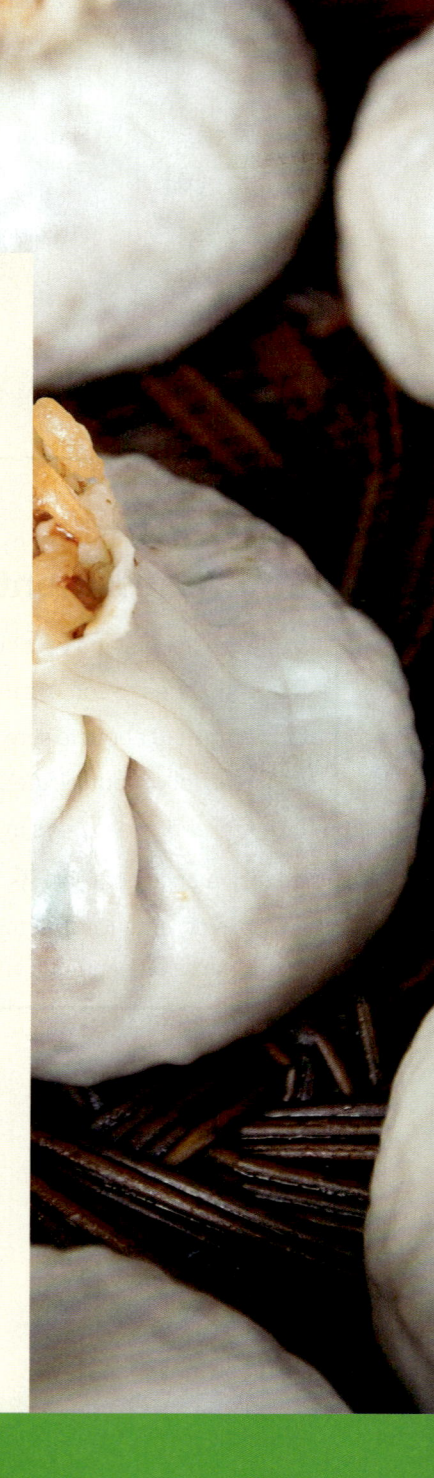

Cambridge IGCSE Mandarin as a Foreign Language

一 温故知新
1 'Before starting' activities

一、说出下面水果的名称。

1 Identify the different kinds of fruit in the picture.

词语 VOCABULARY

1	水果	shuǐ guǒ	fruit
2	香蕉	xiāng jiāo	banana
3	苹果	píng guǒ	apple
4	葡萄	pú táo	grape
5	橙子	chéng zi	orange

补充词语 SUPPLEMENTARY VOCABULARY

| 1 | 草莓 | cǎo méi | strawberry |
| 2 | 西瓜 | xī guā | watermelon |

二、下面这些食物,哪些是可以"吃"的?哪些是可以"喝"的?

2 Do you EAT or DRINK the following foods?

吃	喝
e.g. 米饭	水

词语 VOCABULARY

1	喝	hē	to drink
2	米饭	mǐ fàn	rice
3	面包	miàn bāo	bread
4	鸡蛋	jī dàn	egg
5	蔬菜	shū cài	vegetable
6	水	shuǐ	water
7	牛奶	niú nǎi	milk
8	果汁	guǒ zhī	juice
9	茶	chá	tea

Unit A 5 Everyday activities: Eating and drinking

文化 wén huà
CULTURE

筷子 kuài zi

中国人用筷子吃饭。
Zhōng guó rén yòng kuài zi chī fàn

筷子是用木头、竹子做的。西方人用刀和叉吃饭。
kuài zi shì yòng mù tóu zhú zi zuò de xī fāng rén yòng dāo hé chā chī fàn

词语 cí yǔ
VOCABULARY

1 筷子 kuài zi chopsticks
2 用 yòng to use
3 刀 dāo knife
4 叉 chā fork

补充词语 bǔ chōng cí yǔ
SUPPLEMENTARY VOCABULARY

1 木头 mù tou wood
2 竹子 zhú zi bamboo

三、选择合适的助词填空。每个词可以用多于一次。
sān xuǎn zé hé shì de zhù cí tián kòng měi gè cí kě yǐ yòng duō yú yí cì

3 Choose the most appropriate particles to fill in the gaps. Each word may be used more than once.

A 呢 ne   B 吧 ba   C 了 le

1 明天我们一起去看电影_____。
míng tiān wǒ men yì qǐ qù kàn diàn yǐng

2 他会打篮球,你_____?
tā huì dǎ lán qiú nǐ

3 好久不见_____,你好吗?
hǎo jiǔ bú jiàn nǐ hǎo ma

4 我来介绍一下我的爱好_____。
wǒ lái jiè shào yí xià wǒ de ài hào

5 我正在睡觉_____。
wǒ zhèng zài shuì jiào

词语 cí yǔ
VOCABULARY

好久不见 hǎo jiǔ bú jiàn long time no see;
久 long

句型 jù xíng
LANGUAGE

1 The particle 吧 is used for expressing a request, consultation or proposal. It can be used to soften the tone of a sentence or even turn a command into a suggestion, e.g.

我们去打网球吧。 Let's play tennis, shall we?

吧 can also be used to express an assumption, e.g.

你是中国人吧? I guess you are Chinese?

2 The particle 呢 is often used to follow up a question with another question. It is used to ask the same question as the first one, but about another subject or object, e.g.

A:你好吗? How are you?
B:我很好,谢谢,你呢? I'm fine. Thank you. And you?
A:我也不错。 Not bad.

呢 can be also used in a sentence to indicate an action in progress. It is usually used with 正在 / 正 / 在; however, these can also be omitted from the sentence, e.g.

a 我正在做作业呢。 I am doing homework.
b 我吃饭呢。 I am eating.

3 The particle 了 is often used at the end of a sentence indicating a change of status or the completion of an event, e.g.

a 人多了。 There are more people now.
b 他老了。 He is getting older.

Cambridge IGCSE Mandarin as a Foreign Language

二 听力（一）
2 🔊 Listening (1)

qǐng tīng xià miàn de lù yīn. xuǎn zé zhèng què de dá àn huí
请听下面的录音。选择正确的答案回
dá wèn tí
答问题。

Listen to the recording and choose the correct answers.
CD 01, Track 13

xiǎo yīng zǎo fàn chī shén me
1 小英早饭吃什么？
　　guǒ zhī　　　　miàn bāo　　　　miàn tiáo
　A 果汁　　B 面包　　C 面条

zhāng lǎo shī wǔ fàn hē shén me
2 张老师午饭喝什么？
　　guǒ zhī　　　suān là tāng　　　chéng zi zhī
　A 果汁　　B 酸辣汤　　C 橙子汁

Tiān tiān jīn wǎn xiǎng chī shén me
3 天天今晚想吃什么？
　　miàn tiáo　　　miàn bāo　　　shǔ tiáo
　A 面条　　B 面包　　C 薯条

词语 cí yǔ
VOCABULARY

1	面条	miàn tiáo	noodles
2	酸	suān	sour
3	辣	là	hot, spicy
4	汤	tāng	soup
5	酸辣汤	suān là tāng	sour and spicy soup
6	饱	bǎo	to be full (eating)
7	橙子汁	chéng zi zhī	orange juice
8	想	xiǎng	to want to
9	薯条	shǔ tiáo	chips

三 阅读（一）
3 📖 Reading (1)

yuè dú yǐ xià de wén zì, tián kòng, huí dá wèn tí yī
阅读以下的文字，填空，回答问题一
zhì wǔ
至五。

Read the following and answer each question by filling the gap. **CD 01, Track 14**

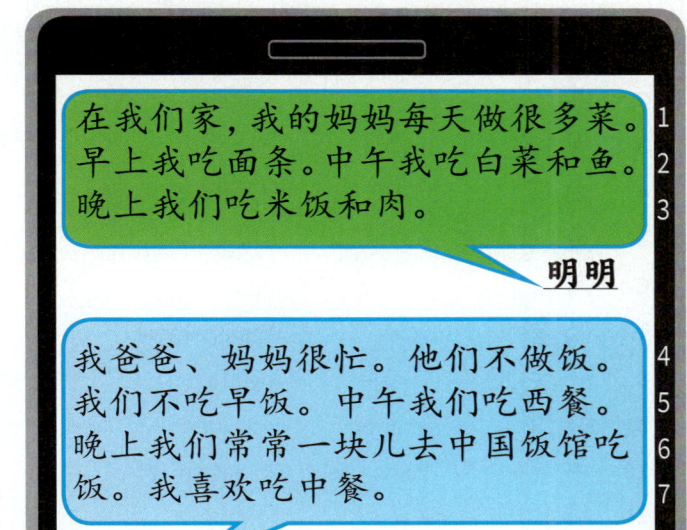

在我们家，我的妈妈每天做很多菜。　1
早上我吃面条。中午我吃白菜和鱼。　2
晚上我们吃米饭和肉。　3

明明

我爸爸、妈妈很忙。他们不做饭。　4
我们不吃早饭。中午我们吃西餐。　5
晚上我们常常一块儿去中国饭馆吃　6
饭。我喜欢吃中餐。　7

英英

我们家有时候在家吃饭，有时候在　8
饭馆吃饭。我们早上吃面包，喝牛　9
奶。中午我和弟弟吃热狗。爸爸、　10
妈妈喜欢喝咖啡，但是我们不喜欢，　11
我们觉得咖啡很苦。晚上我们吃蔬　12
菜和水果　13

美美

43

Unit A 5 Everyday activities: Eating and drinking

1 在<u>明明</u>家，_____（谁？）做饭。
2 <u>明明</u>早上吃_____（什么？）。
3 <u>英英</u>中午吃_____（什么？）。
4 _____（谁？）的爸爸妈妈喜欢喝咖啡。
5 <u>美美</u>晚上吃_____（什么？）。

cí yǔ 词语 VOCABULARY

1	餐	cān	meal
2	菜	cài	dish, vegetable
3	做饭	zuò fàn	to cook
4	白菜	bái cài	Chinese cabbage
5	鱼	yú	fish
6	肉	ròu	meat
7	西餐	xī cān	Western meal
8	一块儿	yí kuàir	together
9	饭馆	fàn guǎn	restaurant
10	中餐	Zhōng cān	Chinese meal
11	热狗	rè gǒu	hot dog
12	咖啡	kā fēi	coffee
13	苦	kǔ	bitter

bǔ chōng cí yǔ 补充词语 SUPPLEMENTARY VOCABULARY

一日三餐	yī rì sān cān	three meals a day

yǔ fǎ 语法 GRAMMAR

Use of cài 菜

菜 has different meanings, depending on context:

1 'vegetable', e.g. 我喜欢吃菜，也喜欢吃肉。
2 'dishes', e.g. 我妈妈每天做很多菜。
3 'cuisine', e.g. 中餐 can also be 中国菜.

sì　　shuō huà　 yī 四　说话（一）
4 🗨 Speaking (1)

yòng xià miàn de wèn tí cǎi fǎng liǎng wèi tóng xué　jiāng dá àn
用下面的问题采访两位同学，将答案
xiě zài biǎo gé lǐ
写在表格里。

Interview two of your classmates and record the information in the table below.

		同学一	同学二
1	nǐ jīn tiān zǎo fàn chī shén me 你今天早饭吃什么？		
2	nǐ měi tiān wǔ fàn chī shén me 你每天午饭吃什么？		
3	nǐ zài nǎr chī wǎn fàn 你在哪儿吃晚饭？		
4	nǐ xǐ huān hē shén me 你喜欢喝什么？		
5	nǐ xǐ huān chī shén me shuǐ guǒ 你喜欢吃什么水果？		

五 阅读（二）
5 Reading (2)

请阅读下面的文字，然后用中文回答问题。

Read the blog below and answer the questions in Chinese. **CD 01, Track 15**

王大朋

2016年8月30日　星期六

你好，我叫王大朋。我住在中国。这是我的博客。在这儿，我介绍两家餐厅。

一、好朋友小吃店
这个餐厅叫"好朋友小吃店"。
他们那儿有美味可口的包子和牛肉汤。
他们的包子有猪肉的、鸡肉的和羊肉的。
我觉得他们的猪肉包子很好吃。但是，
他们的牛肉汤不好喝。

二、欧美西餐厅
"欧美西餐厅"有很多好吃的点心。
我很爱吃那儿的糖果、
蛋糕和冰淇淋。
但是我不喜欢他们的饼干，不好吃。

1 王大朋觉得好朋友小吃店的猪肉包子怎么样？
2 王大朋觉得好朋友小吃店的牛肉汤怎么样？
3 在欧美西餐厅，王大朋很爱吃什么？
4 在欧美西餐厅，王大朋不爱吃什么？

cí yǔ 词语 VOCABULARY

1	这儿	zhèr	here
2	餐厅	cān tīng	canteen
3	小吃店	xiǎo chī diàn	snack bar
4	包子	bāo zi	steamed bun
5	猪肉	zhū ròu	pork; 猪 pig
6	牛肉	niú ròu	beef
7	羊肉	yáng ròu	lamb
8	好吃	hǎo chī	tasty to eat
9	咸	xián	salty
10	好喝	hǎo hē	tasty to drink
11	点心	diǎn xīn	snack, Dim Sum
12	爱吃	ài chī	to like to eat (爱 to love)
13	糖果	táng guǒ	sweets, candy
14	蛋糕	dàn gāo	cake
15	冰淇淋	bīng qí lín	ice cream; 冰 ice
16	饼干	bǐng gān	biscuit
17	怎（么）样	zěn (me) yàng	how (for opinions)

yǔ fǎ 语法 GRAMMAR

家 is a measure word for a type of establishment, e.g. 一家饭店 a restaurant.

bǔ chōng cí yǔ 补充词语 SUPPLEMENTARY VOCABULARY

1	博客	bó kè	blog
2	美味可口	měi wèi kě kǒu	delicious

wén huà 文化 CULTURE

Xiānggǎng de diǎn xīn 香港的点心 Dim Sum in Hong Kong

Xiāng gǎng de diǎn xīn yǒu   chā shāo bāo   shāo mài
香港的点心有：叉烧包、烧卖、
jiǎo zi děng děng   xīng qī tiān   rén men xǐ huān hé
饺子等等。星期天，人们喜欢和
jiā rén yì qǐ   yì biān hē chá yì biān chī diǎn
家人一起，一边喝茶一边吃点
xīn
心。

bǔ chōng cí yǔ 补充词语 SUPPLEMENTARY VOCABULARY

1	叉烧包	chā shāo bāo	barbecue pork bun
2	烧卖	shāo mai	siu mai dumplings

yǔ fǎ 语法 GRAMMAR

1 这儿 and 那儿 mean 'here' and 'there'. We can use 在 with them. We can also use 这里 and 那里, e.g.

   wǒ zài zhèr
a 我在这儿。I am here.

   zài nà lǐ   nǐ kě yǐ hé péng yǒu yì qǐ chī bīng
b 在那里，你可以和朋友一起吃冰
   qí lín
淇淋。You can eat ice cream with your friends there.

Cambridge IGCSE Mandarin as a Foreign Language

2 这儿 and 那儿 can be used with places and names of people, e.g.

    a 你们来我们这儿。 You come to our place (here).

    b 他在<u>王</u>老师那儿。 He is at Mr Wang's place (there).

句型
LANGUAGE

Question word 怎么样 is used for asking opinions, e.g.

这个餐厅怎么样？ What do you think about this restaurant?

It can also be used with 觉得……, e.g.

你觉得这个菜怎么样？ What do you think about this dish?

练习：Translate the following into Chinese, using 怎么样 in your questions.

1 What do you think about this restaurant?
2 What do you think about this movie?

小贴士
TOP TIP

When you are asked a 怎么样 question, try to add more descriptions on top of your general opinions such as 很好, 很不错 to make your answer more detailed, e.g.,

问：你觉得这块蛋糕怎么样？

答：我觉得这块蛋糕很好吃，有水果，也有糖果，我很喜欢。

六 阅读（三）
6 Reading (3)

请阅读下面的菜单，然后选择正确的答案。

Read the menu below and choose the correct answer to each question.

好朋友饭店
菜单

A 套餐一
一碗米饭、一碗鸡汤
一盘白菜、土豆和牛肉
饮料：一杯咖啡

B 套餐二
一盘面条（有虾和猪肉）
一碗羊肉汤
甜点：一盒冰淇淋

C 套餐三
一杯酸奶、一包薯条
一块汉堡包
饮料：一瓶啤酒/一瓶可乐
甜点：一块水果蛋糕

D 套餐四
一个苹果
一碗鸡蛋白菜面条汤
一瓶汽水、一包糖果

Unit A 5 Everyday activities: Eating and drinking

A 套餐一 B 套餐二 C 套餐三 D 套餐四

1 哪个套餐没有饮料？ ☐
2 <u>小王</u>喜欢吃米饭。他要哪个套餐？ ☐
3 <u>天天</u>喜欢吃西餐。他要哪个套餐？ ☐
4 <u>李亚美</u>的爸爸喜欢喝啤酒。
  他要哪个套餐？ ☐
5 哪个套餐有水果和蔬菜？ ☐

cí yǔ
词语
VOCABULARY

1	菜单	cài dān	menu
2	碗	wǎn	bowl
3	鸡	jī	chicken
4	盘	pán	plate, dish
5	土豆	tǔ dòu	potato
6	饮料	yǐn liào	beverage
7	甜	tián	sweet
8	杯	bēi	cup
9	虾	xiā	prawn, shrimp
10	盒（子）	hé (zi)	box
11	酸奶	suān nǎi	yogurt
12	包	bāo	bag, pack
13	块	kuài	piece, slice
14	汉堡包	hàn bǎo bāo	hamburger
15	瓶	píng	bottle
16	啤酒	pí jiǔ	beer; 酒 alcohol
17	可乐	kě lè	coke

bǔ chōng cí yǔ
补充词语
SUPPLEMENTARY VOCABULARY

1 套餐　tào cān　set meal
2 甜点　tián diǎn　dessert

yǔ fǎ
语法
GRAMMAR

liàng cí
量词 Measure words

包，盒，盘，碗，块，杯，瓶 are measure words indicating the shapes or containers of substances, especially food, e.g.

一包糖果 (a pack of candies), 一包薯片 (a pack of chips), 一杯水 (a cup of water), 一杯茶 (a cup of tea)

Depending on the types and shapes of containers, some nouns can be described by more than one measure word, e.g.

一瓶水 (a bottle of water), 一杯水 (a cup of water)

qī　tīng lì　(èr)
七　听力（二）
7 🔊 Listening (2)

nǐ zài xī cān tīng,　hé fú wù yuán shuō huà
你在西餐厅，和服务员说话。

You are in a Western restaurant and talking to a waitress.

qǐng tīng duì huà,　xuǎn zé zhèng què de cí yǔ tián kòng
请听对话，选择正确的词语填空。

Listen to the dialogue and choose words from the box to fill the gaps. **CD 01, Track 16**

糖	一个汉堡包	杯子	牛肉
汉堡包	冰淇淋	咖啡	牛奶

Cambridge IGCSE Mandarin as a Foreign Language

A: 你好，服务员，我要点菜。

B: 好的。菜单在这儿。你想吃什么？

A: 我要一个汉堡包和一包薯条。

B: 你要牛肉汉堡包还是鸡肉汉堡包？

A: 我要____1____。

B: 你要喝什么？我们的葡萄酒、白酒和橙子汽水很好喝。

A: 我不喜欢喝酒，也不爱喝汽水。我想喝____2____。

B: 要加糖和牛奶吗？

A: 要加____3____，不要加糖。

B: 好的。

(菜来了。 *The food is coming.*)

B: 你的菜来了。

A: 我没有____4____。

B: 对不起，我帮你拿。

A: 谢谢。

(十五分钟以后，服务员拿了一盒冰淇淋。 *15 minutes later, the waitress comes with an ice cream.*)

B: 请你来尝尝我们自己做的冰淇淋吧。

A: 谢谢你！

B: 你觉得我们的餐厅怎么样？

A: 我觉得这家餐厅不错。我很喜欢你们的____5____。你们服务员也很友好。

B: 谢谢你！请你的朋友一起来吧！

词语
VOCABULARY

1	服务员	fú wù yuán	waiter/waitress
2	点菜	diǎn cài	to order food
3	要	yào	to want
4	还是	hái shì	or
5	葡萄酒	pú táo jiǔ	wine
6	白酒	bái jiǔ	white wine
7	汽水	qì shuǐ	soft drink
8	加	jiā	to add
9	糖	táng	sugar
10	杯子	bēi zi	cup
11	帮	bāng	to help
12	拿	ná	to fetch
13	请你来	qǐng nǐ lái	to invite you to come
14	友好	yǒu hǎo	friendly

补充词语
SUPPLEMENTARY VOCABULARY

尝尝　cháng chang　to taste

Unit A 5 Everyday activities: Eating and drinking

jù xíng
句型
LANGUAGE

┌──────────────┐
│ hái shì   │
│……还是……│ means 'either …… or …… '; it is used
└──────────────┘
in questions which ask you to choose between two options.

When answering such a question, you choose one of the options.

Alternatively, 都 + Verb means both are okay, while 都 不 + Verb means neither of them.

e.g.

问：nǐ yào niú ròu hàn bǎo bāo hái shì jī ròu hàn bǎo bāo
你要牛肉汉堡包还是鸡肉汉堡包？
Do you want a beef burger or a chicken burger?

答1：wǒ yào niú ròu hàn bǎo bāo
我要牛肉汉堡包。 I want a beef burger.

答2：wǒ dōu yào
我都要。 I want both.

答3：wǒ dōu bú yào wǒ yào
我都不要。我要…… Neither of them. I want (something else).

xiǎo tiē shì
小贴士
TOP TIP

还是 means 'or' only in a question. If you want to express 'or' in a statement, you should use huò zhě 或者, which will be explained in Chapter 25.

---

bā   shuō huà   èr
八 说话（二）
8 Speaking (2)

shì yǔ tóng xué liǎng rén yì zǔ liàn xí tīng lì èr
试与同学两人一组，练习听力（二）
zhōng de duì huà
中的对话。

Work in pairs to practise the dialogue in Listening (2).

cí yǔ
词语
VOCABULARY

与 yǔ with

jiǔ   xiě zuò
九 写作
9 Writing

yī   piān páng bù shǒu
一、偏旁部首 (4)：将下面的汉字按部首分类，填入表格

1 Radicals (4): Sort the following characters by radicals.

想 错 过 欢 忙 桌 凉

	piān páng bù shǒu 偏旁部首 Radicals	yì si 意思 Meanings	hàn zì 汉字 Characters
1	冫	ice	
2	钅	metal	
3	辶	walking	
4	木	wood	
5	欠	to owe	
6	忄	emotion	
7	心	heart	

CAMBRIDGE IGCSE Mandarin as a Foreign Language

二、请读一读下面的"食评",然后给一个餐馆写一个"食评"。

2 Read the food reviews below then write your own review for a restaurant.

大为 ★★★★★ 味道3（很好吃） 环境3（很好） 服务员4（非常好）

吃的人很多，就是牛肉面很不好吃。

喜欢的菜：鸡肉汉堡包

08-30 小王的饭店点评　　　　　　　　　　赞 ｜ 回应 ｜ 收藏 ｜ 不当内容

黄一心 ★★★★☆ 味道1（不好吃） 环境3（很好） 服务员3（不错）

以前听说很不错，但其实一般，很多菜很咸，吃了以后觉得口渴。以后不会去了。

喜欢的菜：没有

08-29 小王的饭店点评　　　　　　　　　　赞 ｜ 回应 ｜ 收藏 ｜ 不当内容

词语 VOCABULARY

| 口渴 | kǒu kě | thirsty; same as 渴 |

补充词语 SUPPLEMENTARY VOCABULARY

1	食评	shí píng	food review
2	新鲜	xīn xiān	fresh
3	味道	wèi dào	taste, flavour
4	就是	jiù shì	just, only

考试练习题
Exam-style question

说话
🗨 Speaking

情景对话

Role play

A 老师：你的中国朋友

B 你：在中国学习的学生

情景：你在中国。你第一次和你的中国朋友见面。你们谈在中国的生活。

Scenario: You are in China. You are meeting your Chinese friend for the first time. You are talking about life in China.

A1: 你是哪国人？

A2: 现在你住在哪儿？

A3: 你每天几点上课？几点下课？

A4: 不上课的时候，你有什么爱好？

A5: 你觉得中国菜怎么样？

Unit A 5 Everyday activities: Eating and drinking

zì wǒ píng gū
自我评估
Self-Assessment

- ☐ I know food and drink vocabulary
- ☐ I can read menus in a restaurant
- ☐ I can order food in a restaurant
- ☐ I understand how to use 这儿 / 那儿 to indicate positions
- ☐ I can understand questions with 怎么样 and express my opinions about food
- ☐ I can write a food review to describe and comment on a restaurant
- ☐ I understand the use of measure words 包，盒，盘，碗，块，杯 and 瓶
- ☐ I understand the uses of particles 吧，呢 and 了
- ☐ I understand how to use the sentence structure ……还是……and how to answer such questions

B Personal and social life

个人与社会

gè rén yǔ shè huì

jiàn kāng yǔ yùn dòng
健康与运动
6 Health and fitness

Learning objectives

This unit will concentrate on learning vocabulary about health and fitness. You will:

- Understand the key vocabulary for body parts
- Read and write sick leave notes
- Talk about how well/unwell you feel and your symptoms to a doctor
- Describe appearances

In addition, you are going to learn:

- Use of the verbal measure word 次
- Adverbs for frequency 常常, 总是, 经常
- Question word 怎么（了）/ 怎么样
- The sentence structure 又……又……

学习目标

本单元，你会：

- 学习"身体部位"的词语
- 读和写病假条
- 和医生讨论你的病情
- 描述一个人的外貌

你还会学到：

- 动量词"次"的用法
- 频度副词"常常"、"总是"、"经常"
- 疑问词"怎么（了）/ 怎么样"
- 句型"又……又……"的用法

Cambridge IGCSE Mandarin as a Foreign Language

一 温故知新
1 'Before starting' activities

一、标出下面的身体部位。

1 Label the body parts.

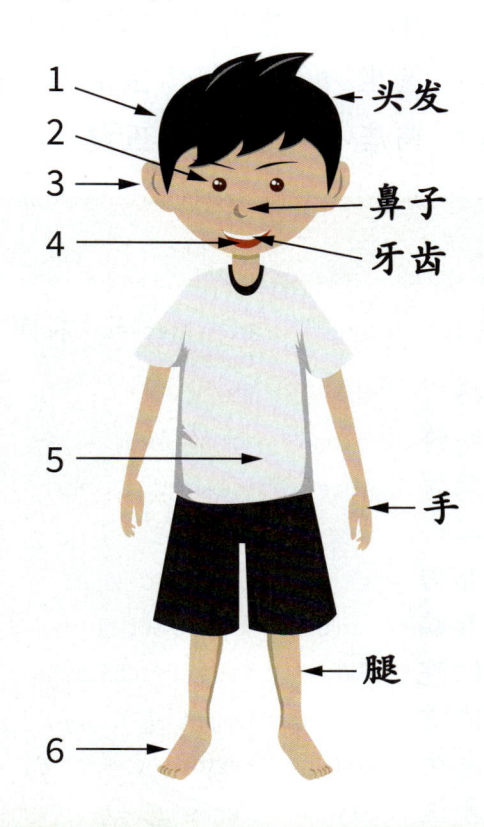

1 → 头发
2
3
4 → 牙齿
   → 鼻子
5 → 手
6 → 腿

词语
VOCABULARY

1	手	shǒu	hand
2	头	tóu	head
3	眼睛	yǎn jing	eye
4	牙齿	yá chǐ	tooth
5	耳朵	ěr duo	ear
6	鼻子	bí zi	nose
7	嘴	zuǐ	mouth
8	腿	tuǐ	leg
9	头发	tóu fa	hair (on the head)
10	肚子	dù zi	tummy, stomach
11	脚	jiǎo	foot

二、读下面的词，哪些对身体好？哪些对身体不好？

2 Read the words below. Which are good for your health? Which are bad for your health?

| A 吸烟 | B 跑步 | C 游泳 | D 晚睡晚起 |
| E 运动 | F 不吃早饭 | G 饭前洗手 |

对身体好	对身体不好
B 跑步	A 吸烟

词语
VOCABULARY

1	吸烟	xī yān	smoking
2	身体	shēn tǐ	body
3	对……好 / 不好	duì……hǎo/ bù hǎo	good/not good to/for…

延伸活动
AIM HIGHER

你还知道哪些活动对身体好吗？试和同学讨论一下。

What other activities do you know that are good for your health? Discuss with your classmates.

Unit B 6 Personal and social life: Health and fitness

文化 CULTURE

饭后百步走，活到九十九

中国人常常说："饭后百步走，活到九十九。"意思是，吃完饭以后去散步，锻炼身体，对身体好。中国人喜欢吃完晚饭以后，和家人到公园一边散步，一边聊天。真开心！

词语 VOCABULARY

1	散步	sàn bù	to stroll, to walk
2	到	dào	to go to
3	公园	gōng yuán	park
4	真	zhēn	really, true

补充词语 SUPPLEMENTARY VOCABULARY

1	饭后百步走，活到九十九	fàn hòu bǎi bù zǒu, huó dào jiǔ shí jiǔ	'Take a walk after dinner, live to ninety-nine'
2	锻炼身体	duàn liàn shēn tǐ	to do exercise
3	聊天	liáo tiān	to chat
4	开心	kāi xīn	happy

三、选出不同类的词。

3 In each question, select the odd one out.

1 A 头   B 手   C 病   D 腿
2 A 发烧 B 头发 C 感冒 D 牙疼
3 A 开刀 B 看病 C 住院 D 体重
4 A 医生 B 牙医 C 医院 D 西医
5 A 药店 B 药房 C 医院 D 医生

词语 VOCABULARY

1	同	tóng	to be the same (不同 not the same)
2	病	bìng	ill
3	发烧	fā shāo	to have fever
4	感冒	gǎn mào	to catch a cold, flu
5	疼	téng	pain
6	开刀	kāi dāo	operation
7	看病	kàn bìng	to see a doctor
8	住院	zhù yuàn	to be hospitalised
9	体重	tǐ zhòng	weight; 重 heavy
10	医生	yī sheng	doctor
11	牙医	yá yī	dentist
12	医院	yī yuàn	hospital
13	西医	xī yī	(doctor of) Western medicine
14	药店	yào diàn	pharmacy
15	药房	yào fáng	= 药店

四、看图，选择正确的词语，完成句子。

4 Look at each picture and choose the correct word to complete the sentence.

| A 高 | B 矮 | C 胖 | D 瘦 | E 长 | F 短 |

Cambridge IGCSE Mandarin as a Foreign Language

他很_____1_____。  她很_____2_____。
她的头发很_____3_____。

他很_____4_____。  她很_____5_____。
她的头发很_____6_____。

二 听力（一）
2 🔊 Listening (1)

王明生病了，他要打电话给护士预约看病。请听下面的录音，选择正确的答案回答问题。

Wang Ming is sick and he is calling to a nurse to make an appointment. Listen to the recording and choose the correct answers. **CD 01, Track 17**

护士：喂，你好。马力医院。
王明：喂，你好。我想看 1(**A** 王医生 **B** 李医生)。
护士：你叫什么名字？
王明：我叫王明。
护士：请问你的生日是几月几号？
王明：我的生日是二零零一年 2(**A** 八月十日 **B** 十月八日)。
护士：你哪儿不舒服？
王明：我感冒了，3(**A** 头疼 **B** 发烧)，嗓子疼。
护士：你想什么时候来？
王明：____4(**A** 星期一 **B** 星期五)____ 上午，可以吗？
护士：好的，上午 5(**A** 十点半 **B** 十点)。
王明：好的，谢谢你。再见。
护士：再见。

词语 VOCABULARY

1	矮	ǎi	short (height)
2	胖	pàng	fat
3	瘦	shòu	slim
4	长	cháng	long
5	短	duǎn	short (length)

句型 LANGUAGE

We learnt some stative verbs in Chapter 1. In this chapter, we learn more of them, including 矮, 胖, 瘦, 长, 短 etc.

As we mentioned in Chapter 1, when using a declarative sentence Subject ＋很 (hěn) ＋ Stative Verb, to negate the sentence just replace 很 with 不. 是 should NOT be used in such sentences.

e.g. **a** 他很高。He is tall.
　　b 她不胖。She's not fat.

词语 VOCABULARY

1	生病	shēng bìng	to get sick
2	打电话	dǎ diàn huà	to make a phone call; 电话 telephone
3	给	gěi	to give
4	护士	hù shi	nurse
5	喂	wéi	hello (for starting telephone conversation)
6	舒服	shū fu	comfortable; 不舒服 to not feel well/be under the weather
7	嗓子	sǎng zi	throat
8	可以	kě yǐ	can

57

Unit B 6 Personal and social life: Health and fitness

补充词语
SUPPLEMENTARY VOCABULARY

预约　yù yuē　to make an appointment, to book

小贴士
TOP TIP

"打篮球"、"打电话"

The verb 打, which literally means 'to hit', is used in various contexts with different meanings, e.g. 打篮球 means 'to play basketball' while 打电话 is 'to make a phone call'. These expressions are fixed, so do not misunderstand them as 'to hit a basketball' or 'to hit the phone'!

三　说话（一）
3　Speaking (1)

试与同学两人一组，练习听力（一）中的对话。

Work in pairs to act out the dialogue in Listening (1).

延伸活动
AIM HIGHER

Replace 感冒 with another symptom, e.g. 牙疼, 头疼, 肚子疼, and complete the dialogue.

好词好句
USEFUL EXPRESSIONS

- 我肚子疼，不想吃饭。
- 我牙疼，很不舒服。
- 我想看医生。

四　阅读（一）
4　Reading (1)

阅读以下的对话，然后回答问题。

Read the following dialogue, then answer the questions.
CD 01, Track 18

王明在医院看病。

A 李医生　B 王明

A: 你哪儿不舒服？

B: 我发烧，头疼，嗓子也疼。

A: 你什么时候开始不舒服？

B: 昨天下午。

A: 你睡觉睡得好吗？

B: 昨天晚上睡得不好。我咳嗽。

A: 你感冒了。要多喝水，多休息，少说话。

B: 我要打针吗？

A: 对，你要打针。也要吃药。这是你的药。一天吃三次。

B: 谢谢医生。

A: 祝你早日康复。

Cambridge IGCSE Mandarin as a Foreign Language

1 <u>王明</u>怎么了？
2 他什么时候开始不舒服？
3 他睡觉睡得好吗？
4 他要打针吗？
5 他一天要吃几次药？

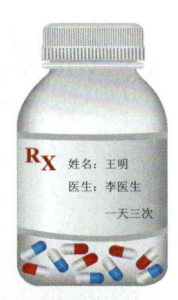

词语
VOCABULARY

1	咳嗽	ké sou	to cough
2	多	duō	many, more
3	少	shǎo	few, fewer, little, less (amount of)
4	打针	dǎ zhēn	injection
5	吃药	chī yào	to take medicine
6	药	yào	medicine
7	次	cì	time
8	怎么了	zěn me le	what happened

补充词语
SUPPLEMENTARY VOCABULARY

早日康复　zǎo rì kāng fù　get better soon

语法
GRAMMAR

1 次 is a verbal measure word. Verb + Number + 次 is used to indicate the frequency of an action, e.g.
   a 一天吃三次 eat three times a day
   b 我去了两次 I've been there twice

2 多 and 少 are opposite words meaning 'more' and 'less'. 多 + action is a pattern used to advise doing an action more, while 少 + action is to advise doing something less, e.g.
   a 多喝水。Drink more water.
   b 多看书。Read more.
   c 少说话。Speak less.
   d 少看电视。Watch less TV.

Note: when using this pattern, be mindful that 多 and 少 should be ALWAYS come **before** the actions.

句型
LANGUAGE

Question words 怎么了 / 怎么样

Both can be used when asking 'how' and to show concern for something or someone.

e.g. 你怎么了 / 怎么样？ What's wrong with you? What happened to you?

Note: 怎么样 can also be used when asking for one's opinions. But 怎么了 cannot be used in that case.

五　写作（一）
5　Writing (1)

填空，帮助<u>王明</u>完成病假条。
Fill in the gaps to help Wang Ming complete a sick leave email.

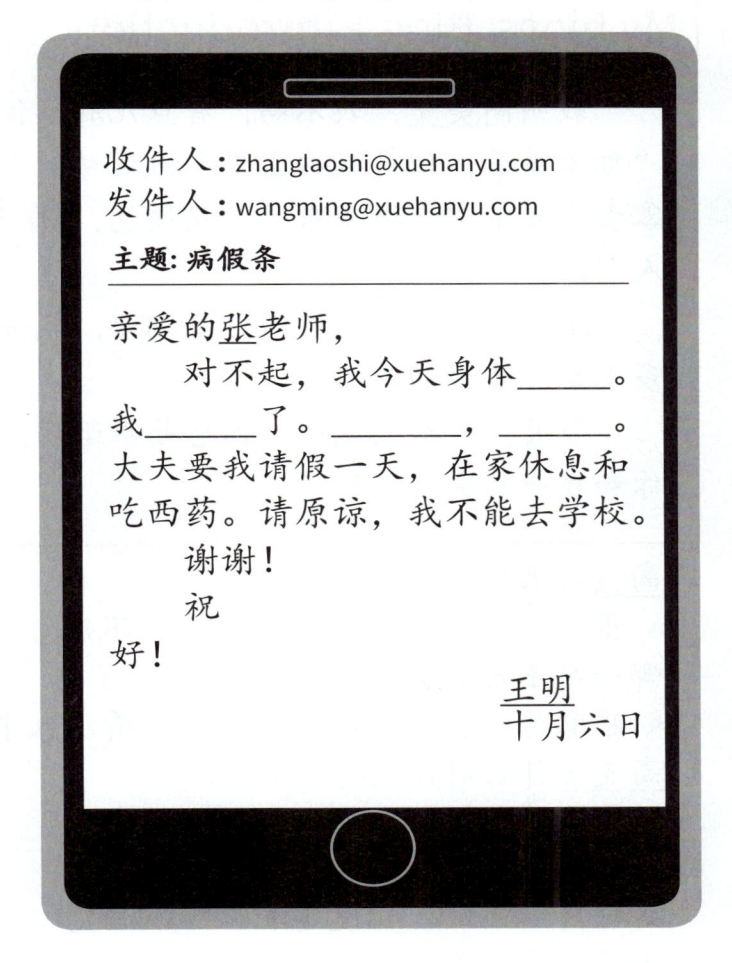

收件人：zhanglaoshi@xuehanyu.com
发件人：wangming@xuehanyu.com

主题：病假条

亲爱的<u>张</u>老师，
　　对不起，我今天身体＿＿＿＿。
我＿＿＿＿了。＿＿＿＿＿，＿＿＿＿。
大夫要我请假一天，在家休息和吃西药。请原谅，我不能去学校。
　　谢谢！
　　祝
好！
　　　　　　　　　　<u>王明</u>
　　　　　　　　　　十月六日

Unit B　6　Personal and social life: Health and fitness

词语
VOCABULARY

1 帮助　bāng zhù　to help
2 大夫　dài fu　doctor (more colloquial than 医生)
3 原谅　yuán liàng　to forgive
4 西药　xī yào　Western medicine

补充词语
SUPPLEMENTARY VOCABULARY

1 收件人　shōu jiàn rén　recipient
2 发件人　fā jiàn rén　sender
3 主题　zhǔ tí　subject, topic
4 病假条　bìng jià tiáo　sick note
5 请假　qǐng jià　to ask for leave

六 阅读（二）
6 Reading (2)

请阅读下面的文字，然后选择正确的答案。
Read the text below and choose the correct answers. CD 01, Track 19

Blogger

My blogs　Blog > introduction

　　我叫高美美，我不高，有点儿胖，但是我觉得自己不难看。妈妈常常说："你不难看，但是我希望你多做运动。"可是，我不爱运动，我的爱好是吃零食。我常常吃很多东西：汉堡包，薯条，蛋糕……我也喜欢睡觉和看小人书。

　　上个星期五，我胃疼。星期六，我去看医生。医生说："你要少吃零食，多喝水，多运动。"

　　今天，爸爸也说："你总是不运动，又经常吃零食，对身体不好，明天你和我一起去爬山！"

1 高美美长什么样？
　A 很高　　B 不美　　C 不瘦　　D 很瘦
2 哪一个不是高美美的爱好？
　A 睡觉　　B 运动　　C 看小人书　D 吃零食
3 高美美什么时候觉得不舒服？
　A 上个星期五　B 星期六　C 今天　D 昨天
4 医生要高美美做什么？
　A 吃药　　B 吃零食　　C 睡觉　　D 运动
5 爸爸要高美美做什么？
　A 吃汉堡包　B 睡觉　　C 爬山　　D 玩电脑游戏

Cambridge IGCSE Mandarin as a Foreign Language

词语
VOCABULARY

1	美	měi	beautiful, pretty
2	难看	nán kàn	not good looking, ugly
3	胃	wèi	stomach
4	上个星期	shàng gè xīng qī	last week
5	健康	jiàn kāng	health, healthy
6	希望	xī wàng	to hope
7	经常	jīng cháng	often
8	长	zhǎng	to grow

补充词语
SUPPLEMENTARY VOCABULARY

1	零食	líng shí	snack
2	丑	chǒu	ugly

句型
LANGUAGE

1 长什么样 is used to ask about someone's appearance,

e.g. 高美美长什么样？ What does Gao Meimei look like?

2 又……又…… (yòu…yòu…) is a sentence structure indicating two similar properties about a subject. 又 must be followed by an adjective or a verb.

e.g.
a 我又矮又胖。I am both short and fat.
b 妹妹又唱歌又跳舞，很高兴。My sister is singing and dancing happily.

语法
GRAMMAR

1 常常, 总是 and 经常 are adverbs describing frequency. They should be placed before verbs.

e.g.
a 我常常吃很多东西。I often eat a lot.
b 你总是玩电脑游戏。You always play computer games.
c 经常吃汉堡包对身体不好。Eating burgers often is bad for your health.

练习：Translate the sentences into Chinese, using the sentence structures given in the brackets.

1 My elder brother is both tall and slim. (又……又……)
2 Swimming is both healthy and fun. (又……又……)
3 I often get sick. (常常/经常)
4 What does your elder brother look like? (长什么样？)
5 My mum always said that doing sports is good for health. (总是)

小贴士
TOP TIP

Using adverbs indicating frequency in your writing will help you express your ideas more clearly and precisely.

七 阅读（三）
7 Reading (3)

一、请阅读下面的文字，选择正确的句子，完成对话。

1 Read the text below, and choose the correct sentence to complete the dialogue.

情景：刘山的手指受伤了，流血，很疼。他打电话叫救护车。

Scenario: Liu Shan has injured his finger and it is bleeding and hurts. He is calling for an ambulance.

Unit B 6 Personal and social life: Health and fitness

A 医生   B 刘山

A	我的手疼了一天了。
B	我的手指受伤了。
C	请你帮助我。我想叫救护车。
D	我的手指非常疼。流血。
E	我打篮球受伤的。

A1: 你好，这里是112急救中心。　　B1: ___1___
A2: 你怎么了？　　B2: ___2___
A3: 你的手指疼吗？流血吗？　　B3: ___3___
A4: 你怎么受伤的？　　B4: ___4___
A5: 疼了多长时间了？　　B5: ___5___
A6: 救护车十分钟以后到。　　B6: 谢谢。

二、刘山在医院。下面是他的病历卡。
　　请读一读，选择"是"或"非"。

2　Liu Shan is in hospital now. Below is his hospital report. Choose 'true' or 'false' for each statement.

112急救中心病历卡

姓名：刘山　　性别：男
年龄：15岁　　生日：六月七日

看病日期：	一月七日
症状	1 手指受伤了。很严重。 2 打篮球受的伤 3 很疼 4 流血 5 要住院一天。明天可以出院。 6 吃药：五天。每天三次。 7 打针：三天

		是	非
1	刘山是女孩。	☐	☐
2	刘山的生日是一月七日。	☐	☐
3	刘山的手指受伤了。不很严重。	☐	☐
4	刘山不用开刀。	☐	☐
5	刘山要住院一天。	☐	☐

词语
VOCABULARY

1	手指	shǒu zhǐ	finger
2	受伤	shòu shāng	to get injured
3	流血	liú xuè	to bleed
4	救护车	jiù hù chē	ambulance; 车 car, see 汽车
5	严重	yán zhòng	serious, severe
6	出院	chū yuàn	to discharge from hospital

补充词语
SUPPLEMENTARY VOCABULARY

1	急救中心	jí jiù zhōng xīn	emergency centre
2	病历卡	bìng lì kǎ	hospital report
3	症状	zhèng zhuàng	symptom

八　说话（二）

8　Speaking (2)

和你的同学两人一组，练习阅读（三）的对话。

Work in pairs to practise the dialogue in Reading (3).

九 听力（二）
9 Listening (2)

李文在介绍他的女朋友。请听介绍，填表。

Li Wen is talking about his girlfriend. Listen to the introduction and complete the table. **CD 01, Track 20**

姓名	国籍	年龄	长什么样?	爱好
Zhāng xiǎo míng 张小明	1	2	3	4

词语 VOCABULARY

1	年轻	nián qīng	young
2	皮肤	pí fū	skin
3	漂亮	piào liang	beautiful
4	心	xīn	heart

补充词语 SUPPLEMENTARY VOCABULARY

爱心　ài xīn　love, kindness

小贴士 TOP TIP

长 has two pronunciations with different meanings.

1 When it is pronounced '**zhǎng**', it is a verb and means 'to grow' or 'to look like', e.g.

你的姐姐长什么样？ What does your elder sister look like?

我的妈妈长得很好看。 My mum looks pretty.

2 When it is pronounced '**cháng**', it is an adjective meaning 'long', e.g.

她的头发很长。 Her hair is long.

十 写作（二）
10 Writing (2)

一、偏旁部首 (5)：将下面的汉字按部首分类，填入表格。

1 Radicals (5): Sort the following characters by radicals.

床　病　花　疼　坏　碗　糕　饭　糖

	piān páng bù shǒu 偏旁部首 Radicals	yì si 意思 Meanings	hàn zì 汉字 Characters
1	疒	disease	____ , ____
2	米	rice	____
3	石	stone	____
4	艹	grass	____
5	饣	food	____
6	土	earth	____
7	广	dotted cliff	____

二、给你的博客写一个自我介绍，谈谈：

2 Write a self-introduction for your blog. You should talk about:

1 你叫什么名字？
2 你是哪国人？
3 你长什么样？
4 你有什么爱好？
5 你家有几口人？他们长什么样？

好词好句 USEFUL EXPRESSIONS

To respond to the question 长什么样? you can use sentences like the following ones:

a 我又高又瘦。
b 我有大大的眼睛，高高的鼻子，长长的头发。

Unit B 6 Personal and social life: Health and fitness

自我评估
Self-Assessment

- [ ] I understand the key vocabulary for body parts
- [ ] I can read and write sick leave notes
- [ ] I can talk about my symptoms and how well/unwell I feel to a doctor
- [ ] I can describe a person's appearance
- [ ] Use of measure word 次
- [ ] Adverbs for frequency 常常，总是，经常
- [ ] Use of question word 怎么（了）/ 怎么样
- [ ] Sentence structure 又……又……

jiā jū shēng huó

家居生活
7 Home life

Learning objectives

This unit will concentrate on learning vocabulary relating to houses, furniture and household appliances. You will:

- Learn key vocabulary for houses, furniture and household appliances

- Understand the use of 有 in a sentence

- Use localisers, e.g. 左边, 上边, to describe location by using the two sentence structures subject 在 + localiser and A 在 B（的）+ localiser

In addition, you are going to learn:

- Measure words 朵，棵，张，台，部

- The reduplication of verbs, e.g. 看看，听听

学习目标

本单元，你会：

- 学习关于房子、家具、家用电器的词语

- 明白"有"在句子中的用法

- 使用方位词和句型 subject 在 + localiser 和 A 在 B（的）+ localiser 描述方位

你还会学到：

- 量词：朵、棵、张、台、部

- 动词叠用：看看、听听……

Unit B 7 Personal and social life: Home life

一 温故知新

1 'Before starting' activities

一、这是林英爱家的房子。请标出下面房间的名称。

1 This is Lin Ying Ai's home. Label the rooms using the words provided in the Vocabulary boxes.

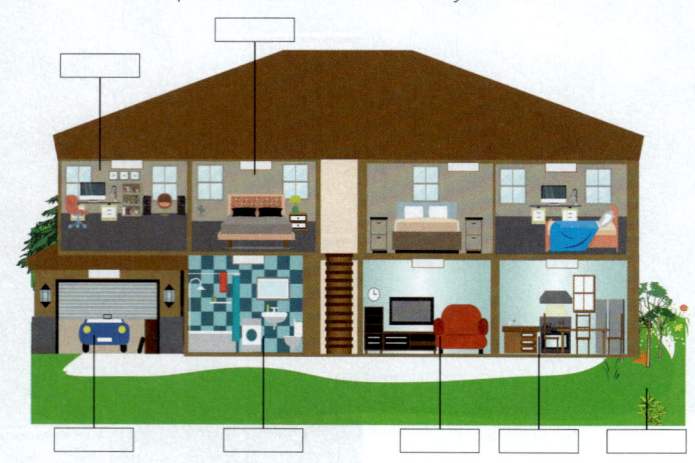

词语
VOCABULARY

1	房子	fáng zi	house
2	房间	fáng jiān	room
3	厨房	chú fáng	kitchen
4	花园	huā yuán	garden
5	车房	chē fáng	garage
6	厕所	cè suǒ	toilet
7	客厅	kè tīng	living room
8	书房	shū fáng	study room

补充词语
SUPPLEMENTARY VOCABULARY

| 卧室 | wò shì | bedroom |

二、林英爱一家人在说他们星期五晚上要做什么。请读下面的句子，他们应该在哪儿做这些活动？请填空。

2 Lin Ying Ai and her family are talking about what they are going to do on Friday evening. Read the text and complete the sentences to say where they can go for the activities.

1 妈妈：

> 我在做饭。

妈妈在_____做饭。

2 爸爸：

> 我想看看电视。

爸爸可以去_____看电视。

3 哥哥：

> 我想看看书。

哥哥可以去_____看书。

4 爷爷：

> 我想种种花儿。

爷爷可以去_____种花儿。

5 我：

> 我想听听音乐，唱唱歌。

我可以去_____听音乐，唱歌。

Cambridge IGCSE Mandarin as a Foreign Language

词语
VOCABULARY

1. 花儿 huār flower
2. 种 zhòng to plant

语法
GRAMMAR

Reduplication of verbs

In Chinese, some one-syllable verbs such as 看, 听, 想, 说, 讲, 写 can be reduplicated to express the meaning of attempting to do something or doing something casually, e.g.

a 看看书 do some reading casually
b 看看电视 watching TV casually
c 听听音乐 listen to music casually

三、选择正确的量词完成句子。

3 Read the uses of the measure words in the grammar box, then choose the most appropriate one for the following phrases.

1 一____花儿   2 三____桌子
3 那____树   4 这____床
5 哪____电影   6 几____电脑

语法
GRAMMAR

duǒ 朵	for flowers	kē 棵	for plants, e.g. trees
zhāng 张	for flat things, such as tables, beds, and sheets of paper	tái 台	for machines
bù 部	for series of books, films, machines and cars		

词语
VOCABULARY

1 桌子 zhuō zi table
2 树 shù tree
3 床 chuáng bed
4 电脑 diàn nǎo computer

二 阅读（一）
2 Reading (1)

读下面的一段话，完成活动一和活动二。

Read the paragraph and complete Activities 1 and 2.
CD 01, Track 21

我的家
2016年9月1日 21:03

1 我叫林小。我的家住在一幢三
2 十层楼高的单元房里。我家很干净。
3 不大不小，六十平方米左右，三室
4 一厅。一进门，厨房在右边，洗手
5 间在左边。阳台在客厅的外边。一
6 间大卧室是爸爸妈妈的，里边有一
7 张大床和一个大衣柜。床的前边有
8 一台电视机。还有一间大卧室是哥
9 哥的，里边也有一个大衣柜。衣柜
10 旁边有一张书桌，哥哥在这张桌子
11 上写作业。桌子的下边有一个收音
12 机，但是收音机坏了。我的小卧室
13 在中间。我的卧室里面只有一张床，
14 妈妈说我的床像"狗窝"，因为很
15 乱。

Unit B 7 Personal and social life: Home life

词语
VOCABULARY

1	层	céng	floor, level
2	楼	lóu	building
3	单元	dān yuán	unit
4	干净	gān jìng	clean
5	进	jìn	to enter
6	门	mén	door
7	右边	yòu biān	right
8	左边	zuǒ bian	left
9	外边	wài bian	outside
10	前边	qián bian	front
11	间	jiān	measure word for rooms
12	里边	lǐ bian	inside
13	电视机	diàn shì jī	TV
14	旁边	páng bian	adjacent, side
15	收音机	shōu yīn jī	radio
16	坏	huài	broken
17	中间	zhōng jiān	between, centre
18	只有	zhǐ yǒu	only
19	乱	luàn	messy; disorder
20	后面	hòu mian	behind
21	上边	shàng bian	over/above
22	下边	xià bian	below/under

补充词语
SUPPLEMENTARY VOCABULARY

1	平方米	píng fāng mǐ	square metre
2	左右	zuǒ yòu	approximately
3	三室一厅	sān shì yì tīng	three bedrooms and one living room
4	狗窝	gǒu wō	kennel

一、回答问题。

1 Answer the questions.

1 厨房在哪儿?
2 客厅的外面是什么?
3 电视机在谁的房间?
4 收音机怎么了?
5 小卧室是谁的?

词语
VOCABULARY

谁的   shuí de   whose

二、选择正确的答案

2 Choose the correct answer.

1 <u>林小</u>住的那幢楼有多少层?
   A 30 **B** 13 **C** 15 **D** 50

2 <u>林小</u>的家怎么样?
   A 很大 **B** 很小 **C** 不大不小
   D 不干净

3 <u>林小</u>的家有几间卧室?
   A 2 **B** 3 **C** 1

4 <u>林小</u>的卧室怎么样?
   A 很大 **B** 很乱 **C** 不大不小
   D 干净

语法
GRAMMAR

方位词 Localisers

Localisers are words indicating locations or directions. The most common localisers are:

前边/面 in front of	后边/面 behind	左边/面 left	右边/面 right	旁边 next to
上边/面 over/above	下边/面 under	里边/面 in(side)	外边/面 outside	中间 between	对面 across from

Cambridge IGCSE Mandarin as a Foreign Language

练习：Match the Chinese with the English.

1. on the table
2. under the table
3. in the kitchen
4. next to my bedroom
5. to the left of the bathroom
6. outside of the house

A 桌子上
B 房子外
C 卫生间的左边
D 厨房里
E 桌子下
F 我卧室旁边

词语 VOCABULARY

卫生间　wèi shēng jiān　bathroom

句型 LANGUAGE

1. Subject 在 + Localiser indicates the location of the subject.

2. A 在 B（的）+ Localiser indicates the location of A with respect to a reference, B.

   Note: 的 can be omitted from the sentence. For localisers 里边, 外边, 上边, 下边, 旁边, the 边 can be omitted. In such cases, 的 should not be written in the sentence.

3. Place + Localiser 有 + Object indicates the presence of the object at the location. The most common translation is 'there is' or 'there are'.

练习：Follow the examples and fill in the gaps to translate the sentences.

Subject	在	Localiser	Meaning
厨房	在	右边。	The kitchen is on the right.
洗手间	1	2	The toilet is on the left.

A	在	B	（的）Localiser	Meaning
阳台	在	客厅	（的）外边。	The balcony is outside the living room.
电视机	在	3	4	The TV set is on the table.

Place	Localiser	有	Object	Meaning
书房	里（边）	有	一张书桌。	There is a desk in the study.
厨房	5	有	6	There is a washing machine in the kitchen.
客厅	7			There are a table, a sofa and a TV in the living room.
8				There are many books on the shelf.

三　听力（一）
3　Listening (1)

马小天和朋友在说他家的房子。请听录音，填表。

Ma Xiaotian is talking about his house with his friend. Listen to the recording and fill in the table. **CD 01, Track 22**

1 客厅里有什么？	2 厨房里有什么？	3 书房里有什么？	4 马小天的卧室里有什么？	5 爸爸妈妈的卧室里有什么？
例：一张沙发，……				

Unit B　7　Personal and social life: Home life

词语
VOCABULARY

1	沙发	shā fā	sofa
2	椅子	yǐ zi	chair
3	冰箱	bīng xiāng	fridge
4	洗衣机	xǐ yī jī	washing machine
5	书架	shū jià	book shelf
6	台灯	tái dēng	reading lamp
7	书桌	shū zhuō	desk
8	梳子	shū zi	comb
9	衣柜	yī guì	wardrobe

A5: 你爸爸妈妈的卧室里有书桌吗?

B5: _____

小贴士
TOP TIP

1 In a 有 sentence, 边 can be omitted.
2 As you know, the negative of a 有 sentence is 没有. However, if you mean that there isn't a washing machine in the kitchen, rather than saying 厨房里没有一台洗衣机, you should say 厨房里没有洗衣机. That is, the measure word should NOT be used when talking about the absence of something.

四 说话 (一)
4 Speaking (1)

假设你是马小天,你的同学是你的朋友。两人一组,根据听力(一)完成下面的问答。

Pretend that you are Ma Xiaotian and your classmate is your friend. Work in pairs, according to the table in Listening (1), and complete the dialogue.

A 朋友　B 马小天

A1: 洗衣机在哪儿?
B1: _____

A2: 客厅里有什么?
B2: _____

A3: 书房里有什么?
B3: _____

A4: 你的卧室里有衣柜吗?
B4: _____

五 写作 (一)
5 Writing (1)

按照下面的结构,写一段话,介绍你家的房子。

Use the structure provided to write a paragraph introducing where you live.

我的家有_____口人,他们是 _____。我们家住在_____(平房/公寓/楼房)。我家的房子_____(不大不小/很小/很大/很宽敞/很干净),有_____个房间。一进门,_____在(左边/右边/前边)。_____在_____的_____边。_____上有_____。……每天晚上,爸爸在客厅_____。我在_____(a room) _____ (activity)……

我很喜欢我家的房子,因为_____。/ 我不喜欢我家的房子,因为_____。

1
2
3
4
5
6
7
8
9
10
11
12
13

Cambridge IGCSE Mandarin as a Foreign Language

词语
VOCABULARY

平房　píng fáng　bungalow; 平 flat

补充词语
SUPPLEMENTARY VOCABULARY

1　楼房　lóu fáng　building
2　公寓　gōng yù　apartment
3　宽敞　kuān chǎng　spacious

好词好句
USEFUL EXPRESSIONS

- 我们家的房子很宽敞。
- 一进门，客厅在左边，厨房在右边。
- 我不喜欢我家的房子，因为我觉得太小了。

文化
CULTURE

There are generally three types of houses in China: 公寓, 楼房 and 平房. In cities, most people live in 公寓, which tend to be more and more in high-rises. 楼房 are houses usually seen in the countryside. There are usually two or three floors in a 楼房. 平房 can be found in some rural areas where the population is low.

公寓

楼房

平房

六　阅读（二）
6　Reading (2)

请阅读下面的租房广告，然后选择正确的答案。
Read the renting advertisements below and choose the correct answers. **CD 01, Track 23**

租房广告 A
1
三十层，公寓，有电梯　　　　　　2
两房一厅，客厅里有卫星电视　　　3
一个洗手间　　　　　　　　　　　4
家具有：床、电视、冰箱　　　　　5
在大有街的中心，买东西很方便　　6

租房广告 B
7
平房　　　　　　　　　　　　　　8
一个大客厅，一个卧室，一个花园　9
厨房里有洗衣机　　　　　　　　　10
家具有桌子、椅子和沙发　　　　　11
房子旁边是公园路。公园路上有很多 12
饭店　　　　　　　　　　　　　　13
很热闹，方便　　　　　　　　　　14

租房广告 C
15
两层楼房，有车房　　　　　　　　16
一楼有一个大客厅和一个饭厅，一个 17
洗手间　　　　　　　　　　　　　18
二楼有四个卧室，两个洗手间　　　19
门口有一个小花园　　　　　　　　20
没有家具，但是有空调和暖气　　　21
不在大街旁边，很干净和安静　　　22

71

Unit B　7　Personal and social life: Home life

词语
VOCABULARY

1	电梯	diàn tī	lift, escalator
2	街	jiē	street
3	中心	zhōng xīn	centre
4	路	lù	road
5	家具	jiā jù	furniture
6	卫星电视	wèi xīng diàn shì	satellite TV
7	买东西	mǎi dōng xi	to shop, to buy something
8	饭厅	fàn tīng	dining room
9	门口	mén kǒu	entrance, doorway
10	空调	kōng tiáo	air-conditioner
11	暖气	nuǎn qì	heating
12	安静	ān jìng	quiet
13	方便	fāng biàn	convenient

补充词语
SUPPLEMENTARY VOCABULARY

1	租	zū	to rent
2	租房	zū fáng	to rent a flat
3	两房一厅	liǎng fáng yì tīng	two bedrooms, one living room
4	适合	shì hé	suitable

读下面三个人的租房要求，看看哪一个广告适合他们。

Read the requirements each person has and choose which advertisement is most suitable for them.

1 <u>张文</u>：我家有五口人。我们想租一个有花园的房子。我们想住在安静的地方。我们有车。
哪一个房子适合我？_____

2 <u>李明</u>：我家有三口人。我们不想买家具。我们喜欢看电视和买东西。
哪一个房子适合我？_____

3 <u>陈平</u>：我和丈夫想租一个有花园的房子。我们常常在饭店吃饭。我爸爸妈妈家在公园路。我们常常去爸爸、妈妈家。
哪一个房子适合我？_____

七 听力（二）
7 🎧 Listening (2)

<u>林有朋</u>搬家了。他和朋友小吴谈他的新家。请听录音，回答问题。

Lin Youpeng has moved. He is talking to his friend Xiao Wu about his new house. Listen to the recording and answer the questions. **CD 01, Track 24**

1 <u>林有朋</u>什么时候搬家了？
2 <u>林有朋</u>搬去哪儿了？
3 <u>林有朋</u>的新家怎么样？
4 <u>林有朋</u>家有阳台吗？
5 大花园在哪儿？

词语
VOCABULARY

1	搬	bān	to move
2	搬家	bān jiā	to move house
3	窗户	chuāng hu	window
4	看见	kàn jiàn	to see

八 阅读（三）
8 📖 Reading (3)

请阅读下面的信，选择唯一正确的答案，在方格里打勾（✓）。

Read the letter below, and answer the questions by ticking the appropriate box. **CD 01, Track 25**

亲爱的<u>刘音</u>：

好久不见了，你好吗？我搬家了。

我家在<u>公园路</u>中心的一个公寓里。

Cambridge IGCSE Mandarin as a Foreign Language

我们家有两个卧室，一个客厅，一个厨房，一个厕所，一个洗澡间。我爸爸、妈妈的卧室在客厅的左边。我的在客厅的右边。

　　我的卧室不大不小。一进屋子，就可以看到一张单人床。床的前面是一个大衣柜。衣柜的对面是一张书桌。书桌上有一台收音机，一个台灯和一台电脑。书桌旁边有一个书架。书架里有很多书和光盘。书桌前边有一个大窗户。窗户外边是一个大花园。

　　我很喜欢我的新家。我想请你来我家玩儿。你下个星期有时间吗？你可以来我家玩电脑游戏。我住在二十六楼，2603房，在电梯的左边。你来的时候给我打电话。

　　　　祝
　　好！

林有朋
十月十三日

		是	非
1	林有朋的新家在公园路中心的一个公寓里。	☐	☐
2	他没有自己的卧室。	☐	☐
3	大衣柜在床的后边。	☐	☐
4	书桌在衣柜的对面。	☐	☐

词语 VOCABULARY

1	洗澡间	xǐ zǎo jiān	bathroom
2	屋子	wū zi	room
3	一……就……	yī……jiù……	as soon as…
4	光盘	guāng pán	CD
5	下个星期	xià ge xīng qī	next week

补充词语 SUPPLEMENTARY VOCABULARY

| 单人床 | dān rén chuáng | single bed |

九　说话（二）
9　Speaking (2)

根据阅读（三），完成情景对话。
Complete the role play based on Reading (3).

A　林友朋　　B　刘英

情景：林有朋想请刘英去他的新家。他们在打电话。

A: 喂，你好，是刘英吗？我是林有朋。
B: 对。我是刘英。你好，有朋。
A: 我搬家了。想请你去我家。
B1: 你什么时候搬家的？
A1: _____
B2: 你家住在哪儿？
A2: _____
B3: 你家在几楼？
A3: _____
B4: 你家有几个房间？
A4: _____

Unit B　7　Personal and social life: Home life

十 写作（二）
10 Writing (2)

一、偏旁部首 (6)：将下面的汉字按部首分类，填入表格。

1. Radicals (6): Sort the following characters by radicals.

烧 矮 轻 双 房 和 胖 短

	piān páng bù shǒu 偏旁部首 Radicals	yì si 意思 Meanings	hàn zì 汉字 Characters
1	矢	arrow	_____ _____
2	火	fire	_____
3	车	car, vehicles	_____
4	又	again	_____
5	户	window	_____
6	禾	crops	_____
7	月	flesh, moon	_____

二、写一封信给你的笔友。介绍一下你的卧室。信中说一说：

2. Write a letter to your pen pal and describe your bedroom. In the letter, talk about:

1. 你的家有几个房间？
2. 你的卧室里有什么家具？
3. 你在卧室里做什么？
4. 你喜欢你的卧室吗？为什么？

词语 VOCABULARY

为什么　wèi shén me　why

好词好句 USEFUL EXPRESSIONS

- 我的卧室不大不小，四四方方，干干净净。
- 我和妹妹一起住这个卧室。
- 我喜欢我的卧室，因为这是我自己的小天地（my own space）。
- 我不喜欢我的卧室，因为太小了。

自我评估
Self-Assessment

☐ I know the basic vocabulary for houses, furniture and household appliances

☐ I can describe a house and its rooms by using the sentence structure Place ＋ Localiser 有 ＋ Object

☐ I can use localisers to describe the location of something using the two sentence structures Subject 在 ＋ Localiser and A 在 B（的）＋ Localiser

☐ Use of measure words 朵，棵，张，台，部

☐ Use of reduplication of verbs, e.g. 看看，听听

yī fu
衣服
8 Clothes

Learning objectives

This unit will concentrate on learning vocabulary about colours and clothes. You will:

- Describe a person's appearance and outfit
- Understand the units of money
- Listen to conversations in a clothes shop
- Talk about school uniforms

In addition, you are going to learn:

- Question word 什么样的
- Measure words 件，条，套，对，双
- The difference between 穿 and 戴
- Nominalising in noun phrases with 的

学习目标

本单元，你会：

- 描述一个人的外貌和穿着
- 明白表示"钱"的单位
- 听关于在服装店购物的对话
- 讨论校服

你还会学到：

- 疑问词：什么样的
- 量词：件、条、套、对、双
- "穿"和"戴"的分别
- 用"的"名词化短语

Unit B 8 Personal and social life: Clothes

一 温故知新
1 'Before starting' activities

一、这是哪一个国家的国旗？国旗上有哪些颜色？和老师、同学们讨论一下，填表。

1. What countries do these flags represent? What colours can you see in each flag? Discuss with your teacher and classmates and fill in the table.

	e.g.	1	2	3	4
国家	中国				
颜色	红色, 黄色				

词语 VOCABULARY

1. 颜色　　yán sè　　colour
2. 红（色）　hóng (sè)　red
3. 白（色）　bái (sè)　white
4. 黄（色）　huáng (sè)　yellow
5. 蓝（色）　lán (sè)　blue
6. 橙色　　chéng sè　orange
7. 黑（色）　hēi (sè)　black
8. 绿（色）　lǜ (sè)　green

补充词语 SUPPLEMENTARY VOCABULARY

国旗　guó qí　flag

延伸活动 AIM HIGHER

根据活动一，两人一组，问答。
问：**中国**国旗是什么颜色的？
答：**中国**国旗是**红色和黄色**的。
……

Replace the words in bold, and ask and answer as many questions as you can.

二、他们穿什么衣服？请你说一说。

2. What are they wearing? List the items of clothing and say them out loud.

1　张红
2　李冰
3　刘文
4　黄一心

Cambridge IGCSE Mandarin as a Foreign Language

词语
VOCABULARY

1	上衣	shàng yī	upper clothes (top, jacket)
2	大衣	dà yī	overcoat
3	衬衣	chèn yī	T-shirt
4	衬衫	chèn shān	shirt
5	鞋	xié	shoe
6	运动鞋	yùn dòng xié	trainer, sneaker
7	裤子	kù zi	trousers, pants
8	短裤	duǎn kù	shorts
9	牛仔裤	niú zǎi kù	jeans
10	裙子	qún zi	skirt
11	袜子	wà zi	sock
12	手套	shǒu tào	glove
13	围巾	wéi jīn	scarf

补充词语
SUPPLEMENTARY VOCABULARY

1	长袖	cháng xiù	long sleeve
2	短袖	duǎn xiù	short sleeve

延伸活动
AIM HIGHER

翻译句子 Translate these sentences:

1 She is wearing white trainers and black socks.
2 My younger brother is wearing a red scarf.
3 My mum likes wearing jeans.
4 I do not like wearing ties.
5 My school uniform is a white shirt, blue pants and black shoes.

词语
VOCABULARY

1	带	dài	belt; to bring, to carry
2	领带	lǐng dài	tie
3	帽子	mào zi	cap, hat
4	手表	shǒu biǎo	watch
5	眼镜	yǎn jìng	glasses

补充词语
SUPPLEMENTARY VOCABULARY

校服	xiào fú	school uniform

语法
GRAMMAR

Both 穿 and 戴 mean 'to wear, to put on'.

穿 is used when you talk about clothing items in which you can put parts of your body, e.g. 上衣, 裤子, 鞋子, 袜子.

戴 is used for most accessories which can be attached to you, e.g. 领带, 围巾, 手套, 帽子, 手表, 眼镜.

三、根据活动二，填空，完成句子。

3 According to Activity 2, fill in the gaps to complete the sentences.

谁 who	穿 / 戴 chuān / dài to wear	颜色 + 的 colour	衣服 clothing item
1 张红		白色的	
2 李冰		黑色的	
3 刘文			袜子
4 黄一冰			手套

Unit B 8 Personal and social life: Clothes

四、选择正确的量词完成句子。

4 Choose the most appropriate measure word for the following phrases.

1. 一____外衣
2. 这____灰色的衬衫是谁的？
3. 两____短裤
4. 一____运动鞋
5. 三____西装
6. 我很喜欢这____围巾。
7. 这____红色的帽子是谁的？

语法
GRAMMAR

jiàn 件	for clothes that go on the upper half of the body	duì 对	meaning *a pair of*. It emphasises the complementarity, e.g. earrings, twins
tiáo 条	for trousers, skirts, scarfs, etc.	shuāng 双	meaning *a pair of*. It indicates that the two function together, e.g. shoes, socks
tào 套	for a set of clothes, such as a suit	dǐng 顶	for hats

Note:

1. 对 and 双 both mean *a pair of* and are only used for separable items existing in dual form.
   There is a minor difference between 对 and 双: 对 emphasises the complementarity while 双 indicates functioning together. e.g. 一 对 耳环 a pair of earrings, 一 双 鞋 a pair of shoes.
2. For a pair of things which are physically inseparable, e.g. 裤子, 眼镜, we cannot use 对 or 双.

补充词语
SUPPLEMENTARY VOCABULARY

1. 西装 xī zhuāng suit
2. 耳环 ěr huán earring

文化
CULTURE

旗袍和唐装

旗袍和唐装是一种用丝绸制作的中国传统服装。旗袍和唐装有红色的、金色的、蓝色的等等。女孩穿上旗袍很好看。男孩可以穿唐装打太极拳。

旗袍　　　唐装

补充词语
SUPPLEMENTARY VOCABULARY

1. 旗袍 qí páo cheongsam
2. 唐装 táng zhuāng Tang suit
3. 丝绸 sī chóu silk
4. 传统 chuán tǒng traditional
5. 服装 fú zhuāng costume

二 阅读（一）
2 Reading (1)

读下面的文字，回答问题。

Read the text and answer the questions. **CD 01, Track 26**

我叫大为，今年十五岁。我的生日是八月九日。我是美国人。我有蓝色的眼睛，金色的头发。我的个子很高。我的爱好是打篮球。我喜欢穿白色的衬衣、蓝色的牛仔裤和黑色的运动鞋。

Cambridge IGCSE Mandarin as a Foreign Language

我叫王西，今年五十六岁。我的生日是十一月三十日。我是中国人。我有黄皮肤、灰白色的头发。我不胖不瘦。我的爱好是画画儿和听音乐。我喜欢穿红色的上衣和黑色的裙子。

我叫李山，今年二十一岁。我的生日是六月二日。我是印度人。我有高高的鼻子，黑色的头发。我又高又瘦。我的爱好是唱歌和跳舞。我喜欢穿西装、戴领带。

1 大为
  A 年龄：_____
  B 生日：_____
  C 国籍：_____
  D 头发的颜色：_____
  E 身材：_____
  F 爱好：_____
  G 喜欢穿的衣服：_____

2 王西
  A 年龄：_____
  B 生日：_____
  C 国籍：_____
  D 头发的颜色：_____
  E 身材：_____
  F 爱好：_____
  G 喜欢穿的衣服：_____

3 李山
  A 年龄：_____
  B 生日：_____
  C 国籍：_____
  D 头发的颜色：_____
  E 身材：_____
  F 爱好：_____
  G 喜欢穿的衣服：_____

词语
VOCABULARY

1 金（色） jīn (sè) gold; 金色的头发 blond(e) hair
2 灰 huī grey

补充词语
SUPPLEMENTARY VOCABULARY

身材 shēn cái figure, shape of the body

语法
GRAMMAR

Modification of nouns

1 A very common way to modify nouns is to attach an adjective to them using 的:
  Adj. + 的 + Noun e.g.

  a 白色的头发
     Here 的 is used to modify 'hair' with the colour 'white'. It attributes the colour 'white' to the 'hair'.
  b 高高的鼻子
  c 红色的上衣

2 However, 的 can be omitted in following cases:
  a Expressing a close personal relationship, such as for family, close friends, girlfriend/boyfriend, e.g.
     这是我男朋友，我妹妹今年五岁
  b Referring to an institutional/organisational relationship, e.g. 我们公司在上海，我学校很漂亮
  c When the adjective has one syllable, e.g. 红衣服，白袜子

3 Linking a modifier to a noun
   Similar to an adjective, a noun + 的 can act as a modifier to describe a noun, e.g. 美国的衣服 American clothes, 耳环的颜色 earrings' colour.

Unit B 8 Personal and social life: Clothes

4 Verb phrases as modifiers

Unlike in English, Chinese relative clauses precede the noun they modify, e.g.

a 昨天买的衣服贵吗？ Are the clothes you bought yesterday expensive?

b 他喜欢的音乐很不错。 The music that he likes is quite good.

三 写作（一）
3 Writing (1)

一、完成个人资料登记。

1 Complete the personal profile.

姓	名	国籍
年龄	生日	头发的颜色
身高	喜欢的颜色	喜欢的衣服
爱好	喜欢吃的	喜欢喝的

二、写一段话，介绍你自己。

2 Write a paragraph to introduce yourself.

你可以谈谈：
You may talk about:
- 你多大？
- 你长什么样？
- 你喜欢什么颜色？
- 你喜欢穿什么衣服？
- 你的爱好是什么？
- ……

好词好句
USEFUL EXPRESSIONS

- 我有一张圆脸。
- 我有一张瓜子脸。
- 我有高高的鼻子。
- 我有黑眼睛、黄皮肤、黑头发。

四 说话（一）
4 Speaking (1)

猜一猜：我是谁？
Guess who?

三到五人一组，每一个人头上都戴着一张有名字的卡片。每一个人轮流问问题，直到猜出"我是谁？"

Work in groups of three to five. Everyone wears a card with someone's name on their head. Take turns to ask questions about the named person until each of you finds out 'who I am'. You might ask:

我穿红色的裙子吗？
我喜欢唱歌吗？
……

词语
VOCABULARY

到   dào   to

五 听力（一）
5 Listening (1)

林小路在服装店买衣服。请听录音，填空。

Lin Xiaolu is in a clothes shop. Listen to the recording and fill in the gaps. **CD 01, Track 27**

A 林小路   B 售货员

A: 请问，这件____1____打折吗？现在多少钱？

B: 原价七百块，现在打八折，____2____块。

A: 我可以试试吗？

B: 可以。你穿几号？

A: 我穿____3____号。

……

B: 怎么样？

A: 还不错。但是我不喜欢这个颜色。

B: 这件上衣有____4____、红色、黄色和银灰色。你要什么颜色的？

Cambridge IGCSE Mandarin as a Foreign Language

A: 我要___5___的。给你六百。
B: 找你四十块。
A: 谢谢。
B: 不客气。

词语
VOCABULARY

1	服装店	fú zhuāng diàn	clothes shop
2	买	mǎi	to buy
3	售货员	shòu huò yuán	shop assistant
4	请问	qǐng wèn	excuse me
5	打折	dǎ zhé	to give a discount
6	多少钱	duō shǎo qián	how much (money)?; 多少 how many/much? (depending on the combination); 钱 money
7	找（钱）	zhǎo (qián)	to give change
8	试	shì	to try
9	号	hào	size
10	银（色）	yín (sè)	silver

补充词语
SUPPLEMENTARY VOCABULARY

原价　　yuán jià　　original price

语法
GRAMMAR

打折 is not exactly equivalent to the word 'discount' in English. You may need to do some maths when seeing or hearing the word. In Chinese 打折 literally means 'fold up the original price', e.g. 打八折 means the current price is 80% of the original price, that is, 20% off the original price.

练习：Match the discounts.

1　打八折　　A　−20%
2　打七五折　B　25% off
3　打九折　　C　−12%
4　打八八折　D　10% off

文化
CULTURE

钱 Units of Money

The Chinese currency is called 人民币 (Rén mín bì) (RMB). The sign for RMB is ¥. Amounts of money are expressed in terms of the following measure words depending on formal or informal circumstances:

Formal			Informal		
yuán 元 dollar	jiǎo 角 ten cents/dime	fēn 分 cent	kuài 块 dollar	máo 毛 ten cents/dime	fēn 分 cent

e.g.

¥367 = 三百六十七元 or 三百六十七块
¥150.50 = 一百五十元五（角）or
一百五十块五（毛）

Sometimes, the 角 or 毛 can be omitted.

小贴士
TOP TIP

When answering 多少钱, the answer can be the price with the measure word, e.g. 五百块, 一百元, or add 钱 at the end, e.g. 五百块钱, 一百元钱. However, 钱 should not be used if the measure words are omitted.

Unit B 8 Personal and social life: Clothes

六 说话（二）
6 💬 Speaking (2)

<u>假设</u>你是<u>林小路</u>，你的同学是售货员。<u>两人一组</u>，读听力（一）的对话。

Pretend that you are Lin Xiaolu and your classmate is the shop assistant. Work in pairs and read aloud the dialogue in Listening (1).

延伸活动
AIM HIGHER

现在，和你的同学两人一组，假设你去买鞋。仿照听力（一）的对话，完成角色扮演。

Now work in pairs to pretend you are going to buy shoes. Use Listening (1) as an example to create a new dialogue and complete the role play.

好词好句
USEFUL EXPRESSIONS

- 你穿几号？
- 这双鞋打折吗？
- 这双鞋打八五折。
- 我可以试试这双吗？

七 阅读（二）
7 📖 Reading (2)

世界各地的学生在一个论坛上讨论他们的校服。

Students from all over the world are discussing their school uniforms.

请读下面的文字，回答活动一的问题。

Read the text in the forum discussion, and answer the following questions. **CD 01, Track 28**

你的校服是什么样的？

安娜 (Anna)
我的学校在<u>英国伦敦</u> (London)。 1
在我们学校，男生穿白色的衬衫， 2
蓝色的外套，咖啡色的长裤，戴蓝 3
色的领带和帽子。女生穿白色的衬 4
衫，蓝色的外套，咖啡色的长裙。 5
我们都穿黑色的皮鞋。我们天天都 6
要穿校服。我妈妈很喜欢我们的校 7
服，她觉得很传统。但是我不喜因 8
为我觉得老土。 9

山本林子
我的学校在<u>日本东京</u> (Tokyo)。 10
在我们的学校，男生穿蓝色的衬， 11
绿色的短裤，白色的运动鞋。女生 12
白色的上衣，蓝色的短裙，白色的 13
长袜和白色运动鞋。我们每天穿校 14
服上学。我很喜欢我们的校服，因 15
为我觉得很时髦，很酷！ 16

李好
我的学校在<u>中国南京</u> (Nanjing)。 17
在我们的学校，男生和女生都穿灰 18
色的运动服，蓝色的运动鞋。我们 19
每个星期一穿校服。星期二到星期 20
五，我们穿自己的衣服。我不喜欢 21
我们的校服，因为我觉得我们的校 22
服又肥又大。 23

吴小
我的学校在<u>新加坡</u>。在我们学校， 24
女生穿红色的连衣裙，男生穿白色 25
的衬衫和黑色的西装。我们每天穿 26
校服上学。我觉得我们的校服很好 27
看。 28

词语
VOCABULARY

1	咖啡色	kā fēi sè	brown
2	肥	féi	fat; 肥大 loose
3	什么样的	shén me yàng de	how it looks
4	好看	hǎo kàn	good looking
5	酷	kù	cool

补充词语
SUPPLEMENTARY VOCABULARY

1	老土	lǎo tǔ	old-fashioned
2	时髦	shí máo	trendy, fashionable

选择正确的答案，回答问题。

Choose the best answer to each question.

1 谁的学校在英国？
 A 安娜 B 山本林子
 C 李好 D 吴小

2 谁的学校在日本？
 A 安娜 B 山本林子
 C 李好 D 吴小

3 谁的校服有帽子？
 A 安娜 B 山本林子
 C 李好 D 吴小

4 安娜的妈妈觉得校服____？
 A 很传统 B 老土
 C 很时髦 D 很酷

5 谁不要天天穿校服上学？
 A 安娜 B 山本林子
 C 李好 D 吴小

八 听力（二）
8 🔊 Listening (2)

记者在采访陈红。听下面的采访，回答问题。

A journalist is interviewing Chen Hong. Listen to the interview, and answer the questions. **CD 01, Track 29**

1 陈红今年多大？
2 她几点上学？
3 她什么时候要穿校服？
4 她觉得她的校服怎么样？
5 不穿校服的时候，她常常穿什么？

九 写作（二）
9 ✏️ Writing (2)

一、偏旁部首 (7)：将下面的汉字按部首分类，填入表格。

1 Radicals (7): Sort the following characters by radicals.

衬　常　张　裤　玩　绿　问　红　贵

	偏旁部首 Radicals	意思 Meanings	汉字 Characters
1	门	door	
2	衤	clothes	
3	纟	silk	
4	贝	shell, money	
5	弓	bow	
6	王	king, jade	
7	巾	handkerchief	

Unit B 8 Personal and social life: Clothes

二、 给阅读（二）的讨论区写一段话，介绍你们的校服。

2 Write a paragraph for the forum in Reading (2) to talk about your school uniform.

我的学校在＿＿＿＿。在我们的学校，男生穿＿＿＿＿，＿＿＿＿，＿＿＿＿。女生穿＿＿＿＿，＿＿＿＿，＿＿＿＿。我们＿＿＿＿（什么时候）穿校服。我们＿＿＿＿（喜欢／不喜欢）穿校服。因为＿＿＿＿。不穿校服时，我喜欢穿＿＿＿＿。

好词好句
USEFUL EXPRESSIONS

- 男生穿……，戴……。女生穿……，戴……。
- 我喜欢我们的校服，因为我觉得很时髦。／我不喜欢我们的校服，因为很老土。
- 我们天天穿校服上学。
- 不穿校服时，我穿……

自我评估
Self-Assessment

- ☐ I know the basic vocabulary for colours and clothing items
- ☐ I can describe someone's appearance and outfit
- ☐ I understand the units of money and can talk about price
- ☐ I can talk about school uniforms
- ☐ Question word 什么样的
- ☐ Measure words 件，条，套，对，双
- ☐ The difference between 穿 and 戴
- ☐ Nominalising in noun phrases with 的

Cambridge IGCSE Mandarin as a Foreign Language

mǎi dōng xi
买东西
9 Shopping

Learning objectives

This unit will concentrate on learning vocabulary about shopping. You will:

- Listen to conversations about shopping
- Understand an introduction of a shop
- Talk about a shopping experience
- Write about your opinions of online shopping

In addition, you are going to learn:

- Measure words 支, 把, 面
- Post-verbs 在, 到
- Units of length and mass

学习目标

本单元，你会：

- 听得懂关于购物的对话
- 阅读关于商店的介绍
- 谈论购物经历
- 写一写你对网上购物的看法

你还会学到：

- 量词：支、把、面
- 动词后加"在"、"到"
- 长度和重量单位

一 温故知新
1 'Before starting' activities

一、和你的老师、同学们讨论一下，在下面这些地方买东西，你可以买什么？

1 Discuss with your teacher and classmates: what can you buy from the following places?

    bǎi huò shāng diàn
A 百货商店 department store

    shū diàn
B 书店 bookshop

    shì chǎng
C 市场 market

    wén jù diàn
D 文具店 stationery shop

    wǎng shàng shāng diàn
E 网上商店 online shop

词语 VOCABULARY

1	东西	dōng xi	thing, stuff
2	纪念品	jì niàn pǐn	souvenir
3	礼物	lǐ wù	present, gift
4	日常用品	rì cháng yòng pǐn	daily necessities
5	钥匙	yào shi	key
6	镜子	jìng zi	mirror
7	橡皮	xiàng pí	eraser
8	牙刷	yá shuā	toothbrush
9	笔	bǐ	pen
10	玩具	wán jù	toy
11	文具	wén jù	stationery
12	商店	shāng diàn	shop

二、翻译句子。

2 Translate the sentences into English.

1 我住在市场附近。
2 请你写在本子上。
3 照片挂在墙上。
4 我们来到北京。
5 在百货商店，你可以买到各种各样的东西。

词语 VOCABULARY

1	本子	běn zi	notebook, workbook
2	挂	guà	to hang

补充词语 SUPPLEMENTARY VOCABULARY

墙 qiáng wall

Cambridge IGCSE Mandarin as a Foreign Language

句型
LANGUAGE

Verb + 在 + Place/Object (+ Localiser) indicates the final location of an object after the action. Many verbs can be followed by 在, such as 住, 写, 挂, 穿
e.g. 我住在中国。 I live in China.

Verb + 到 + Object indicates the result of the action. Many verbs can be followed by 到, such as 来, 看, 听, 想
e.g. 我可以吃到很多好吃的东西。 I can eat many tasty foods.

语法
GRAMMAR

zhī 支	for pens and pencils	miàn 面	for mirrors
bǎ 把	for things that you can handle, e.g. chair, keys, umbrella, rulers	fù 副	meaning *a set of*. It's usually used to indicate the integration of things, e.g. gloves, glasses

三、选择正确的量词完成句子。

3 Add the correct measure word in each of the sentences below.

1 我喜欢戴这____眼镜。
2 我去超市买一____镜子。
3 这____钥匙是我的。
4 一____雨伞。
5 我想买这____铅笔。

词语
VOCABULARY

1 雨伞　　yǔ sǎn　　umbrella
2 铅笔　　qiān bǐ　　pencil

补充词语
SUPPLEMENTARY VOCABULARY

超市　　chāo shì　　supermarket

文化
CULTURE

文化

文房四宝

毛笔、墨水、宣纸、砚台是中国人书房里常用的文具。人们常常把这四种文具叫做"文房四宝"。人们用"文房四宝"写书法和画国画。

下面是这四种文具的图片，请你把汉字和图片搭配起来。

A 墨水（儿）　B 毛笔　C 宣纸　D 砚台

1  (　)　2  (　)

3 (　)　4  (　)

词语
VOCABULARY

1 毛笔　　　　máo bǐ　　Chinese calligraphy brush
2 墨水（儿）　mò shuǐr　　ink

补充词语
SUPPLEMENTARY VOCABULARY

1 文房四宝　wén fáng sì bǎo　the four treasures of the study room
2 宣纸　　　xuān zhǐ　　rice paper specially made for Chinese calligraphy or painting
3 砚台　　　yàn tái　　ink stone

Unit B　9　Personal and social life: Shopping

二 阅读（一）
2 Reading (1)

三个在中国学习的留学生在谈他们的购物经历。请读下面的文字，回答问题。
Three overseas students who are studying in China are talking about their shopping experiences. Read the following text and answer the questions. **CD 01, Track 30**

安娜：

> 我是马来西亚人，但是我住在北京王府井附近。我喜欢去我家旁边的市场买东西。我觉得中国的市场很有意思。在那里，我可以买到很多便宜的东西。昨天，我去市场买了一斤白菜，一公斤大米和两斤苹果。一共花了50元。

丽丽：

> 我是德国人。我住在市中心以外五公里的地方，我家旁边有一个小超市。昨天，我去超市买了一把牙刷、一个牙膏和一块香皂。一共花了85块。

黄小花：

> 我是中国人。今年十六岁。我的爱好是逛街和画画儿。我常常去市中心的百货公司五楼的一个文具店。那儿有很多好看的笔和本子。昨天，我去那儿买了一个练习本，十张彩色纸，五支圆珠笔，五支彩色铅笔，一瓶墨水儿。一共花了三百块。

1 安娜现在住在哪儿？
2 昨天，安娜买了什么？一共花了多少钱？
3 昨天，丽丽买了什么？
4 黄小花有什么爱好？
5 黄小花常常去哪儿的文具店？

文化 CULTURE

"公斤"和"公里"——中国人用的单位 The units of mass and length in Chinese

1 Units of mass

In China, people use 千克 (qiān kè) (kg) and 克 (kè) (g) for the weight or mass of something. People also use 斤 (jīn) (500 g) and 公斤 (gōng jīn) (kg) when weighing something in markets.

2 Units of length

In China, people use 毫米 (háo mǐ) (mm), 厘米 (lí mǐ) (cm), 米 (mǐ) (m), 千米 (qiān mǐ) (km) for measuring lengths. They also use 里 (lǐ) (500 m), 公里 (gōng lǐ) (1 km) as units of length.

词语 VOCABULARY

1	便宜	pián yi	cheap
2	米	mǐ	rice
3	花	huā	to spend
4	斤	jīn	unit of mass, 500 grams
5	公斤	gōng jīn	unit of mass, 1 kilogram
6	一共	yí gòng	in total
7	市中心	shì zhōng xīn	city centre
8	以外	yǐ wài	outside of…
9	公里	gōng lǐ	unit of length, 1 kilometre

词语
VOCABULARY

10	牙膏	yá gāo	toothpaste
11	香皂	xiāng zào	soap
12	纸	zhǐ	paper
13	圆珠笔	yuán zhū bǐ	ballpoint pen
14	练习本	liàn xí běn	workbook, exercise book
15	单位	dān wèi	unit

补充词语
SUPPLEMENTARY VOCABULARY

1	购物	gòu wù	shopping
2	经历	jīng lì	experience
3	彩色	cǎi sè	colour, colourful

三 写作（一）
3 Writing (1)

按照下面的结构，写一段话，介绍你的购物经历。

Use the structure provided to write a paragraph introducing your shopping experience.

我是____国人。现在我住在_____。
我喜欢去_____(place) 买东西。因为我
觉得_____(your opinion about the shopping
place)。在那里，我可以买到_____。
_____(when?)，我去那儿买了____，
____，和____。一共花了____。

好词好句
USEFUL EXPRESSIONS

- 现在我住在市中心以外五公里的地方。
- 我喜欢去超市买东西，因为我觉得超市很方便。
- 在那里，我可以买到各种各样的东西。

小贴士
TOP TIP

Use a good variety of tenses to demonstrate your writing skills. In Chinese, you can use different time phrases to indicate tenses, e.g. 昨天，现在，明天，常常.

四 听力（一）
4 🔊 Listening (1)

万新百货公司昨天开业了。你将听到一个介绍这个百货公司的广告。

Wanxin Department Store opened yesterday. Listen to the advertisement that introduces the store and complete Activities 1 and 2. **CD 01, Track 31**

一、填空。

1 Fill in the store's floor plan.

四 楼
(5)____ (6)____ (7)____
三 楼
(3)____ 和 (4)____
二 楼
(2)____
一 楼
(1)____

营业时间：____(8)____ AM - ____(9)____ PM

地址：上三路____(10)____号

Unit B 9 Personal and social life: Shopping

二、请再听一遍录音，填空。

2 Listen to the recording again and fill in the gaps.

在一楼，你可以买到___1___、女装、童装、毛巾等等。在三楼，你可以买到___2___、杂志、___3___、橡皮、___4___等。四楼有___5___，方便您取钱。旁边也有三个___6___和一个超市。

词语 VOCABULARY

1	毛巾	máo jīn	towel
2	等（等）	děng (děng)	etc.
2	尺子	chǐ zi	ruler
3	银行	yín háng	bank
4	取钱	qǔ qián	to withdraw money
5	营业时间	yíng yè shí jiān	open hours
6	地址	dì zhǐ	address

补充词语 SUPPLEMENTARY VOCABULARY

| 1 | 开业 | kāi yè | to start business |
| 2 | 名牌 | míng pái | famous brand |

五 说话（一）
5 Speaking (1)

两人一组，完成情景对话。

Work in pairs to complete the role plays.

A 你的朋友 **B** 你自己

情景 1：你要买一个生日礼物给妈妈。你和你的朋友在讨论送什么礼物给你的妈妈。

Scenario 1: You are going to buy a birthday present for your mum, and you are discussing with your friend what present to buy.

A1: 你妈妈的生日是几月几号？

B1: _____

A2: 你妈妈有什么爱好？

B2: _____

A3: 你妈妈喜欢什么颜色？

B3: _____

A4: 她喜欢穿什么衣服？

B4: _____

A5: 买_____ (present) 吧，怎么样？

B5: _____

延伸活动 AIM HIGHER

Think about any other questions you could ask for this discussion.

CAMBRIDGE IGCSE Mandarin as a Foreign Language

好词好句
USEFUL EXPRESSIONS

- 你想买多少钱的礼物?
- 你妈妈喜欢花儿吗?

A 服务员　B 顾客（你自己）

情景 2：现在你想买一个钱包送给妈妈。你在百货公司，和服务员在说话。

Scenario 2: Now you would like to buy a wallet for your mum. You are talking to a shop assistant in a department store.

A1: 你想买什么?

B1: _____

A2: 你要什么颜色的?

B2: _____

A3: 你是要用现金还是用信用卡付钱?

B3: _____

词语
VOCABULARY

1 顾客　gù kè　customer
2 钱包　qián bāo　wallet

六　阅读（二）
6　Reading (2)

一、三个同学在网上买东西。请看下面的网页，选择正确的答案。

1 Three students are doing online shopping. Read the webpage below and choose the correct answers.

购物网 Shopping
宝贝　电器店 文具店 玩具店 书店 服装店 鞋店

主题市场
女装 >
鞋靴 >
童装玩具 >
家电 >
美妆 >

BIG SALE　SALE 30%

1 王明要买毛笔，她要点击哪一个?
A 电器店　B 书店　C 文具店　D 玩具店

2 李平要买一部手机，他要点击哪一个?
A 电器店　B 书店　C 文具店　D 玩具店

3 大卫要买一个书包，他要点击哪一个?
A 鞋店　B 书店　C 文具店　D 玩具店

4 大卫想买打折的东西。他可以点击哪一个?
A 大减价　B 登陆　C 付钱　D 注册

词语
VOCABULARY

1 手机　shǒu jī　mobile phone
2 书包　shū bāo　school bag, satchel
3 减价　jiǎn jià　deduction
4 付钱　fù qián　to pay

Unit B　9　Personal and social life: Shopping

补充词语
SUPPLEMENTARY VOCABULARY

1	电器	diàn qì	electronic devices, electrical appliances
2	点击	diǎn jī	to click
3	登陆	dēng lù	to log in
4	注册	zhù cè	to register

词语
VOCABULARY

1	照相机	zhào xiàng jī	camera
2	游戏机	yóu xì jī	game player
3	方式	fāng shì	way
4	现金	xiàn jīn	cash
5	信用卡	xìn yòng kǎ	credit card
6	支票	zhī piào	cheque
7	卖	mài	to sell
8	这个月	zhè ge yuè	this month

补充词语
SUPPLEMENTARY VOCABULARY

1	联系	lián xì	to contact
2	联系人	lián xì rén	contact person
3	美金	Měi jīn	US dollar
4	港币	Gǎng bì	Hong Kong dollar
5	英镑	Yīng bàng	British pound sterling

二、李平在网上购物 (online shopping)。他看到这个页面 (webpage)。请读下面的文字，选择"是"或者"非"。

2 Li Ping is shopping online and he sees the page below. Read the text and answer the questions.

---

http://www.maidongxi/hongpingguo.com

红苹果电器店   搜索

欢迎来到红苹果电器店。
我们卖电视、冰箱、电脑、手机等等。
这个月，我们的照相机、手机和游戏机
大减价！快来买！

联系人：小美
联系电话：3874-9936
你也可以到我们的商店。我们的商店地址是：
市中心国立百货公司三楼。
营业时间：11:00 AM – 10:30 PM
付钱方式：现金（人民币，美金，港币，英镑都可以）
，信用卡
对不起，不可以用支票付款

		是	非
1	这个商店卖电器。	☐	☐
2	这个月，电视、冰箱、电脑大减价。	☐	☐
3	你可以在网上买这个商店的电器，也可以在市中心商店买。	☐	☐
4	这个商店早上十点营业。	☐	☐
5	你不可以用信用卡付钱。	☐	☐

三、李平在找他想要买的商品。读下面的表格，选择正确的答案。

3 Li Ping is looking for what he wants to buy. Read the tables below and choose the correct answers.

商品	小面照相机	三元照相机	国美照相机	乐听照相机
价钱	8999 元	10 000 元（打八折）	9000 元	7899 元
信息	送一个书包，免费送货	送货费：20 元	免费送货	免费送货

Cambridge IGCSE Mandarin as a Foreign Language

商品	苹果手机	天想手机	一心手机	思可手机
价钱	5000元（打八折）	3000元（打七五折）	4800元（打六折）	6780元
信息	免费送货	免费送货	送货费：5元	免费送货

商品	开心游戏机	蓝猫游戏机	加能游戏机	金英游戏机
价钱	原价：5090元 减价以后：4999元	原价：5888元 减价以后：5800元	原价：7500元 减价以后：7000元	原价：8800元 减价以后：6880元
信息	送纪念品，免费送货	送一个玩具，送货费：20元	送货费：30元	送货费：35元

1 买哪一个照相机有礼物送？
 A 小面照相机 B 三元照相机
 C 国美照相机 D 乐听照相机

2 哪一个手机没有打折？
 A 苹果手机 B 天想手机
 C 一心手机 D 思可手机

3 哪一个手机要送货费？
 A 苹果手机 B 天想手机
 C 一心手机 D 思可手机

4 哪一个游戏机的原价在八千元以上？
 A 开心游戏机 B 蓝猫游戏机
 C 加能游戏机 D 金英游戏机

5 哪一个游戏机和送货费减价以后的价钱在5000元以下？
 A 开心游戏机 B 蓝猫游戏机
 C 加能游戏机 D 金英游戏机

词语 VOCABULARY

1 找　zhǎo　to look for
2 价钱　jià qián　price
3 送　sòng　to give as a present, to deliver
4 以上　yǐ shàng　above, more than
5 以下　yǐ xià　below, fewer/less than, lower than

补充词语 SUPPLEMENTARY VOCABULARY

1 费　fèi　fee, fare
2 免费　miǎn fèi　free of charge
3 送货　sòng huò　to deliver goods

七 听力（二）
7 Listening (2)

李平要在网上买一个手机。他在和联系人小美打电话。请听录音，将对话重组。

Li Ping wants to buy a phone from Hong Ping Guo Electronic Appliances online shop. He is making a phone call to the contact person Xiao Mei. Listen to the recording and rearrange the dialogue by putting the correct letters into each dialogue box. **CD 01, Track 32**

A 下个星期三送货。
B 你喜欢什么牌的？
C 好的。你可以用现金付款，也可以用信用卡付款。
D 你好，这里是红苹果电器店服务台。
E 可以。
F 我想买你们的手机。
H 我喜欢天想手机。请问，怎么付款。
I 什么时候送货？
J 可以给我收据吗？

Unit B 9 Personal and social life: Shopping

小美：

D
1
3
5
7

李平：

F
2
4
6

词语
VOCABULARY

1 零钱　líng qián　change
2 商场　shāng chǎng　shopping centre, mall

补充词语
SUPPLEMENTARY VOCABULARY

排队　pái duì　to queue, to line up

自我评估
Self-Assessment

- ☐ I can listen to conversations about shopping
- ☐ I understand an introduction of a shop
- ☐ I can talk about my shopping experiences
- ☐ I can write about my opinions of online shopping
- ☐ Measure words 支，把，面
- ☐ Post-verbs 在，到
- ☐ Units of length and mass

词语
VOCABULARY

1 服务台　fú wù tái　service counter, helpdesk
2 收据　shōu jù　receipt

补充词语
SUPPLEMENTARY VOCABULARY

牌　pái　brand

八　写作（二）
8　Writing (2)

朋友们在讨论网上购物。请先读一读他们的看法，然后写下你自己的看法。

Some friends are discussing their views about online shopping. Read the text below first, and then write down your own opinions.

李国新：我平时很忙，没时间买东西。网上购物真方便，价钱便宜，还可以送货。不用带零钱去买东西，也不用排队付款。

黄红英：我喜欢逛街。我觉得去商场买东西又可以逛街，又可以锻炼身体，对身体好。我不喜欢在家里一边看电脑，一边买东西。

吴冰：我不会用网上购物。我觉得网上银行很不方便。

我：＿＿＿＿＿＿＿＿＿＿＿＿＿＿＿＿＿＿

CAMBRIDGE IGCSE Mandarin as a Foreign Language

jū zhù huán jìng
居住环境
10 Living environment

Learning objectives

This unit will concentrate on vocabulary to describe your living environment. You will:

- Listen to and read descriptions about living environments

- Read a map in Chinese and ask for/give directions

- Write about your living environment

In addition, you are going to learn:

- Localisers (2): 东方，北边

- Prepositions (1): 在，从，到 to express location/direction

- Simple directional complements: 来，去

- Sentence structure: ……离…… + adjective

学习目标

本单元你会：

- 阅读和听到关于居住环境的描述

- 用中文指路、问路

- 写一写你的居住环境

你还会学到：

- 方位词（2）：东方、北边

- 介词（1）：在、从、到

- 趋向动词：来、去

- 句型：……离……+形容词

Unit B 10 Personal and social life: Living environment

一 温故知新
1 'Before starting' activities

一、请在适当的地方填写正确的答案。

1 Write the correct directions around the compass below.

| 东 | 西北 | 北 | 东南 | 南 | 西南 | 东北 | 西 |

方向

> **小贴士**
> **TOP TIP**
>
> For intermediate directions, 'north' or 'south' comes first in English but second in Chinese, e.g. 东南 (southeast) and 西北 (northwest).

> **语法**
> **GRAMMAR**
>
> Localisers (2)
>
> 1 To refer to the 'northern part' or 'western part', the character 方 is used, e.g. 东方, 南方, 西方 and 北方.
> 2 Putting a direction before the character 边 has a similar meaning to 方, e.g. 北京的西边 'the west side of Beijing', 学校的东边 'the east side of the school'. Another character, 面, has the same function. For example, 东边 and 东面 are interchangeable.
> 3 There is no 中边 for 'middle' or 'in the centre', just 中间。

二、请看表格，回答问题。

2 Read the table, and answer the questions.

一个在北京的商场

五楼	日常用品店
四楼	时装店
三楼	服装店
二楼	文具店
一楼	西餐厅

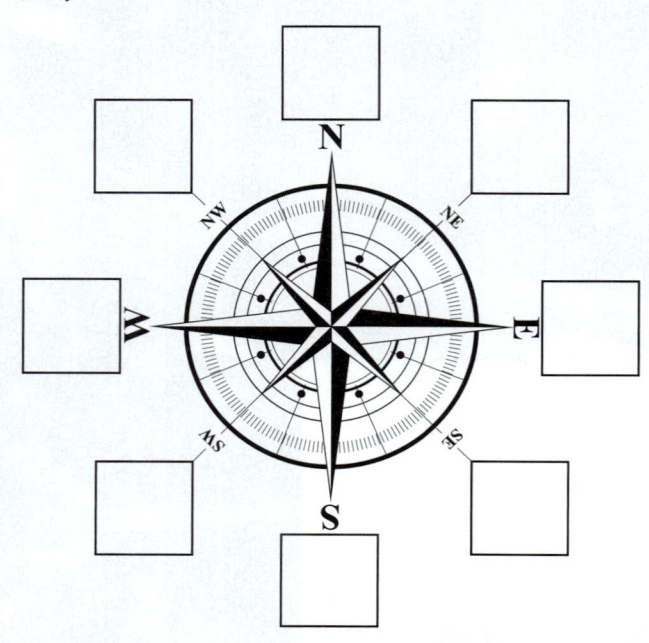

词语
VOCABULARY

1	北	běi	north
2	东	dōng	east
3	东北	dōng běi	northeast
4	东边	dōng biān	the east side
5	东南	dōng nán	southeast
6	南	nán	south
7	西	xī	west
8	西北	xī běi	northwest
9	西方	xī fāng	the west
10	西南	xī nán	southwest
11	方向	fāng xiàng	directions

词语
VOCABULARY

1	楼上	lóu shàng	upstairs/one floor up
2	楼下	lóu xià	downstairs/one floor down
3	时装店	shí zhuāng diàn	boutique
4	钢笔	gāng bǐ	fountain pen

Cambridge IGCSE Mandarin as a Foreign Language

例：买薯条要到<u>一</u>楼的<u>西餐厅</u>。

1 小美想买一条裙子,可以去___楼的_____。
2 王明要买一支钢笔,他要去___楼的_____。
3 要吃热狗要去___楼的_____。
4 在文具店,可以买到_____、_____、_____、_____。
5 从服装店到楼上,是_____。
6 时装店在_____的楼下。

语法
GRAMMAR

Prepositions (1): 在、从、到

1 在 is very similar to the English preposition 'in' or 'at', e.g. 在文具店 'in the stationery shop'.
2 从……到…… is similar to 'from … to …' in English. It can express time or direction in Chinese, e.g.
   a 从十二点到一点我们在餐厅吃饭。 From twelve to one o'clock we have lunch at a restaurant.
   b 从南到北 from south to north

练习：Translate the following sentences into English.

1 坐飞机(plane)从上海到北京要两个多小时。
   fēi jī
2 在小吃店可以买汉堡包和咖啡。
3 从你家到饭馆可以坐公车(take a bus)。
   zuò gōng chē

二 阅读（一）
2 Reading (1)

请看图回答问题,选择"是"或"非"。
Read the map below and choose 'true' or 'false' for each sentence.

王城小区的设施

图书馆	电影院	广场
警察局	公园	医院
	体育场	

		是	非
1	体育场在北边。	☐	☐
2	电影院的对面是公园。	☐	☐
3	广场在图书馆的旁边。	☐	☐
4	医院的附近是体育场。	☐	☐
5	图书馆的东边是公园。	☐	☐
6	图书馆在警察局的南边。	☐	☐
7	公园在小区的中心。	☐	☐
8	广场的北边是医院。	☐	☐

词语
VOCABULARY

1	设施	shè shī	facilities
2	电影院	diàn yǐng yuàn	cinema
4	体育场	tǐ yù chǎng	sports stadium
5	图书馆	tú shū guǎn	library
6	警察局	jǐng chá jú	police station; 警察 police
7	广场	guǎng chǎng	plaza/square
8	对面	duì miàn	opposite
9	附近	fù jìn	nearby

Unit B 10 Personal and social life: Living environment

补充词语
SUPPLEMENTARY VOCABULARY

小区　　xiǎo qū　　housing estate

文化
CULTURE

广场舞 Chinese Fitness Dancing

在中国,很多人在广场一起跳舞,又可以做运动,保持身体健康。看他们跳舞十分有意思。

C 汽车站　　D 警察局

E 电影院　　F 游泳池

G 停车场　　H 游乐场

I 邮局

三 听力
3 🔊 Listening

你到了一个小区,邻居给你介绍设施。请看图片。

You just arrived in a new neighbourhood and a neighbour talks to you about the facilities there.

请听录音,将图片旁的字母分别填入适当的方格内。

Listen to the recording, and put the correct letter in the appropriate box on the map. **CD 01, Track 33**

A 图书馆 　　B 诊所

例:"邮局在图书馆的东边。" 所以 I 在 A 的东边。

		A 图书馆	I

N

Cambridge IGCSE Mandarin as a Foreign Language

词语 VOCABULARY

1	邻居	lín jū	neighbour
2	诊所	zhěn suǒ	clinic
3	汽车站	qì chē zhàn	bus stop; 汽车 car, bus
4	游泳池	yóu yǒng chí	swimming pool
5	停车场	tíng chē chǎng	car park
6	游乐场	yóu lè chǎng	playground
7	邮局	yóu jú	post office

四 阅读（二）
4 Reading (2)

一、请阅读下面介绍白城小区的传单。

1 Read the leaflet below about a neighbourhood called Baicheng. **CD 01, Track 34**

白城小区——一个你爱的家

环境干净、设施齐全、空气清新

1 白城小区在南红市的郊区。小区有很多花草树木，空气清新，人口不多，小区也很安全。

2 东边有一个汽车站。

3 小区设施齐全。小区的中心是俱乐部。它的南面有一个足球场，足球场的左边有四个网球场。网球场的北边有一个室外游泳池。

4 停车场在小区北边的地方，汽车站在邮局的南面，小区还有一个医务所。

5 最大的商城"白城购物城"在小区的南边，离小区很近。商城里面有很多时装店，可以跟朋友一起逛街。

6 附近还有一个游乐场，小朋友会很喜欢的。

7 郊区没有工厂，这个地区很舒服。

8 娱乐中心在游乐场的旁边。

词语 VOCABULARY

1	环境	huán jìng	environment
2	空气	kōng qì	air
3	人口	rén kǒu	population
4	安全	ān quán	safe
5	郊区	jiāo qū	suburb
6	草	cǎo	grass
7	俱乐部	jù lè bù	clubhouse
8	近	jìn	close
9	地方	dì fang	place
10	商城	shāng chéng	a commercial area which has a large number of department stores
11	离	lí	to be away from
12	近	jìn	close
13	工厂	gōng chǎng	factory
14	地区	dì qū	district, zone; 地 land, field
15	娱乐中心	yú lè zhōng xīn	recreation centre
16	远	yuǎn	far

补充词语 SUPPLEMENTARY VOCABULARY

1	设施齐全	shè shī qí quán	fully equipped
2	空气清新	kōng qì qīng xīn	fresh air
3	花草树木	huā cǎo shù mù	flowers and trees, lots of plants
4	室外游泳池	shì wài yóu yǒng chí	outdoor pool
5	医务所	yī wù suǒ	clinic, same as 诊所

Unit B 10 Personal and social life: Living environment

二、王先生想搬到白城小区。他想知道小区是否适合他和他的家人。请选择"适合"或"不适合"。

2 Mr Wang wants to move to Baicheng neighbourhood. He wants to know if it is the right place for him and his family. Choose 'suitable' or 'not suitable' for the following sentences.

		适合	不适合
1	王先生的儿子大王经常生病，他要住在空气好的地方。	☐	☐
2	王太太有汽车，小区要有一个停车的地方。	☐	☐
3	王先生要电影院离家不远。	☐	☐
4	王太太觉得买衣服的地方要在家附近。	☐	☐
5	大王喜欢小区附近没有工厂。	☐	☐

词语 VOCABULARY

知道　zhī dào　to know

句型 LANGUAGE

Expressing distance with 离

To say that something is far or close (distance), you can use the word 离 in the following basic pattern:

> Place 1 + 离 + Place 2 + 很远 / 近

e.g.
a 商场离图书馆很近。 The shopping mall is close to the library.
b 我家离游泳池很远。 My house is far from the swimming pool.

五 阅读（三）
5 Reading (3)

文化 CULTURE

微博 Weibo
Wēi bó

"微博"在英文是 'microblog' 的意思，是中国的 'Twitter'。

请阅读下面的两则微博，然后回答问题。
Read the Weibo entries below, and then do the activities.
CD 01, Track 35

李小天 @Lixiaotian

【#乡下 郊区很好# 城市】这是我来 1
到上海的第三个星期。我从乡下来， 2
以前住在郊区。上海是一个大城市， 3
市中心环境和我以前的家很不一样。 4
以前我住在乡下的村子里，有很多花 5
草树木，风景很好。村子附近有树林， 6
空气很清新。但是好玩儿的地方不多， 7
附近没有电影院、商场。医院也离我 8
们家很远。 9

2016-10-11 20:04 上海

收藏　　转发 0　　评论 2　　点赞 3

陈白雪 @Snowchen

【#新加坡#城市】我上个星期搬到 1
新加坡。我的房子在海边，可以看见 2
大海。这里的邻居都很友好，早上都 3
跟我说"你好"。这里的设施都很齐 4
全。我喜欢去家附近的一个商场，里 5
边有餐厅、电影院、时装店。我常常 6
到那儿去买衣服。不过这里的居民都 7
觉得绿色的地方不多。我家对面的路 8
口有一个汽车站，去上学很方便。 9

2016-02-20 08:35 新加坡

收藏　　转发 0　　评论 4　　点赞 1

Cambridge IGCSE Mandarin as a Foreign Language

词语
VOCABULARY

1	乡下	xiāng xià	countryside
2	村子	cūn zi	village
3	风景	fēng jǐng	scenery
4	树林	shù lín	forest
5	海边	hǎi biān	seaside
6	海	hǎi	sea
8	居民	jū mín	residents
9	路口	lù kǒu	junction, intersection (of roads)
10	多久	duō jiǔ	how long

补充词语
SUPPLEMENTARY VOCABULARY (FOR 'WEIBO')

1	收藏	shōu cáng	to save
2	转发	zhuǎn fā	to retweet
3	评论	píng lùn	to comment
4	点赞	diǎn zàn	to like

一、请用下列词组填空。

1 Use the words provided to fill in the gaps.

村子　风景　树林　海边　邻居
里边　居民　路口

1 我不住在城市，我住在_____里。
2 在_____人们可以钓鱼。
3 住在这个小区的____觉得这里绿色的地方不多。
4 这里有很多花草树木，____很美。
5 我家附近的____都很友好。
6 这个小区____有很多设施，比如娱乐中心、图书馆等。

二、请阅读上面的微博，然后回答问题。

2 Read the Weibo entries, and then answer the questions below.

1 李小天来了上海多久？
2 李小天从哪里来？
3 上海的环境跟他的家一样吗？
4 李小天以前住在乡下的什么地方？
5 他以前的家空气怎么样？
6 陈白雪的房子在哪里？
7 那里的邻居怎么样？
8 那里的居民觉得环境怎么样？

语法
GRAMMAR

Simple directional complements: 来、去

1 The basic meaning of 来 is '(coming) from' and 去 is 'going to', e.g. 我从中国来 'I come from China', 我去中国 'I am going to China'.

2 来 and 去 are also used as directional complements to describe the direction of a verb. The basic pattern is:

Verb + 来 or 去

It is important to consider the position of the speaker. 来 is used when the action involves coming closer to the speaker, and 去 when the action means moving away from the speaker, e.g.

a 你上去。You go up.
b 我下来。I am coming down.
c 李小天今天在上海，明天回去乡下。 Li Xiaotian is in Shanghai today. He is going back to the countryside tomorrow.

3 Adding a place with 到

到 + place + 来 or 去

e.g.

a 小天的哥哥到上海来了。Xiaotian's elder brother has arrived in Shanghai.
b 我住在香港，明天到马来西亚去。I live in Hong Kong and will go to Malaysia tomorrow.

Unit B 10 Personal and social life: Living environment

六 说话
6 Speaking

两人一组，回答以下问题。

Work in pairs to ask and answer the following questions.

1 你家附近有什么公共设施？
2 你喜欢住在市中心还是郊区？为什么？
3 住在市中心有什么好处？有什么坏处？
4 住在郊区有什么好处？有什么坏处？

词语 VOCABULARY

1 好处　hǎo chù　advantage
2 坏处　huài chù　disadvantage, harm

七 写作
7 Writing

李小天的朋友陈友给他发了一条短信：

主题: 上海市中心

李小天：

1
2　知道你现在住在上海的市中心。
3　市中心有什么设施？住在市中心
4　有什么好处、坏处？以前住在郊
5　区有什么好处、坏处？你喜欢哪
6　一个？给我写一封电邮。
7　　谢谢
8　　祝
9　好！
10　　　　　　　　　　　陈友

给陈友回信，不少于 150 个汉字。

! 小贴士 TOP TIP

1 Most of the materials you prepared in the Speaking activity can be used in this task.
2 Include some idiomatic expressions, such as 花草树木, 设施齐全.
3 Include sentence structures such as '……离…… + adjective' and '到……来 / 去', too.

八 阅读（四）
8 Reading (4)

一、朗读以下词语。

1　Read aloud the following words.

1	2	3	4
wǎng yòu guǎi 往右拐	xiàng zuǒ guǎi 向左拐	hóng lǜ dēng 红绿灯	shí zì lù kǒu 十字路口

词语 VOCABULARY

拐　guǎi　to turn (to another direction)

! 小贴士 TOP TIP

The two phrases 往……拐 and 向……拐 have the same meaning, i.e. you can also say 往左拐 or 向右拐.

二、陈小红要去找王一好。请看一看以下的对话。在地图上找出王一好的家在哪里。

2 Chen Xiaohong will go to Wang Yihao's home. Read their conversation, then find Wang's house on the map.

陈小红

一好,我明天来你家玩儿,你家离汽车站有多远?

王一好

我家离汽车站不远,走五分钟左右。

陈小红

从汽车站到你家怎么走?

王一好

我家离汽车站不远。从汽车站出去后往南走,你会路过一个公园,然后往右拐,右边是文具店,左边是电影院。

陈小红

然后呢?

王一好

顺着马路一直走,到了第三个路口再转右,我家就在你右边了。我家对面是诊所。

陈小红

我迷路的话怎么办?

王一好

可以打公用电话。

陈小红

好,麻烦你了!

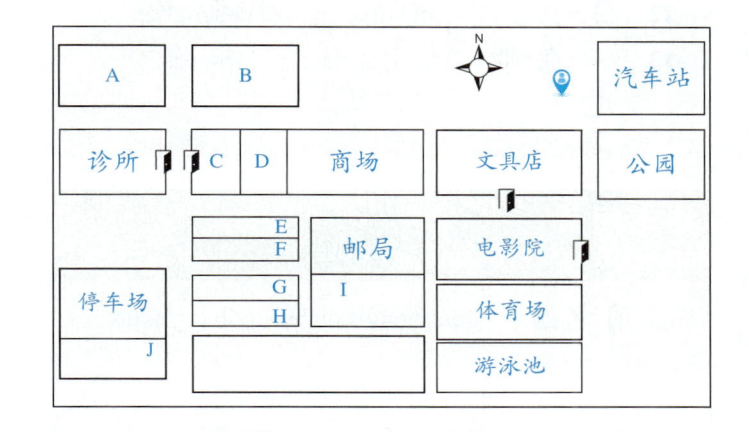

	A	B			汽车站
诊所	C	D	商场	文具店	公园
	E / F		邮局	电影院	
停车场	G / H		I	体育场	
	J			游泳池	

词语
VOCABULARY

1	……离……有多远?	……lí……yǒu duō yuǎn?	How far is (Place 1) from (Place 2)?
2	到……怎么走?	dào……zěnme zǒu?	How do you get to …?
3	出去	chū qù	to go out
4	往……走	wǎng……zǒu	to go towards/in the direction of, e.g. in the text 往南走 means 'to go south'; 走 to walk
5	路过	lù guò	to pass through/by
6	过马路	guò mǎ lù	to cross the road; 过 to cross; 马路 road
7	一直	yì zhí	all the way; 直 straight
8	顺着	shùn zhe	along; 顺着马路一直走 go straight ahead along this road
9	在……边	zài……biān	on the (right/left) side

Unit B 10 Personal and social life: Living environment

103

词语
VOCABULARY

10	迷路	mí lù	to get lost
11	麻烦你了	má fan nǐ le	sorry to bother you; 麻烦 to trouble (someone)
12	目的地	mù dì dì	destination
13	……在哪儿?	……zài nǎr?	Where is…?

补充词语
SUPPLEMENTARY VOCABULARY

| 公用电话 | gōng yòng diàn huà | public phone |

延伸活动
AIM HIGHER

Work in pairs and try to ask each other for the directions below:

	目的地
1 诊所	体育场
2 电影院	汽车站
3 文具店	停车场
4 C	游泳池

You can use the question patterns:

a 体育场在哪儿?
b 从诊所到体育场怎么走?

Use the phrases in Reading (4) to help you answer the questions.

句型
LANGUAGE

……离……有多远?

To ask how far one place is from another place, you can use the question pattern 离……有多远?

e.g. 球场离这儿有多远? 'How far is the stadium from here?' A possible answer is 不远, 要走五分钟 'Not far, it takes 5 minutes to walk'.

自我评估
Self-Assessment

☐ I can listen to and read descriptions about living environments
☐ I can read a map in Chinese and ask for/give directions
☐ I can write about my living environment
☐ Prepositions 在, 从, 到
☐ Simple directional complements 来 and 去
☐ Sentence structure ……离…… + adjective
☐ Localisers such as 东, 南

Cambridge IGCSE Mandarin as a Foreign Language

xué xiào shēng huó
学校生活
11 School routine

Learning objectives

This unit will concentrate on talking about the subjects you take in school and describing a school day. In particular, you will:

- Describe what subjects are offered in a school

- Respond to questions about the subjects you like and do not like

- Read a letter about subject options

- Talk about your school routine

In addition, you will learn:

- Measure words: 些，门，节

- Word order: 跟 + (whom)

- Question word: 为什么

- Sentence structure: 因为……所以……

- Use of 一点儿

学习目标

本单元你会：

- 说一说学校有什么科目

- 回答你喜欢、不喜欢什么科目

- 阅读一封跟选课有关的信

- 描述你上学的每一天

你还会学到：

- 量词：些、门、节

- 语序：跟 + 谁

- 疑问词：为什么

- 句型：因为……所以……

- 怎么用"一点儿"

Unit B 11 Personal and social life: School routine

一　温故知新
1　'Before starting' activity

说一说你学校有什么科目。

> 我们学校有英语、数学、美术课，我最喜欢汉语课。

> 我们学校有＿＿＿、＿＿＿、＿＿＿课，我最喜欢＿＿＿。

词语
VOCABULARY

1	科目	kē mù	subject
2	英语	Yīng yǔ	English
3	汉语	Hàn yǔ	Chinese
4	地理	dì lǐ	geography
5	科学	kē xué	science
6	数学	shù xué	mathematics
7	体育	tǐ yù	physical education
8	法语	Fǎ yǔ	French
9	德语	Dé yǔ	German
10	历史	lì shǐ	history
11	美术	měi shù	art
12	音乐	yīn yuè	music
13	日文	Rì wén	Japanese
		wén yǔ	

In Chinese, 文 and 语 are mostly interchangeable. For example, 英文 = 英语; 德文 = 德语; 法语 = 法文.

However, the only exception is the word 'Chinese'. It is either 中文 or 汉语 never 中语 / 汉文.

小贴士
TOP TIP

Try to put the vocabulary items into different categories such as 'languages' and 'science subjects'. It will help you remember them, e.g. 'languages' include 法语, 英语, 汉语.

二　听力（一）
2　Listening (1)

一、八个朋友在谈论他们的学校科目。请看以下的词语。

1　Eight friends are talking about their school subjects. Look at the words below.

请听下面的录音，选择唯一正确的答案，将字母填入方格中。

Listen to the recording, choose the only correct answer for each person and put the letter in the box.
CD 01, Track 36

A 音乐	B 数学	C 美术	D 历史
E 科学	F 地理	G 法语	H 体育

1 小青	2 小天	3 王红	4 小王
A			
5 小刘	6 小马	7 小乐	8 小中

好词好句
USEFUL EXPRESSIONS

- 我喜欢数学，所以选择了这一科。
- 我想做医生，所以要学习科学。

词语
VOCABULARY

1	学习	xué xí	to learn
2	选择	xuǎn zé	to choose
3	所以	suǒ yǐ	so/therefore

Cambridge IGCSE Mandarin as a Foreign Language

句型
LANGUAGE

……所以……

所以 is a conjunction which means 'so' or 'therefore'. It is used to explain results in the following pattern:

Reason, 所以 + Result

e.g.

a 她长得漂亮，所以很多人都喜欢她。
She is pretty, so many people like her.

b 白菜很咸，所以我不想吃。
That Chinese cabbage is very salty, so I do not want to eat it.

小贴士
TOP TIP

Remember to put a comma before 所以.

音乐是很多学生喜欢的一课

很多学生都喜欢体育课，因为可以做运动

二、请听小张每天的课程表，选择唯一正确的答案，将字母填入方格中。

2 Listen to the description of Xiao Zhang's timetable. Choose the only correct answer for each class period, numbered 1–5, and put the letter in the box.
CD 01, Track 37

A 中文	B 体育	C 历史	D 体育
E 地理	F 法语	G 英语	H 数学

小张的星期二 Xiao Zhang's Tuesday

第一节课	第二节课	休息	第三节课	第四节课	午饭	第五节课
1	2	—	3	4	—	5

词语
VOCABULARY

1 课程表 kè chéng biǎo timetable
2 节 jié a measure word for class periods; 第一节课 dì yī jié kè Period 1

三 说话（一）
3 Speaking (1)

一、朗读。

1 Read aloud the following dialogue.

问：学校有哪些课？

答：中文、英语、数学等等。你呢？

问：你喜欢哪门课？

答：我喜欢中文。

问：你不喜欢哪门课？

答：我不喜欢数学。

Unit B 11 Personal and social life: School routine

词语
VOCABULARY

1. 些　xiē　a measure word, meaning 'some' or 'a little'; 哪些 nǎ xiē which
2. 门　mén　a measure word for lessons, subjects

二、练一练。

2 Practise talking about school subjects.

你的同学学习什么课？喜欢什么？不喜欢什么？请用活动（一）的句型，跟你的同学练一练。

Familiarise yourself with all the sentence structures and questions in Activity 1. Practise them with your classmates.

语法
GRAMMAR

Measure words: 些, 门, 节

1. 些 is a measure word for multiple objects with unspecified number; it means 'some' or 'a little' in English, e.g.
   王明带了一些书本来。Ming Wang brought some books.
2. When 些 combines with the question word 哪, it means 'which', e.g.
   哪些国家的人说英文？Which countries speak English?
3. As explained in the previous Vocabulary box, 门 is a measure word for lessons and subjects, e.g.
   我学习五门课。I study five subjects.
   节 is used to describe a lesson period, e.g.
   这一节课是中文。This period/class is Chinese.

四　阅读（一）
4　Reading (1)

请阅读下面的信，然后回答问题。
Read the letter below, and then answer the questions.
CD 01, Track 38

小明： 1
　你好！最近我搬到一个新的小区， 2
也到了一个新的学校上课，所以一直 3
都很忙，我没给你写信，请原谅。 4
　在新的学校，我认识了很多新的朋 5
友，他们都很友好。我常常跟朋友在 6
校园打乒乓球和踢足球。这里的课外 7
活动都很好玩儿。 8
　这个星期过得很不错。我在这个学 9
期一共学九门课：英文、数学、汉语、 10
经济、地理、戏剧、日语、化学和物理。 11
　学校的课程很难，每个人要学三 12
门外语，我选择了汉语、日语和法语。 13
我选了汉语，因为它很有用。日语和 14
法语比汉语容易。我学会了很多法语 15
的字。我很喜欢戏剧，因为上课时可 16
以演戏，老师上课常常开玩笑，所以 17
我们都对戏剧感兴趣。 18
　我不喜欢英文，因为要常常看书。 19
我的英文老师常常说，阅读可以提升 20
我们的语文水平，所以每个星期我们 21
都得到图书馆看书。 22
　你在北京国际学校学哪些课呢？写 23
信给我吧。 24
　祝 25
好！ 26
　　　　　　　　你的朋友 小王 上 27
　　　　　　　　　　　　三月十五日 28

Cambridge IGCSE Mandarin as a Foreign Language

词语
VOCABULARY

1	最近	zuì jìn	recently
2	跟	gēn	with
3	校园	xiào yuán	school campus
4	课外活动	kè wài huó dòng	extracurricular activities
5	这个星期	zhè ge xīng qī	this week
6	不错	bú cuò	not bad
7	学期	xué qī	term, semester
8	化学	huà xué	chemistry
9	日语	Rì yǔ	same as 日文
10	物理	wù lǐ	physics
11	课程	kè chéng	curriculum
12	难	nán	difficult, hard
13	外语	wài yǔ	foreign language
14	有用	yǒu yòng	useful
15	字	zì	word
16	容易	róng yì	easy
17	对……感兴趣	duì…… gǎn xìng qù	to be interested in…
18	阅读	yuè dú	reading
19	提高	tí gāo	to increase, to raise
20	语文	yǔ wén	language
21	水平	shuǐ píng	level, standard
22	得	děi	need to, must
23	国际	guó jì	international

补充词语
SUPPLEMENTARY VOCABULARY

1	演戏	yǎn xì	to act
2	开玩笑	kāi wán xiào	to make jokes

语法
GRAMMAR

Word order: Subject + 跟 + Person + Verb + Object

1 To express 'with + person', the preposition 跟 is used in Chinese. The basic pattern is:

  Subject + 跟 + Person + Verb + Object

  e.g. 我常常跟朋友打乒乓球和踢足球。 I often play table tennis and football with my friends.

2 Sometimes the word 一起 (together) is used with 跟, e.g. 我跟小红一起逛商场。 I go shopping with Xiao Hong.

3 If the sentence involves time and place, the word order is:

  Subject + Time (or it can be put before the subject) + 跟 + Person + Place + Verb + Object

  e.g. 我今天跟朋友一起在公园踢足球。 I play football with my friends in a park today.

The use of 跟 will be explained in detail with another preposition, 给, in Chapter 18.

句型
LANGUAGE

为什么 and 因为

为什么 is a question word which is used to ask 'why';

因为 is used to answer the question and to explain why, e.g.

a 为什么他没上学？因为他发烧了。
Why was he absent from school today? Because he had a fever.

b 为什么小王一直都很忙？ Why was Xiao Wang always busy?

c 我不喜欢英文，因为要常常看书。
I do not like English, because I often have to read books.

Unit B 11 Personal and social life: School routine

1 为什么小王一直都很忙？
2 小王常常跟他的新朋友做什么？
3 他在新学校学习多少门课？
4 小王会说什么外语？
5 为什么他学了汉语？
6 小王觉得哪两种外语容易？
7 为什么小王喜欢戏剧？
8 为什么小王不喜欢英文？
9 为什么多阅读对小王好？
10 小明在哪个学校上学？

五 阅读（二）
5 Reading (2)

一、以下是一些对科目意见的词语。试把他们分类。

1 Categorise the following words for expressing opinions of some subjects.

不错	对……感兴趣	好玩儿	进步
困难	难	容易	水平	有趣
有意思	愉快	没意思	差	还可以

不好	中性	好
		例：有意思

词语 VOCABULARY

1	进步	jìn bù	to improve
2	愉快	yú kuài	happy
3	困难	kùn nán	difficult
4	差	chà	poor, bad
5	还可以	hái kě yǐ	not too bad, acceptable
6	有趣	yǒu qù	interesting

二、请阅读下面的短文，选择唯一正确的答案，在方格里打勾。

2 Read the short passage below. Choose the correct answer for each question by ticking the box.
CD 01, Track 39

林明的学校生活

林明是北京国际学校的学生，是王小明的同学。两年前，他们在七年级的时候认识，他们都觉得，上课是一天中最愉快的事情。

林明每天八点钟上课，每节课是一个小时，一天有六节课。星期一的第一节课是音乐课，他喜欢一边唱歌，一边学习。音乐课之后是化学课，也是他最不喜欢的课，因为他觉得做实验没意思。他跟王小明都觉得，学化学比学汉语还难。因为下周他有化学考试，所以他每天放学后都做化学作业。做完作业后，林明觉得自己的化学好了一点儿。

十二点到十二点半，林明会跟王小明一起吃午饭。休息的时候还会跟朋友们一起打篮球，有时候一起去图书馆看书。两点半是西班牙语课，林明也喜欢这门课，因为他觉得上课很好玩儿。他的西班牙语成绩很好。化学考试后是学校假期，他会去马来西亚看爷爷奶奶，因为他的家就在那儿。

Cambridge IGCSE Mandarin as a Foreign Language

1 林明和王小明今年是 ____ 年级的学生。
   A 七 ☐   B 八 ☐   C 九 ☐

2 林明和王小明都觉得上课是一件 ____ 的事情。
   A 开心 ☐   B 不愉快 ☐   C 没意思 ☐

3 林明一天要上几个小时的课？
   A 1 ☐   B 6 ☐   C 16 ☐

4 为什么林明喜欢音乐课？
   A 可以唱歌、跳舞 ☐
   B 可以唱歌、写字 ☐
   C 可以学东西、唱歌 ☐

5 哪一个是林明不喜欢化学的原因？
   A 因为实验有点儿难 ☐
   B 因为化学有家长会 ☐
   C 因为这一课没意思 ☐

6 哪一个不是林明的语言课？
   A 日语 ☐   B 西班牙语 ☐   C 中文 ☐

7 林明的午饭有多长时间？
   A 一个小时 ☐   B 三十分钟 ☐
   C 十五分钟 ☐

8 在假期的时候，林明会做什么？
   A 带爷爷奶奶去马来西亚 ☐
   B 在学校做化学考试 ☐
   C 回家 ☐

词语
VOCABULARY

1	事情	shì qing	things; same as 事
2	点钟	diǎn zhōng	an expression for o'clock e.g. 8:00 is 八点钟
3	假期	jià qī	holiday, vacation
4	考试	kǎo shì	examination
5	成绩	chéng jì	results, scores
6	家长会	jiā zhǎng huì	parents' meeting
7	语言	yǔ yán	language
8	贵	guì	expensive

语法
GRAMMAR

The use of 一点儿

一点儿 is placed after an adjective, often to make a comparison or a request, e.g.

a 这件衣服太贵了，便宜一点儿吧。
   This piece of clothing is too expensive; cheaper, please!

b 吃了药后，他的身体好一点儿了。
   After taking his medication, he feels better.

Remember 一点儿 cannot be put before an adjective.

六 说话（二）
6 Speaking (2)

一、你的老师怎么样？试找出以下词语的意思。

1 What is your teacher like? Look these words up in a dictionary and find out their meanings.

yán gé	yǒu qù	hǎo wánr	yǒu hǎo
严格	有趣	好玩儿	友好

你的老师怎么样？

我觉得体育老师很友好，因为他经常都很关心我们。

你的老师怎么样？

我觉得汉语老师很严格，因为上课不可以聊天儿。

Unit B 11 Personal and social life: School routine

> 你的老师怎么样？

> 我觉得科学老师很认真，因为她每天都很认真教学生。

词语
VOCABULARY

| 1 | 认真 | rèn zhēn | to take something seriously; serious |
| 2 | 教 | jiāo | to teach |

补充词语
SUPPLEMENTARY VOCABULARY

| 关心 | guān xīn | to care |

二、短讲准备。

2 Topic conversation.

做一个两分钟以内的短讲，讲一讲"学校的一天"：

Give a two-minute talk about your school routine:

- 你今年学几门课？
- 你们每天几点钟上课？每节课多长？一天有多少节课？
- 你为什么选中文课？
- 你最喜欢哪一课？为什么？老师怎么样？
- 你最不喜欢哪一课？为什么？老师怎么样？

七 听力（二）
7 🔊 Listening (2)

林明妈妈在家长会跟王老师谈林明在学校的生活。请先阅读一下问题。

Lin Ming's mother is talking to Mr Wang about Lin Ming's life at school. Read the questions first.

请听谈话，用中文或拼音回答问题。

Listen to the conversation, and answer the questions in Chinese. You may write your answers in Chinese characters or pinyin. **CD 01, Track 40**

1. 王老师是哪国人？
2. 林明喜欢什么课？
3. 下周林明有什么考试？
4. 林明觉得数学作业怎么样？
5. 林明选择哪一个外语？为什么？

❗ 小贴士
TOP TIP

还是 (or) is a very common question word in Chinese, and there are only two possible answers, e.g. 你喜欢吃鸡还是鸭子？ The only possible answers are 鸡 or 鸭子. Do not confuse with 还有, which means 'also'.

词语
VOCABULARY

| 鸭 | yā | duck |

八 阅读（三）
8 📖 Reading (3)

请阅读北京国际学校的网页，然后回答问题。

Read the following webpage of Xiao Wang's school, then answer the questions.

北京国际学校
愉快学习，提高学生水平

1. 我们的学生一共学习九门课。英文、数学、科学是主要的科目。在科学中，他们会学到生物、物理、化学的东西。我们的学生都对科学很感兴趣，因为他们都喜欢做实验，上课很好玩儿。

2. 每个学生都会说两门外语。很多学生都选了中文，因为他们都住在中国，学习汉语很有用。我们有很多美国学生，他们觉得回去自己国家后，会说西班牙语很有用，所以学习西班牙语的人也有很多。

3. 每一年我们都有三次家长会。在家长会的时候，爸爸妈妈们会知道他们孩子在学校的生活，也可以跟老师说话，看看怎么样可以在家里帮忙提高学生的水平。

4. 在休息、午饭的时间，很多学生都会有课外活动。有很多学生也喜欢去图书馆，因为他们都知道，多看自己喜欢的书能够提高自己的语文水平。

北京国际学校相关资讯　　二〇一六年三月二十八日

词语 VOCABULARY

1 生物　shēng wù　biology
2 孩子　hái zi　child
3 够　　gòu　　enough

补充词语 SUPPLEMENTARY VOCABULARY

主要　zhǔ yào　major

1 什么课是学生的主要科目？
2 科学可以学到什么东西？
3 为什么学生都对科学很感兴趣？
4 哪两门外语最多学生学习？
5 为什么学生住在中国，但是想学西班牙语？
6 在家长会的时候，可以跟谁说话？
7 为什么学生在午饭时候去图书馆看书？

文化 CULTURE

中国的教育制度 Education in China

中国有九年的义务教育 yì wù jiào yù (compulsory education)。在中国，学生要学习语文、数学、英语、物理、化学、历史、地理、体育等等。

Unit B 11 Personal and social life: School routine

九 写作
9 Writing

一、写出五个科目的词语。

二、写出五个形容老师的词语。

三、试再读阅读（一）(<u>小王</u>的信) 的作文。你是<u>小明</u>，请给<u>小王</u>回信，说一说：

- 你今年学几门课？
- 你为什么选中文课？
- 你最喜欢哪一课？为什么？老师怎么样？
- 你最不喜欢哪一课？为什么？老师怎么样？
- 你们每天几点钟上课？每节课多长？一天有多少节课？

自我评估
Self-Assessment

- ☐ I can describe what subjects are offered in a school
- ☐ I can respond to questions about the subjects I like or do not like
- ☐ I can read a letter about one's subject options
- ☐ I can express opinions on why I like or do not like a subject
- ☐ I can talk about my school routine
- ☐ Measure words 些，门，节
- ☐ Word order when using 跟
- ☐ Question word 为什么
- ☐ Sentence structure 因为……所以……
- ☐ Use of 一点儿

Cambridge IGCSE Mandarin as a Foreign Language

xué xiāo shè shī
学校设施
12 School facilities

Learning objectives

This unit will concentrate on learning vocabulary about school facilities. You will:

- Listen to an introduction about schools
- Talk about different school facilities and their functions
- Read a map of a school

In addition, you are going to learn:

- Sentence structure
  一……就……
- Connective
  虽然……但是……
- Compound directional complements
- Use of 地 to form adverbs

学习目标

本单元，你会：

- 听关于学校的介绍
- 介绍学校的不同设施及功能
- 明白学校的地图

你还会学到：

- 句型"一……就……"
- 关联词"虽然……但是……"
- 趋向补语
- 方式副词＋地

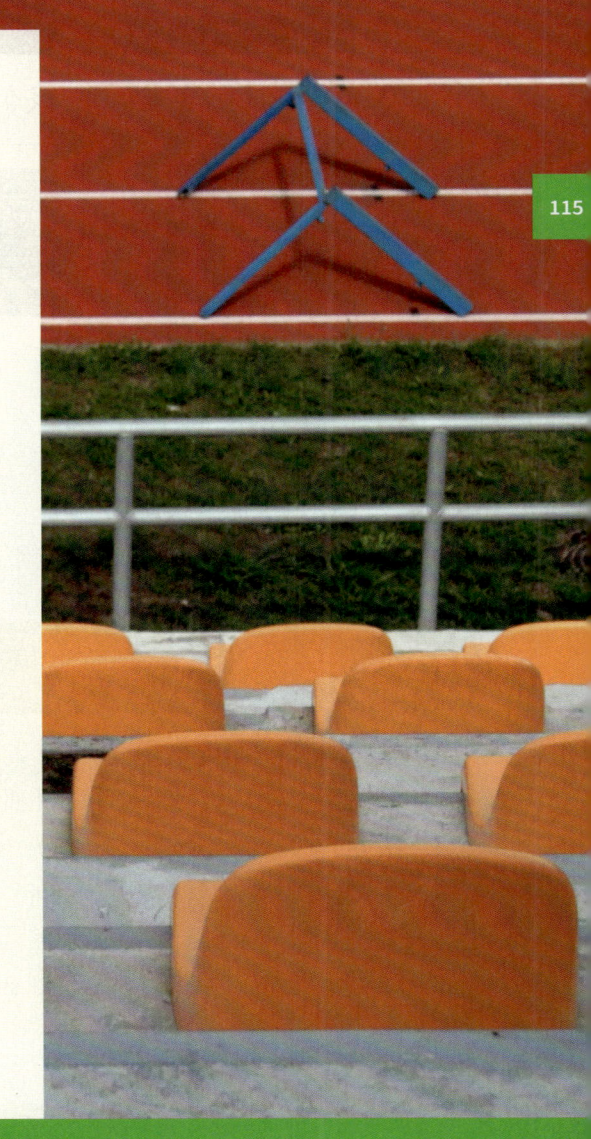

Unit B 12 Personal and social life: School facilities

一 温故知新
1 'Before starting' activities

一、和同学讨论一下，在这些地方，你们可以做什么？选择正确的词语，完成句子。

1 Discuss with your classmates: what can you do in the following places? Fill in the gaps with the most appropriate words.

A 上课	B 踢足球	C 看表演
D 做实验	E 吃饭	

1 同学们在教室里_____。 
2 老师们在礼堂里_____。 
3 学生们在实验室里_____。 
4 我们在食堂里_____。 
5 他们在球场上_____。

词语
VOCABULARY

1	教室	jiào shì	classroom
2	礼堂	lǐ táng	assembly hall
3	实验室	shí yàn shì	laboratory
4	实验	shí yàn	experiment
5	食堂	shí táng	canteen
6	球场	qiú chǎng	sports field, stadium

二、翻译句子。

2 Translate the sentences below.

1 上课了，学生们都走进教室。
2 爸爸从新加坡回来了。
3 演出开始了，我们都坐了下来。
4 妹妹从学校里走出来。
5 妈妈不在家，她出去了。

词语
VOCABULARY

1	回	huí	to return
2	来	lái	to come
3	出	chū	to exit

语法
GRAMMAR

趋向补语 Compound directional complements

When expressing directions, we usually use directional complements after a verb. Also, we can use some compound directional complements in the following way.

	上	下	进	出	回	过	起
来	上来	下来	进来	出来	回来	过来	起来
去	上去	下去	进去	出去	回去	过去	

Note:
1 来 and 去 can only be used after the other directional complements.
2 We never say 起去.

e.g.
a 他上来。 He comes up.
b 他下去。 He goes down.
c 妈妈走出去。 Mum went out. (exit)
d 妈妈走进去。 Mum went in. (enter)
e 妹妹跑进来。 The younger sister comes running in.
f 妹妹跑出来。 The younger sister comes running out.

Cambridge IGCSE Mandarin as a Foreign Language

三、按照英文意思，选择正确的词完成句子。

3 Choose the most appropriate words to complete the sentences.

| A 认真地 | B 很快地 | C 高兴地 |
| D 大声地 | | |

1 我正在_____唱歌。 I am singing happily.

2 他_____跑过来。 He runs here fast.

3 老师们正在_____开会。 The teachers are having a meeting seriously.

4 爷爷_____笑了起来。 Grandpa laughed loudly.

词语 VOCABULARY

1 开会 kāi huì to have a meeting
2 笑   xiào   to smile, to laugh
3 快   kuài   fast

补充词语 SUPPLEMENTARY VOCABULARY

大声 dà shēng loud

语法 GRAMMAR

de
地 is a particle word used after an adjective to form an adverb before the verb, indicating the manner in which the action occurs.

e.g. 高兴地笑 laugh loudly

二 听力（一）

2 🔊 Listening (1)

听问题，选择正确的答案。

Listen to the questions and choose the correct answers.
CD 01, Track 41

1 ____ A 我们学校设施齐全，有游泳池、操场、食堂、足球场等等。
2 ____ B 我们学校一共有八十个老师。
3 ____ C 校长办公室在地下层。
4 ____ D 我的学校叫蓝山中学。
5 ____ E 往左走，游泳池在门的右边。
6 ____ F 我们教学楼一共有六层楼。

词语 VOCABULARY

1 操场 cāo chǎng playground
2 要   yào   to need to

语法 GRAMMAR

往……走 is used when talking about 'going towards' a certain direction.

e.g. 往左走 turn left, 往右走 turn right, 往前走 go ahead

三 听力（二）

3 🔊 Listening (2)

一、听录音，填空。

1 Listen to the recording and fill in the gaps. CD 01, Track 42

Unit B 12 Personal and social life: School facilities

我的学校叫蓝山中学。这所学校很大，有____1____老师和____2____个学生。我们学校设备齐全，历史悠久。

一进门，左边就是一个很大的足球场。右边是一个____3____。中间是一座教学楼。足球场的后边有一个____4____，体育馆旁边有一个小卖部。游泳池的后边有一个____5____。教学楼里有礼堂、办公室、教室、实验室等等。教学楼的前边有一个小花园。

词语
VOCABULARY

1	所	suǒ	measure word for institution, e.g. school
2	设备	shè bèi	equipment
3	体育馆	tǐ yù guǎn	gym
4	小卖部	xiǎo mài bù	tuckshop
5	办公室	bàn gōng shì	office
6	校长	xiào zhǎng	head teacher, principal

补充词语
SUPPLEMENTARY VOCABULARY

1	历史悠久	lì shǐ yōu jiǔ	having a long history
2	教学楼	jiào xué lóu	teaching and learning building

二、请再听一遍录音，根据录音内容，将不同的设施填入地图内。

2　Listen to the recording again and fill in the gaps with the different facilities according to what you hear.

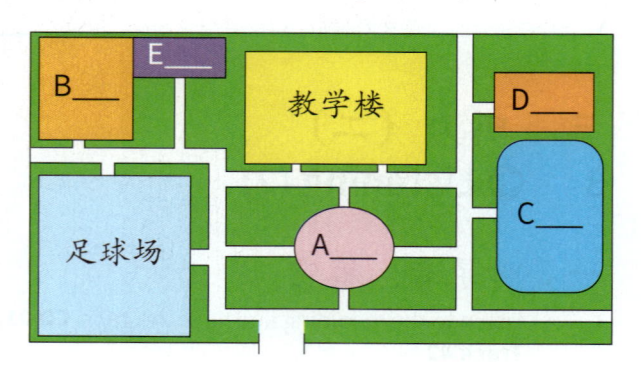

B___　E___　教学楼　D___　足球场　A___　C___

句型
LANGUAGE

一……就…… As soon as …

This structure is used to express that as soon as one event occurs the other event takes place, e.g.

一进门，左边就是一个很大的球场。 As soon as you enter the room, you will find a big field on your left.

我一下课就去吃午饭。 As soon as I finished school I went to have lunch.

我们一回到学校就要交作业。 As soon as we return to school we have to hand in our homework.

他们正在唱歌。妈妈一走进去，他们就停了下来。 They were singing. When my mum came in they stopped immediately.

练习：Translation practice

1 As soon as I am back home I watch TV.

2 As soon as we sat down（坐下）the teacher came in（进来）.

3 As soon as my younger brother finishes（做完）his homework he plays computer games.

Cambridge IGCSE Mandarin as a Foreign Language

词语
VOCABULARY

停　tíng　to stop

小贴士
TOP TIP

When 一 occurs immediately before a verb, it always means 'as soon as'. When 一 occurs immediately before a measure word, it is always the number one.

e.g. 我一进学校，就看到一个教学楼。
As soon as I entered the school, I saw a teaching building.

The first 一 means 'as soon as' while the second 一 means 'one'.

四　说话（一）
4　Speaking (1)

做一个学校"开放日"的演讲。画一张学校参观路线图，并讲解给你的同学听。

Prepare a presentation for Open Day at your school. Create a visitors' route and explain it to your classmates.

好词好句
USEFUL EXPRESSIONS

- 欢迎来到我们学校。
- 这是参观路线图。
- 一进门，你就可以看到一个体育馆。
- 往前走，游泳池在教学楼的后边。
- 教学楼在中间。食堂在教学楼的旁边。

补充词语
SUPPLEMENTARY VOCABULARY

1　开放日　kāi fàng rì　open day
2　路线　lù xiàn　route
3　讲解　jiǎng jiě　to explain

文化
CULTURE

中国的学校

在中国，六岁到十二岁上小学。十二岁到十八岁上中学。一般来说 (in general) 学生们在一个教室里上所有的 (all) 课。一个教室就是一个班 (class/form)。一个班有四十到五十个学生和一个班主任 (form tutor)。

图片上，你可以看到一间中学的教室。你看，教室的前面有一个黑板，中间有一张老师的桌子，中文叫"讲台"。教室里有二十张桌子和四十把椅子。

词语
VOCABULARY

小学　xiǎo xué　primary/elementary school

Unit B 12　Personal and social life: School facilities

延伸学习
AIM HIGHER

讨论，填表 Discuss with your classmates and fill in the table.

	中国的学校	我的学校
1 学生几岁上小学？几岁上中学？		
2 学生在一个教室里上所有的课吗？		
3 一个班有多少学生？		
4 用白板还是黑板？		
5 学生们有班主任吗？		

词语
VOCABULARY

| 1 | 白板 | bái bǎn | whiteboard |
| 2 | 黑板 | hēi bǎn | blackboard |

五 阅读（一）
5 📖 Reading (1)

读下面的课程广告，选择唯一正确的答案，回答问题。

Read the advertisements below and choose the correct answers.

A 寒假外语课程

你想学一门外语吗？在这里，小朋友们可以一边玩游戏，一边学英语、德语、法语、日语、西班牙语等等。 1
 2
 3
适合人群：5-11 岁的小学生 4
地点：广州大学外文系 5
时间：2 月 1 日 - 2 月 15 日 6
　　　上午 8:00 - 9:00，下午 3:00 - 4:00 7
学费：1890 元 8

B 暑假游泳课程

你想让你的孩子快乐地学会游泳吗？快来我们的游泳班吧！ 1
 2
本课程适合 5 岁以上的中小学生。 3
地点：蓝山中学游泳池 4
时间：7 月 1 日 - 8 月 1 日每天上午 5
　　　10:00 - 12:00 6
学费：1000 元 7

C 中文夏令营

这个暑假，你想去西安一边旅游，一边学中文吗？在这个中文夏令营，你可以参观中国的中学，认识中国朋友，也可以读很多中文书，看中文电影。在这里，你每天都要说中文。 1
 2
 3
 4
 5
适合人群：15-20 岁中文学生 6
地点：西安 7
时间：7 月 3 日 - 7 月 13 日 8
学费：8000 元 9

词语
VOCABULARY

1	寒假	hán jià	winter holidays/vacation
2	地点	dì diǎn	venue
3	广州	Guǎng zhōu	Guangzhou
4	大学	dà xué	university
5	外文	wài wén	foreign language
6	系	xì	department
7	学费	xué fèi	tuition fee
8	让	ràng	to let
9	暑假	shǔ jià	summer holidays/vacation
10	旅游	lǚ yóu	to travel
11	夏令营	xià lìng yíng	summer camp

Cambridge IGCSE Mandarin as a Foreign Language

补充词语
SUPPLEMENTARY VOCABULARY

人群　rén qún　group of people

1　谁可以去寒假外语课程？
　A　明明（15 岁）　　B　张红（20 岁）
　C　英英（4 岁）　　D　冰冰（6 岁）

2　谁不可以去暑假游泳课程？
　A　明明（15 岁）　B　明明的弟弟（14 岁）
　C　英英的妈妈（35 岁）　D　冰冰（6 岁）

3　在中文夏令营，学生不可以做什么？
　A　认识中国朋友　　B　每天说英文
　C　看中文书　　　　D　看中文电影

4　哪一个课程下午不上课？
　A　寒假外语课程　　B　暑假游泳课程
　C　中文夏令营　　　D　没有

六　阅读（二）
6　Reading (2)

马力是英国人，她参加了西安的中文夏令营。下面是她的日记，请读一读，回答问题。

Mary is from Britain. She participated in a summer camp in Xi'an. Read her diary and answer the questions.
CD 01, Track 43

七月十三日　星期五

　　今天是我在西安中文夏令营的最后一天。明天我就要回英国了。我哭了，哭得很厉害，因为舍不得我的老师和同学。
　　今年暑假，参加这个夏令营的学生有英国的、美国的、德国的、韩国的和日本的。一共有三十人。米那是美国人，她今年十六岁。我们现在是好朋友。我们都喜欢唱歌，特别是中文歌。
　　每天，我们都去西安外文大学学习中文。我们的中文老师叫张银，今年三十岁。张老师个子高高的，脸圆圆的，很可爱。她十五岁的时候，在英国当交换学生。她说，去英国以前，她的妈妈担心她不习惯英国的生活。但是她很担心自己的英文不好，害怕自己不明白英国人说什么。为了提高英文水平，她每天都读英文书。现在她的英文非常好。我很喜欢张老师，因为她的课很有意思。今天，我和张老师说："张老师，我喜欢你！我可以给你写信吗？"没想到张老师笑了。她说："我会记住回信的！"

1　参加夏令营的学生有多少人？
2　"我"和米那都喜欢做什么？
3　张老师什么时候在英国？
4　去英国之前，张老师担心什么？
5　"我"为什么喜欢张老师？

词语
VOCABULARY

1	最后	zuì hòu	last, final
2	哭	kū	to cry
3	厉害	lì hai	terribly, terrible
4	韩国	Hán guó	Korea
5	特别	tè bié	especially
6	圆	yuán	round, circle
7	当	dāng	to act as

Unit B　12　Personal and social life: School facilities

词语
VOCABULARY

8	交换学生	jiāo huàn xué shēng	exchange student
9	担心	dān xīn	to worry
10	习惯	xí guàn	to get used to
11	害怕	hài pà	to be afraid; same as 怕
12	明白	míng bai	to understand
13	为	wèi	for; 为了 in order to
14	没想到	méi xiǎng dào	not to have been expected
15	记住	jì zhù	to remember; 记 to remember

补充词语
SUPPLEMENTARY VOCABULARY

舍不得 shě bu dé   not want to be parted with

七 写作
7 Writing

回到英国以后，马力写了一封信给张老师。请读一读，然后代表张老师，写一封回信。

When she returned to Britain, Mary wrote a letter to Ms Zhang. Read the letter and write a reply to Mary on behalf of Ms Zhang.

亲爱的张老师：

　　你好吗？虽然中文夏令营结束了，我还是很想念你。现在，我的中文水平提高了。昨天，我和爸爸妈妈去中国饭店吃饭。服务员和我说中文，我明白了。爸爸妈妈非常高兴。谢谢你，张老师！

张老师，你中学的时候，喜欢什么课？喜欢哪个老师？你的学校怎么样？有什么设备？

　　虽然我知道你很忙，但是我希望你会回信。

　　祝

好

　　　　　　　　　马力

　　　　　　　　八月一日

张老师的回信

亲爱的马力：

　　你好。谢谢你的来信。我很好。谢谢你。

　　很高兴你的中文水平提高了。

　　中学的时候，我喜欢_____。因为_____。我喜欢我的_____课老师，因为_____。我的学校虽然_____，但是_____。我的学校设备齐全，有_____、_____、_____和_____等等。

　　你喜欢你的学校吗？

　　祝

学习进步！

　　　　　　　　　张老师

　　　　　　　　八月十日

Cambridge IGCSE Mandarin as a Foreign Language

好词好句
USEFUL EXPRESSIONS

- 我喜欢化学课，因为我喜欢做实验。
- 我喜欢美术课，因为我喜欢画画儿。
- 我的学校虽然不大，但是历史悠久。
- 我的学校虽然是新学校，但是有很多好老师。

句型
LANGUAGE

虽然……但是 / 可是…… Although…, but…

This sentence structure is used to link clauses with contrasting meanings. 虽然 and 但是 are both connectors for contrast sentences. 虽然 can sometimes be omitted. 但是 can be replaced by 不过 or 可是.

It expresses that while the former part of the sentence is true, there is a contrasting reaction in the latter part.

虽然 + subject + 但是 / 可是 + contrary reaction

e.g. 虽然他是法国人，但是他不会说法语。

练习：Read the example sentence below and complete your own sentences.

虽然	我知道你很忙，	但是	我希望你会回信。
虽然	中文很难，	但是	
虽然		但是	

词语
VOCABULARY

1	虽然	suī rán	although
2	可是	kě shì	but
3	不过	bú guò	but

小贴士
TOP TIP

虽然……但是…… is a very useful structure for linking complex contrast sentences. Using connectors often will make both your written and your spoken language more interesting.

八 说话（二）
8 Speaking (2)

和同学两人一组，完成情景对话。
Work in pairs and complete the dialogue.

A 老师 B 在中国的交换学生

情景：交换学生在图书馆和一个中国老师说话。

Scenario: An exchange student is talking to a Chinese teacher in the library.

A1: 你是哪国人？
A2: 你来中国多长时间了？
A3: 你会说什么语言？
A4: 你喜欢看什么书？
A5: 你有什么爱好？

自我评估
Self-Assessment

- ☐ I can listen to an introduction about schools
- ☐ I can introduce the different functions of school
- ☐ I can read a map of a school
- ☐ Sentence structure: 一……就……
- ☐ Connective 虽然……但是……
- ☐ Compound directional complements
- ☐ Use of 地 to form an adverb

Unit B 12 Personal and social life: School facilities

考试练习题
Exam-style questions

一、听力
1 🔊 Listening

<u>刘一平</u>是新同学。她想参加学校的课外活动。她在和老师说话。先看图片。

Liu Yiping is a new student. She wants to participate in extracurricular activities. She is talking to a teacher. First look at the pictures.

听下面对话。将图片旁的字母分别填入适当的方格内。

Listen to the dialogue, and put the correct letter in the appropriate box. **CD 01, Track 44**

A   B   C   D

1 星期一 ☐
2 星期三 ☐
3 星期五 ☐

二、阅读
2 📖 Reading

选择唯一正确的答案。

For each of the questions, choose the correct answer.

1 小<u>王</u>买了一瓶墨水。小<u>王</u>买了什么?

A   B   C   D

2 图书馆关门了。哪里关门了?

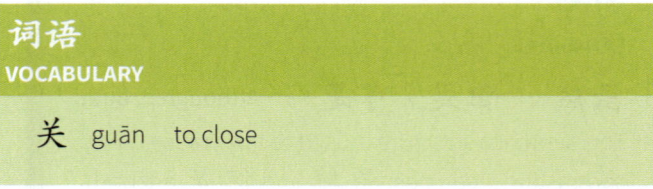

A   B   C   D

词语
VOCABULARY

关　guān　to close

三、阅读
3 📖 Reading

请看图回答问题 1 至 3,选择"是"或"非"。

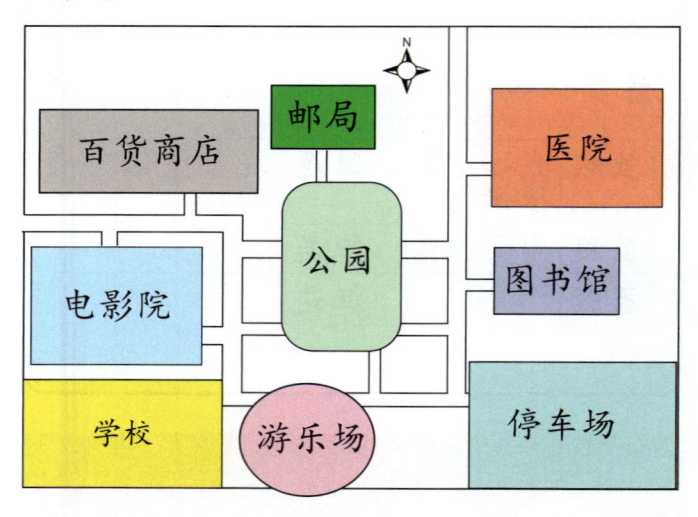

		是	非
1	电影院在西边。	☐	☐
2	去邮局应该从公园一直往北走。	☐	☐
3	学校旁边有停车场。	☐	☐

Cambridge IGCSE Mandarin as a Foreign Language

C The world around us
zhōu yóu shì jiè
周游世界

tiān qì yǔ qì hòu
天气与气候
13 Weather and climate

Learning objectives

This unit will concentrate on weather and climate around the world. You will:

- Read weather forecasts and compare the weather conditions in different cities
- Understand conversations about weather and climate
- Talk about the weather and climate in your own city
- Write a letter to a friend in China about the weather in your city

In addition, you are going to learn:

- Comparisons: ……比……
- Sentence structure: 如果……，就……
- Future (1): 要……了，快要……了，快……了
- The use of verb/adjective + 起来 + 了
- Measure word: 场

学习目标

本单元你会：

- 阅读世界各个城市的天气预报
- 明白有关天气情况的对话
- 说一说你所在城市的天气
- 给一个中国的朋友写一封信，说一说你所住城市的天气

你还会学到：

- 比较：……比……
- 句型：如果……，就……
- 未来 (1)：要……了、快要……了、快……了
- 怎么用"起来＋了"
- 量词：场

Cambridge IGCSE Mandarin as a Foreign Language

一 温故知新
1 'Before starting' activity

把中文和英文搭配起来。
Match the following words with their English meanings.

1	多云 / 阴天	A		cold
2	刮风	B		cloudy
3	晴天	C		windy
4	下雪	D		raining
5	下雨	E		snowing
6	有雾	F		climate
7	热	G		foggy
8	冷	H		sunny
9	天气	I		hot
10	气候	J		weather

词语 VOCABULARY

1	多云	duō yún
2	刮风	guā fēng
3	晴天	qíng tiān
4	下雪	xià xuě
5	下雨	xià yǔ
6	阴天	yīn tiān
7	有雾	yǒu wù
8	热	rè
9	冷	lěng
10	天气	tiān qì
11	气候	qì hòu

延伸活动 AIM HIGHER

还有什么其他"天气与气候"的词语?

二 阅读（一）
2 Reading (1)

请阅读下面的天气预报,然后选择"是"或"非"。

Read the weather forecast below and choose True or False for each sentence.

明天天气预报		
北京	晴	27°C
香港	晴	25°C
上海	下雨	24°C
西安	晴	20°C
南京	有雾	24°C
广州	大风	31°C

		是	非
1	北京比香港热。	☐	☐
2	在上海要用雨衣。	☐	☐
3	上海跟南京的气温一样。	☐	☐
4	广州最热。	☐	☐
5	西安气温在二十一到二十五度之间。	☐	☐

词语 VOCABULARY

1	天气预报	tiān qì yù bào	weather forecast
2	度	dù	degree (temperature)
3	气温	qì wēn	temperature
4	上海	Shàng hǎi	Shanghai
5	西安	Xī'ān	Xi'an
6	南京	Nán jīng	Nanjing
7	晴	qíng	sunny
8	风	fēng	wind

Unit C 13 The world around us: Weather and climate

词语 VOCABULARY

9	……比……	bǐ	a sentence structure for comparison (see Language box below)
10	最	zuì	most
11	凉快	liáng kuai	cool
12	雨衣	yǔ yī	raincoat

补充词语 SUPPLEMENTARY VOCABULARY

| 在 A 和 B 之间 | zài A hé B zhī jiān | between A and B |

小贴士 TOP TIP

A number and 度 are used to tell temperature in Chinese, e.g. 五度, 十三度, 零下三度.

想一想：为什么是"两度"不是"二度"？

文化 CULTURE 文化

在中国，温度一般都用"摄氏度" (Shè shì dù) (Celsius)，而不用"华氏度" (Huá shì dù) (Fahrenheit)。

句型 LANGUAGE

比 is used when two things are being compared.

1 The basic pattern is: A 比 B + adjective,
e.g. 北京比香港热。Beijing is hotter than Hong Kong.

练习：Use the information in the weather forecast to make comparisons about temperature between the following cities.

1 北京、上海（热）
2 上海、香港（热）
3 北京、西安（凉快）
4 西安、广州（热）
5 南京、北京（凉快）

2 A similar structure is ……比……一点儿. 一点儿 was introduced in Chapter 11 and can be used with the sentence structure ……比…… to indicate just a little bit more/less, e.g. 香港比广州热一点儿 Hong Kong is slightly hotter than Guangzhou.

3 A complement of quantity can be added after the adjective to indicate how much/many more/less in comparison, e.g. 香港比北京热三度 Hong Kong is hotter than Beijing by 3 degrees.

三 说话（一）
3 Speaking (1)

请再看阅读（一）的天气预报，然后跟同学练习对话。

Look at the forecast in Reading (1) again and ask your partner about the weather in each city.

1 香港 2 上海 3 西安 4 南京 5 广州

北京明天多少度？

北京明天二十七度。

北京明天天气怎么样？

北京明天晴天。

句型 LANGUAGE

1 怎么样？ (zěn me yàng) how is…?
2 多少度？ (duō shǎo dù) how many degrees?

Cambridge IGCSE Mandarin as a Foreign Language

延伸活动
AIM HIGHER

Go to a weather forecast website and look at the forecasts for different cities. Work in pairs and ask each other about the weather in the cities. The following are some suggestions.

1 雅加达 (Yǎ jiā dá) Jakarta
2 曼谷 (Màn gǔ) Bangkok
3 东京 (Dōng jīng) Tokyo

四 听力（一）
4 🔊 Listening (1)

一、 你将听到几个中文句子。在唯一正确的方格内打勾（✓）回答问题。

1 You will hear some short phrases in Chinese. Answer each question by ticking one box only. **CD 01, Track 45**

1 今天天气怎么样？
 A 下雨 ☐ B 晴天 ☐
 C 阴天 ☐ D 刮风 ☐

2 今天多少度？
 A 32°C ☐ B 23°C ☐
 C 24°C ☐ D 30°C ☐

3 明天天气怎么样？
 A 下毛毛雨 ☐ B 下雪 ☐
 C 有雷雨 ☐ D 晴天 ☐

4 明天多少度？
 A −10°C ☐ B 10°C ☐
 C 7°C ☐ D −7°C ☐

补充词语
SUPPLEMENTARY VOCABULARY

1 零下　línɡ xià　minus, below zero
2 毛毛雨　máo mao yǔ　drizzle
3 雷雨　léi yǔ　thunderstorm

二、 你正在听天气预报。把图片旁的字母分别填入适当的方格内。

2 You will hear a weather forecast. Listen, and put the correct letter in the appropriate box. **CD 01, Track 46**

1 新加坡	2 台北	3 香港	4 北京

A
B
C
D
E

Unit C 13 The world around us: Weather and climate

语法
GRAMMAR

1 To give an approximate temperature, we use the pattern 在……度左右, e.g. 在二十度左右 around 20°C.

2 To give a range of temperature we use 在 number 到 number 之间, e.g. 在二十四到二十六度之间 24°C to 26°C.

五 阅读（二）
5 Reading (2)

请阅读下面的信，然后回答问题。
Read the letter below and answer the questions.
CD 01, Track 47

小王： 1
　　你好！我暑假去了北京看爷爷 2
奶奶。 3
　　我们住在爷爷奶奶的家。北京的房 4
子不便宜，他们的家比我们的家贵。北 5
京夏天的天气很不错，每天太阳都出来， 6
我们都很快乐。如果我们住的地方每天 7
都有阳光，气候就很舒服。我们晚上躺 8
在公园看星星。 9
　　有一天，我跟妹妹一起去了市中心。 10
爷爷要我们带雨伞。他说："天要下雨 11
了！"我们都笑了，太阳都出来了，不可 12
能会下雨的。 13
　　可是，我们走了几分钟就下雨了。 14
我们的衣服都湿透了。我不知道哪条路 15
最好走。我走了十分钟就想："我们迷路 16
了。如果我们听了爷爷的话，衣服就不 17
会湿透了。" 18
　　回家后，妹妹说她不舒服，感觉快 19
要发烧了。奶奶给了她一大碗热汤，让 20

她暖和暖和。晚上妹妹发烧了，体温在 21
39 度左右。妹妹休息了一个星期，没有 22
去玩儿。我们走的时候，天气预报说， 23
北京会多云转晴，但是我们要回家了。 24
　　你在马来西亚怎么样？请给我写信。 25
　　祝 26
好！ 27
　　　　　　　　　　　你的朋友　小田 28
　　　　　　　　　　　九月二十二日 29

1 小田的爷爷奶奶住在哪里？
2 为什么小田在北京很快乐？
3 爷爷为什么要小田带伞？
4 小田走了多久才知道他们迷路了？
5 回家后奶奶做了什么？
6 妹妹发烧时的体温是多少？
7 天气预报说了什么？
8 小王在哪里？

词语
VOCABULARY

1	夏天	xià tiān	summer
2	太阳	tài yang	the sun, sunshine
3	出来	chū lái	to come out
4	阳光	yáng guāng	sunlight
5	如果……就……	rú guǒ……jiù……	if…, then…
6	躺	tǎng	to lie (down)
7	可能	kě néng	possible
8	有一天	yǒu yì tiān	one day
9	快要……了	kuài yào ……le	soon
10	暖和	nuǎn huo	warm
11	云	yún	cloud
12	转	zhuǎn	to change

Cambridge IGCSE Mandarin as a Foreign Language

词语
VOCABULARY

| 13 | 赶 | gǎn | to catch (also see Supplementary Vocabulary) |

补充词语
SUPPLEMENTARY VOCABULARY

1	湿透	shī tòu	wet through; 湿 wet
2	这时候	zhè shí hòu	this time
3	赶快	gǎn kuài	to hurry
4	转晴	zhuǎn qíng	to change to sunny weather

句型
LANGUAGE

如果……，就……

This is the same sentence structure as 'if..., (then)...' in English, e.g. 如果每天都有阳光，气候就很舒服。 If the sun came out every day, the weather would be very pleasant.

Note: remember to use 就 in the second part of the sentence.

语法
GRAMMAR

Future (1): 要……了、快要……了、快……了

要……了, 快要……了 and 快……了 all imply 'about to' or that something is going to happen soon.

Note that 了 is paired up with 快 / 要 / 快要 here; this is different from the single use of 了 to imply a past action, e.g.

a 天快要黑了。 The sky is going to get dark soon.
b 小明要生病了。 Xiao Ming is about to get sick.
c 快到了。 We are almost there.

六 听力（二）
6 🔊 Listening (2)

一个学生和老师在谈天气。
A student is talking about the weather with his teacher.

听录音，用中文或拼音回答问题。
Listen to the recording and write your answers in Chinese characters or pinyin. **CD 01, Track 48**

1 北京春天时，白天的天气怎么样？
2 北京的夏天怎么样？
3 北京的冬天怎么样？
4 冬天去北京时要穿什么？

词语
VOCABULARY

1	季节	jì jié	season
2	春天	chūn tiān	spring
3	秋天	qiū tiān	autumn
4	冬天	dōng tiān	winter
5	夜里	yè lǐ	at night; night time
6	强风	qiáng fēng	strong wind; 强 strong
7	毛衣	máo yī	jumper, sweater

Unit C 13 The world around us: Weather and climate

七 阅读（三）
7 Reading (3)

请阅读下面的新闻报道，然后回答问题。

Read the news article below, and answer the questions.
CD 01, Track 49

北京今年冬天的第一场雪

1. 北京昨天下了冬天的第一场大雪。
2. 北京很多地方都变成了白色的世界。
3. 很多人都在公园里看雪、照相，他们
4. 都上传照片到微博。
5. 因为下雪，人们都穿上了冬天的衣
6. 服。女孩们拿出各式各样的大衣，戴
7. 上五颜六色的帽子、手套，在雪中逛
8. 街。她们都穿得很漂亮，好像一朵花。
9. 男孩子看见女孩子穿得这么漂亮，都
10. 很开心。
11. 天气预报说，冷空气进入北京，明
12. 天的气温最低要降到零下五度了。如
13. 果明天有阳光的话，最高气温是五度。
14. 医生说，天气要转冷了，小孩子要小
15. 心感冒，上学时生病就不好。
16. 李木雷在北京一个卖大衣的时装
17. 店工作。他说，因为冬天来了，他们
18. 店也开始热闹起来了。他们的冬天衣
19. 服都打折了，很多顾客都喜欢买帽子。
20. 李木雷是法国人，每一次下雪他都会
21. 很想家，很想去滑雪。今年，他很想
22. 去日本的郊区滑雪。滑雪又好玩儿又
23. 健康，他最喜欢了。

一、请用下列词组填空。

1 Use the following words to fill in the gaps.

| 照相　戴　逛街　好像　天气预报 |
| 打折　健康 |

1 明天的_____是，最高气温五度，最低零下五度。
2 北京昨天下了雪。北京_____一个白色的世界。
3 在李木雷的商店，大衣_____了。
4 滑雪是一个_____的运动。
5 冬天要_____帽子、手套。

二、选择唯一正确的答案。

2 Choose the correct answer to each question.

1 在公园里，很多人
  A 看微博 □
  B 看白色的北京 □
  C 拍照片 □

2 女孩子戴上的帽子
  A 有十一种颜色 □
  B 有很多颜色 □
  C 有一朵花 □

3 男孩子
  A 喜欢女孩子穿得漂亮 □
  B 喜欢一朵花 □
  C 送女孩子一朵花 □

4 谁要小心感冒？
  A 小学生 □
  B 老师 □
  C 医生 □

5 今年李木雷要做什么？
  A 回法国的家 □
  B 去法国滑雪 □
  C 在郊区滑雪 □

Cambridge IGCSE Mandarin as a Foreign Language

词语
VOCABULARY

1 起来 qǐ lái — a complement used to indicate that an action or state has started and is ongoing
2 好像 hǎo xiàng — to look like
3 低 dī — low

补充词语
SUPPLEMENTARY VOCABULARY

1 场 cháng — a measure word for an event
2 变成 biàn chéng — to become
3 上传 shàng chuán — to upload
4 降 jiàng — to drop, to fall, to lower

语法
GRAMMAR

Measure word: 场

There are two pronunciations for the measure word 场: 'cháng' and 'chǎng'. They have different meanings.

1 场 'cháng' is a measure word for an event, e.g.
   a 今天下了场大雨。 It rained today.
   b 那场比赛很好看。 That competition was good.
2 场 'chǎng' is a measure word for sports and entertainment, e.g.
   a 跳一场舞 a dance
   b 两场足球赛 two football matches

句型
LANGUAGE

Verb/Adjective + 起来

起来 is a complement used to show that an action or state has started and is ongoing. The basic pattern is:

| Verb / Adj. + 起来 + 了 |

e.g.
a 他们店开始热闹起来了。Their shop is getting busier.
b 他身体好起来了。His health is getting better.

文化
CULTURE

tiān yǒu bú cè fēng yún
"天有不测风云"

This is a Chinese saying which means 'something unexpected can happen any time'.

八 说话（二）
8 Speaking (2)

口头回答以下问题。
Answer the following questions orally.

1 今天天气怎么样？
2 今天多少度？
3 (a city name) 的春天怎么样？要穿什么？
4 (a city name) 的夏天怎么样？要穿什么？
5 (a city name) 的秋天怎么样？要穿什么？
6 (a city name) 的冬天怎么样？要穿什么？

Unit C 13 The world around us: Weather and climate

例：
问：

> 北京的冬天怎么样？要穿什么？

答：

> 北京的冬天很冷，有时候有大风雪，气温在零下五到十度左右。出门要穿大衣，戴帽子，围巾和手套。

九 写作
9 Writing

一、 写出五个跟天气有关的词语。

1　Write down five words related to weather and climate.

二、 请再读阅读（二）的信。你是小王，请给小田回信。信里提及：

2　Read the letter in Reading (2) again. You are Xiao Wang and you are writing a letter back to Xiao Tian. Mention the following in your letter:

- 你住在哪里？
- 你住的地方夏天怎么样？
- 你在夏天做了什么？
- 你最喜欢的季节是哪一个？为什么？

自我评估
Self-Assessment

☐ I can read weather forecasts and compare the weather conditions in different cities
☐ I can understand conversations about weather and climate
☐ I can talk about the weather and climate in my own city
☐ I can write a letter about my city's weather to a friend in China
☐ Comparisons: ……比……
☐ Sentence structure: 如果……，就…….
☐ Future (1): 要……了，快要……了，快……了
☐ Use of 起来 + 了
☐ Measure word 场

Cambridge IGCSE Mandarin as a Foreign Language

jiāo tōng gōng jù
交通工具
14 Transportation

Learning objectives

This unit will concentrate on learning vocabulary about different modes of transport. You will:

- Read guidelines on how to get around in a city

- Listen to an announcement on a train

- Talk about the different public and private modes of transport in your city

- Respond to questions when buying train tickets

- Write a letter to a friend to introduce the transportation system in your city

In addition, you are going to learn:

- The measure words 辆, 匹 and 种

- The sentence structures 比……更, 最, ……没有…… and 先……然后……

- Word order: 我坐公共汽车上学

学习目标

本单元你会:

- 阅读交通指南

- 听懂火车上的广播

- 说一说你居住的城市有什么交通工具

- 学习怎么用中文买火车票

- 给朋友写一封信,介绍你城市的交通工具

你还会学到:

- 量词:辆、匹、种

- 句型:比……更、最,……没有……、先……然后……

- 语序:我坐公共汽车上学

135

Unit C 14 The world around us: Transportation

一 温故知新
1 'Before starting' activities

一、从以下图片中找出不同交通工具的名称。

1 Identify the different modes of transport in the image below.

词语
VOCABULARY

1	交通	jiāo tōng	traffic
2	摩托车	mó tuō chē	motorbike
3	还	hái	still, also

补充词语
SUPPLEMENTARY VOCABULARY

1	交通工具	jiāo tōng gōng jù	means of transportation
2	电车	diàn chē	tram
3	缆车	lǎn chē	cable car
4	人力车	rén lì chē	rickshaw
5	校车	xiào chē	school bus

延伸活动
AIM HIGHER

你还能说出多少种交通工具？

语法
GRAMMAR

1 辆 (liàng), 匹 (pǐ)

辆 is a measure word which refers to cars, e.g. 一辆汽车, 两辆校车. 匹 (pǐ) is a measure word for horses only, e.g. 一匹马.

2 种 as a measure word

In the previous Aim Higher question, 种 is a measure word for referring to 'how many different *types*'. A similar usage is 你会说多少种语言? How many different types of languages do you speak?

延伸活动
AIM HIGHER

What is the measure word for 船?

二、什么时候用"坐"？什么时候用"骑"？什么时候用"走"？请填以下的表格。

2 When do we use 坐, 骑 or 走? Enter modes of transportation in the appropriate columns of the table.

词语
VOCABULARY

1	坐	zuò	to travel by
2	骑	qí	to ride (e.g. a horse)

坐	骑	走
例：坐飞机、	例：骑马	
a	b	c
坐_____	骑_____	走_____ (lù)
坐_____		
坐_____		

Cambridge IGCSE Mandarin as a Foreign Language

文化 CULTURE

不同地方对交通工具的叫法

在台湾,"地铁"叫"捷运(jié yùn)"。在香港叫"地铁"。在不同的地方中,香港叫"巴士(bā shì)",中国内地叫"公交车"。在香港,"出租车"也叫"的士",在台湾叫"计程车"。这些都是相通(xiāng tōng)(interchangeable)的。

台湾捷运 　　香港地铁

香港巴士 　　北京公交车

词语 VOCABULARY

出租汽车(chū zū qì chē) / 出租车(chū zū chē) taxi, cab

坐出租车可以说"打车(dǎ chē)",比如"我今天打车上班"。

语法 GRAMMAR

语序:我坐公共汽车上学
Word order: Manner

'Manner' refers to how you do something. In the example 我坐公共汽车上学, it refers to how you get to school. 坐公共汽车 is put before the action 上学 as it is a description of how you get to school. Look at the following examples:

	Subject	Manner	Action	English
1	我	坐公共汽车	到游泳池。	I take a bus to go to the swimming pool.
2	我	坐地铁	到市中心。	I take the underground to the city centre.
3	我	坐飞机	去日本。	I take a plane to Japan.

二 听力(一)
2 Listening (1)

你刚到一个新学校,同学们一起谈他们怎么上学。

You just started at a new school. Your classmates are talking about how they get to school every day.

听录音,选择正确的交通工具回答问题,将字母填入方格内。

Listen to the recording and put the correct letter in the appropriate box. **CD 01, Track 50**

A 出租车　　B 公共汽车　　C 船
D 校车　　　E 飞机　　　　F 自行车
G 地铁　　　H 妈妈开车

晶晶(Jīng jing)	大力(Dà lì)	小王(Xiǎo wáng)	冰冰(Bīng bing)	庭庭(Tíng ting)
D				

Unit C 14 The world around us: Transportation

词语
VOCABULARY

1	先……然后……	xiān…… rán hòu ……	first… then…
2	开车	kāi chē	to drive

补充词语
SUPPLEMENTARY VOCABULARY

小岛	xiǎo dǎo	island

句型
LANGUAGE

先 …… 然后 …… first…then…

This is a sentence structure for describing two actions where one is followed by another, e.g.

我每天都要先坐船，然后坐公交车上学。Every day I take first the ferry, then the bus to school.

三 说话（一）
3 Speaking (1)

一、跟同学练习以下的对话。

1 Read aloud the following dialogue.

你在南京的一个火车站买票。一个售票员跟你讲话。

You are buying train tickets in the Nanjing Train Station. A ticket agent is talking to you.

目的地是哪里？

我要去北京。

你下午出发还是晚上？

我下午去。

你要几张票？

我要一张票。

你要单程票还是来回票？

来回票，谢谢。

你什么时候返回南京？

我明天回来。

二、现在跟同学一起练习，一个当售票员，一个当乘客，把"南京"改为"北京"和"西安"。同时还可以问以下问题：

2 Now practise the dialogue with a classmate, with one of you as the ticket agent and the other as the passenger. Change the city name 'Nanjing' to 'Beijing' and 'Xi'an'. You could also ask the following questions:
1 你行李多吗？
2 你要软卧还是硬卧？

小贴士
TOP TIP

Read the scenario carefully; do not say you want to go to 'Nanjing' if you are buying tickets in Nanjing Station!

词语
VOCABULARY

1	火车站	huǒ chē zhàn	train station
2	售票员	shòu piào yuán	ticket agent
3	出发	chū fā	to set out
4	……张（票）	……zhāng (piào)	measure word for 'tickets'
5	单程票	dān chéng piào	single ticket

CAMBRIDGE IGCSE Mandarin as a Foreign Language

词语
VOCABULARY

6	来回票	lái huí piào	return/round-trip ticket
7	行李	xíng li	luggage
8	软卧	ruǎn wò	soft sleeper
9	硬卧	yìng wò	tourist coach; a hard bed in a carriage

四 阅读（一）
4 Reading (1)

请阅读下面的网页,然后用中文回答问题：
Read the following text and answer the questions in Chinese.
CD 01, Track 51

香港的交通工具
香港这个大城市，有各种各样的交通工具。香港国际机场是很多旅客的第一个到达的地方。飞机场每天的飞机都准时起飞，时刻表的飞机很少有"误点"的出现。从机场到市中心，可以选择坐地铁，也可以选择坐巴士。从机场到市中心的地铁叫"机场快线"，三十分钟就可以到市中心，是最快的选择。你也可以坐巴士，路程大概一个多小时。坐巴士比坐地铁更便宜，但是巴士没有地铁快。你可以在汽车站坐A10路巴士到市中心。

香港的市中心叫"中环"，那里什么时候都是人山人海，车水马龙，非常热闹。从那儿坐地铁到香港每个角落都方便，每天的末班车在凌晨一点左右，要回家的话不要太晚。坐巴士也可以，不过在上班、下班这些繁忙时间都会堵车，约了朋友的人可能会迟到。

1 香港的交通工具多吗？为什么？
2 香港国际机场是一个什么样的地方？
3 从机场到市中心，可以坐什么？（两个答案）
4 机场快线要坐多久？
5 巴士从机场到市中心要多久？
6 巴士跟地铁，哪个更贵？
7 巴士跟地铁，哪个更快？
8 "中环"是怎么样的？（三个答案）
9 末班车在什么时候开出？
10 为什么坐巴士可能会迟到？

词语
VOCABULARY

1	(飞)机场	(fēi) jī chǎng	airport
2	准时	zhǔn shí	on time
3	很少	hěn shǎo	seldom, rarely
4	起飞	qǐ fēi	to take off
5	时刻表	shí kè biǎo	schedule/timetable
6	路程	lù chéng	journey
7	大概	dà gài	probably
8	更	gèng	even more
9	路	lù	route number
10	热闹	rè nao	busy and lively
11	末班车	mò bān chē	the last train/bus
12	回家	huí jiā	to go home
13	晚	wǎn	late
14	上班	shàng bān	to go to work
15	下班	xià bān	to get off work
16	堵车	dǔ chē	traffic jam
17	迟到	chí dào	to be late

Unit C 14 The world around us: Transportation

补充词语
SUPPLEMENTARY VOCABULARY

1	到达	dào dá	to arrive
2	误点	wù diǎn	delay
3	出现	chū xiàn	to appear
4	人山人海	rén shān rén hǎi	sea of people
5	车水马龙	chē shuǐ mǎ lóng	heavy traffic
6	角落	jiǎo luò	corner
7	凌晨	líng chén	before dawn

句型
LANGUAGE

1. ……比……更 + Adjective
   This pattern is similar to the ……比…… + Adjective structure you have learnt in Chapter 13. 更 means 'even more' and it is used here for emphasis. In Reading (1), 坐巴士比坐地铁更便宜 means 'taking a bus is even cheaper than taking the underground'.

2. 最 + Adjective
   In Chinese, you can use 最 to form a superlative, e.g. 最好 'the best', 最高 'the tallest', 最漂亮 'the most beautiful'. In the passage, it says 最快 'the fastest'.

3. ……没有…… + Adjective
   In Chinese you cannot use 不 in a sentence structure containing 比. It is wrong to say 巴士比地铁不快. You can use ……没有…… + adjective instead, e.g. 巴士没有地铁快.

李小红:

　　知道你快要来伦敦，我很高兴。北京和伦敦都是大城市，他们都有各种各样的交通工具。我觉得你会喜欢伦敦的。很多人都喜欢在市中心逛街、买东西。伦敦的地下铁路很方便，在不同的购物大街都有地铁站，从出口一出，就可以看见大大小小的商店，十分热闹。星期六、日，街上人山人海，十分挤，不想去逛街的话可以去公园坐坐，伦敦的海德公园很有名。

　　从你住的地方去海德公园可以坐地铁，也可以坐公共汽车。两种交通工具都可以直接到那里。虽然伦敦的公共汽车很有意思，但是它比地铁更慢了。坐10路公共汽车就可以到海德公园。

　　你到了伦敦以后，要给我打个电话，我们可以一起在伦敦吃中餐。
　　祝
好！
　　　　　　　　　　　　　马田上
　　　　　　　　　　　　　三月三十日

五 阅读（二）
5 Reading (2)

请阅读下面的信，然后回答问题。请选择唯一正确的答案，在方格里打勾。

Read the letter below and answer the questions. Choose the only correct answer to each question by ticking the box.

Cambridge IGCSE Mandarin as a Foreign Language

1 大城市有
　A 很少的交通工具。☐
　B 一个一个的交通工具。☐
　C 很多的交通工具。☐

2 很多人喜欢在伦敦
　A 购物。☐
　B 的超市买东西。☐
　C 坐地铁。☐

3 什么时候街上很挤？
　A 周末 ☐
　B 星期一到五 ☐
　C 每天六点钟 ☐

4 去海德公园坐地铁更好，因为
　A 更快 ☐
　B 更慢 ☐
　C 更有意思 ☐

5 马田和李小红在伦敦最有可能一起吃的是
　A 香肠 ☐　B 汉堡包 ☐　C 饺子 ☐

词语
VOCABULARY

1	地下	dì xià	(adj.) underground
2	铁路	tiě lù	railway; 地下铁路 = 地铁
3	站	zhàn	station, stop
4	出口	chū kǒu	exit
5	挤	jǐ	crowded
6	慢	màn	slow
7	周末	zhōu mò	weekend

补充词语
SUPPLEMENTARY VOCABULARY

1	直接	zhí jiē	directly
2	海德公园	Hǎi dé gōng yuán	Hyde Park
3	有名	yǒu míng	famous

六　听力（二）
6 🔊 Listening (2)

你在中国的高铁上听到一段广播。请用中文或拼音填空。

You are listening to a broadcast on a high-speed train in China. Fill in the gaps with Chinese characters or pinyin.

CD 01, Track 52

在广播中，这一班火车是从＿1＿到＿2＿的。车程一共＿3＿小时三十七分钟。如果乘客想买可乐，可以去＿4＿号车。职员叫我们要把＿5＿和＿6＿放好。

词语
VOCABULARY

1	大家	dà jiā	everybody
2	广播	guǎng bō	broadcast, announcement
3	……班	……bān	measure word for 'train' or 'bus'
4	乘	chéng	to take, same as 坐
5	开往	kāi wǎng	going to
6	手提包	shǒu tí bāo	handbag
7	箱子	xiāng zi	box, suitcase, trunk

Unit C 14 The world around us: Transportation

补充词语
SUPPLEMENTARY VOCABULARY

| 高铁 | gāo tiě | high-speed rail |

七 听力（三）
7 🔊 Listening (3)

王老师是李明的汉语老师。王老师以前住在一个大城市。李明很想知道那里有什么交通工具。

Ms Wang is Li Ming's Chinese teacher and she used to live in a big city. Li Ming wants to know what modes of transport there are in that city.

请听李明的采访，用中文或拼音回答问题。

Listen, and answer the questions in Chinese. You may write your answers in Chinese characters or pinyin.

CD 01, Track 53

1 王老师以前的学校在哪里？
2 她住在哪里？
3 王老师怎么形容那里的交通工具？
4 那里有什么交通工具？
5 为什么王老师觉得那里的地铁很方便？

补充词语
SUPPLEMENTARY VOCABULARY

| 形容 | xíng róng | to describe |

八 说话（二）
8 💬 Speaking (2)

试与同学两人一组，回答一下问题。

Work in pairs to ask and answer the following questions.

1 你每天怎么上学？
2 你家附近交通方便吗？有哪些交通工具？
3 你喜欢坐飞机旅行吗？为什么？
4 你最喜欢的是什么交通工具？为什么？
5 现在很多人都骑自行车上班，你觉得有什么好处？有什么坏处？

词语
VOCABULARY

| 骑自行车 | qí zì xíng chē | to ride a bike |

好词好句
USEFUL EXPRESSIONS

- 我每天坐公共汽车上学。
- 我喜欢坐飞机，因为从香港去北京只需要三个多小时，十分方便。

延伸活动
AIM HIGHER

Try to include the sentence structures you have learnt in this chapter to expand your answers, e.g. 我每天先走路，再坐公共汽车上学。骑自行车比坐地铁更便宜，但是自行车很慢。

九 写作
9 Writing

一、大城市一般有什么主要的交通工具？试写出五个。

二、给中国笔友写一封信，说一说：
- 你住的地方有什么主要的交通工具
- 你怎么上学
- 在学校学什么、做什么
- 你喜欢你的学校吗？为什么？

写不少于 150 个汉字。

好词好句
USEFUL EXPRESSIONS

- 我的学校在市中心，那儿交通很方便。
- 每天我先走路五分钟，去地铁站，然后再坐地铁到学校。
- 坐地铁比坐公共汽车更准时。

自我评估
Self-Assessment

- ☐ I know vocabulary for different modes of transport
- ☐ I can read guidelines on how to get around in a city
- ☐ I can listen to announcements on a train
- ☐ I can talk about the different public and private modes of transportation in a city
- ☐ I can respond to questions when buying train tickets
- ☐ I can write a letter to a friend to introduce the transportation system in my city
- ☐ Measure words 辆，匹 and 种
- ☐ Sentence structures 比……更，最，……没有…… and 先……然后
- ☐ Word order: 'manner'

Unit C 14 The world around us: Transportation

lǚ yóu jīng lì
旅游经历
15 Holidays: Travel experiences

Learning objectives

This unit will concentrate on developing your skills in narrating past travel experiences. You will:

- Learn more vocabulary about travelling in China

- Read a diary and a narrative about travel experiences

- Listen to a dialogue about someone's journey

- Respond to questions and make a two-minute presentation about one of your travel experiences

- Write a letter about a trip you have taken in the past

In addition, you are going to learn:

- 了, 过 and other time expressions indicating past events

- Sentence structures 是……的, 越……越…… and 越来越……。

学习目标

本单元你会：

- 学到更多与<u>中国</u>旅游有关的生词

- 阅读关于旅游经历的日记和叙述

- 聆听别人的旅游经历

- 回答关于旅游经历的问题，并以两分钟说一说自己的旅游经历

- 写一封有关个人旅游经历的信

你还会学到：

- "了"和"过"的分别，和其他与过去叙述的时间词

- 句型："是……的"、"越……越……"和"越来越……"

Cambridge IGCSE Mandarin as a Foreign Language

一 温故知新
1 'Before starting' activities

一、中国旅游景点"是"与"非"
1 Quiz about Chinese tourist attractions

你认识中国吗？请选择"是"或"非"。
How much do you know about China? Look at the statements below and choose 'True' or 'False'.

		是	非
1	中国的首都是北京。	☐	☐
2	兵马俑在南京。	☐	☐
3	故宫是北京的中心。	☐	☐
4	天坛在西安。	☐	☐
5	香港是中国南方的一个城市。	☐	☐

故宫

兵马俑

天坛

词语
VOCABULARY

1	首都	shǒu dū	capital city
2	兵马俑	Bīng mǎ yǒng	terracotta warriors and horses
3	故宫	Gù gōng	The Forbidden City
4	天坛	Tiān tán	The Temple of Heaven

补充词语
SUPPLEMENTARY VOCABULARY

旅游景点 lǚ yóu jǐng diǎn tourist attraction

二、以下的旅游景点是在中国的哪个城市？请在唯一正确的方格内打勾。

2 Where can you find the following tourist attractions in China? Answer each question by ticking one box.

1 北海公园
  A 天津 ☐ B 北京 ☐ C 香港 ☐
2 长城
  A 香港 ☐ B 南京 ☐ C 北京 ☐
3 颐和园
  A 西安 ☐ B 南京 ☐ C 北京 ☐
4 东方明珠塔
  A 香港 ☐ B 上海 ☐ C 北京 ☐
5 水立方
  A 北京 ☐ B 天津 ☐ C 香港 ☐

长城

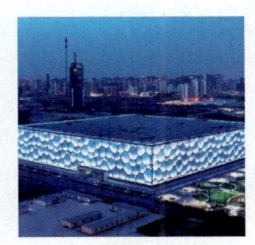

北京的水立方

东方明珠塔

颐和园

Unit C 15 The world around us: Holidays: Travel experiences

> **!**
> 小贴士
> TOP TIP
>
> You can expand your vocabulary of tourist attractions in Chinese by doing research online. Websites such as TripAdvisor (猫图鹰 Māo tú yīng) would be a good place to start. You can type in a Chinese city name and it will show you tourist attractions in Chinese. You can even read reviews, which are a useful source of materials for learning Chinese.
>
> tripadvisor.cn

词语 VOCABULARY

1	北海公园	Běi hǎi gōng yuán	Beihai Park
2	天津	Tiān jīn	Tianjin
3	长城	Cháng chéng	The Great Wall of China
4	颐和园	Yí hé yuán	The Summer Palace

补充词语 SUPPLEMENTARY VOCABULARY

1	东方明珠塔	Dōng fāng míng zhū tǎ	Oriental Pearl TV Tower
2	水立方	Shuǐ lì fāng	the Water Cube; the National Aquatic Center

二 阅读（一）
2 Reading (1)

阅读下面的短文，然后回答问题。

Read Judy's diary below, and write your answers in Chinese.

CD 01, Track 54

《茱迪的日记》 Zhū dí de rì jì 1
九月二十二日　　　　星期一　　　晴 2
　　上个月是我的假期，爸爸妈妈带 3
我去了北京和天津旅行。我以前没有 4
来过中国。我们先去北京，然后坐火 5
车去天津。 6
　　在北京，我最喜欢的是颐和园和 7
北海公园。市中心太热闹了，每一次 8
我看见它人山人海，车水马龙，我都 9
头疼。我们想省钱，所以只好住在亲 10
戚家里，没有住饭店。 11
　　天津天气很好，每天都是晴天。 12
那里好玩儿的地方不多，但是人们很 13
友好。有一天我们想去参观博物馆， 14
忽然发现我们已经迷路了。我们的手 15
机没有地图，心里很着急，只好向过 16
路人问路。我以为我的发音不好，但 17
是他们都明白我的话，还说我的中文 18
很好。 19
　　北京是中国的首都，好玩儿的地 20
方特别多。我在北京的机场买了一本 21
伦敦旅游书，看看我的国家有什么好 22
玩儿的地方。 23

词语 VOCABULARY

1	上个月	shàng gè yuè	last month
2	旅行	lǚ xíng	to travel
3	太	tài	too (+adjective)
4	省钱	shěng qián	to save money; 省 to save
5	只好	zhǐ hǎo	to have no choice but
6	饭店	fàn diàn	hotel
7	参观	cān guān	to visit
8	博物馆	bó wù guǎn	museum

Cambridge IGCSE Mandarin as a Foreign Language

词语
VOCABULARY

9	忽然	hū rán	suddenly
10	发现	fā xiàn	to find out/discover
11	已经	yǐ jīng	already
12	着急	zháo jí	anxious
13	过路人	guò lù rén	person passing by
14	以为	yǐ wéi	to mistakenly think that
15	发音	fā yīn	pronunciation
16	前天	qián tiān	the day before yesterday

补充词语
SUPPLEMENTARY VOCABULARY

| 亲戚 | qīn qi | relatives |

1 莱迪跟谁一起去中国玩儿?
2 莱迪以前去过中国吗?
3 她是怎么去天津的?
4 在"每一次我看见它人山人海"一句中的"它"是指什么?
5 为什么莱迪一家没有住饭店?
6 天津的人怎么样?
7 莱迪发现自己迷路后,做了什么?
8 为什么莱迪买了一本旅游指南?
9 莱迪是哪国人?

语法
GRAMMAR

Expressing the past: Using particles 了 and 过, and using time expressions

1 One of the most common uses of the particle 了 (le) is to show the completion of an action. The basic pattern is:

Verb + 了 (+ Object)

e.g.

a 前天他吃了苹果。 He ate an apple two days ago.

b 小美到了机场。 Xiaomei arrived at the airport.

Note: the concept of using 了 is not the same as past tense in English. 了 indicates completion of an action in a certain time frame, e.g. 我们吃了早餐后去公园逛逛 After breakfast we go to the park for a walk. In Chapter 13 了 is used with 要 / 快 / 快要 to express anticipation of a future event.

练习: Highlight the sentences that include 了 in Judy's diary. Translate those sentences into English and think about whether the grammar rule applies in each case.

2 Similar to 了, the particle 过 (guò) indicates an action that has been experienced in the past. The basic pattern is:

Subject + Verb + 过 + Object

e.g.

a 莱迪吃过中国菜。 Judy has eaten Chinese food before.

b 李红唱过这首歌。 Li Hong has sung this song before.

练习: Highlight the sentences that include 过 in the diary. Translate the sentences into English and think about whether the grammar rule applies in each case.

3 Negation when using 过

没 is used to negate 过 as it is about past experience. The basic pattern is:

Subject + 没 + Verb + 过 + Object

e.g. 小明没看过这个电影。 Xiao Ming has never seen this movie before.

4 Time expressions

Judy mentions in her diary that her travel experience is from 上个月 'last month'. In Chinese, using this kind of time expression shows that it is a completed action and provides more detail on when you did it, e.g. 昨天我们去了公园踢足球,今天早上我们吃了中餐。

Unit C 15 The world around us: Holidays: Travel experiences

5 Questions with 没有 at the end of the sentence
Adding 没有 at the end of a sentence using 了 or 过 indicates a yes-or-no question, asking whether one has done something in the past, e.g.

a 你做了功课没有？ Have you done your homework?

b 你去过马来西亚没有？ Have you been to Malaysia?

三 说话（一）
3 Speaking (1)

两人一组，做角色扮演。

Work in pairs to act out this role play.

你：你自己
同学：你的一个中国朋友
你上个星期去了中国旅游。你的一个中国朋友正在问你的经历。

Last week, you went travelling in China. A Chinese friend is asking about your experience.

1 你什么时候去旅行的？
2 你跟谁一起去旅行？
3 你这是第几次跟家人去中国旅行？
4 你去了哪里？
5 你怎么去那里？
6 你们住在哪里？
7 那里天气怎么样？
8 那里人们怎么样？

小贴士
TOP TIP

To understand questions asked by a native Chinese speaker, it is important to pay attention to the question words he/she has used. Common question words include 什么, 哪儿, 谁, 怎么样, etc.

四 听力（一）
4 Listening (1)

小马与小王正用微信通话。

Xiao Ma and Xiao Wang are chatting on WeChat.

请听下面的对话，用中文或拼音回答问题。

Listen to the conversation and answer the questions in Chinese. You may write your answers in Chinese characters or pinyin. **CD 01, Track 55**

1 小王去了哪里？
2 那里天气怎么样？
3 小王最喜欢做什么？
4 在那儿可以做什么？（两个答案）

词语
VOCABULARY

| 名胜古迹 | míng shèng gǔ jì | historic and scenic sites |

延伸活动
AIM HIGHER

小王参观了很多名胜古迹，请你找一找那儿有什么好玩儿的地方。
答：那儿有很多很多名胜古迹，有_____，_____，_____等等。

五 阅读（二）
5 Reading (2)

茱迪在北京的机场买了一本伦敦旅游指南。以下是其中一页，请先看看。

Judy has bought a travel guidebook about London at the airport in Beijing. Read the following extract from the book. **CD 01, Track 56**

London Travel Guide

伦敦

伦敦不只是有名的旅游城市，也是英国的首都，最近越来越受游客欢迎。以下是伦敦的介绍：

一、交通

伦敦有各种各样的交通工具。公共汽车和地铁都很方便，游客一般都坐这两种交通工具。在市中心，很多人都骑自行车上班，居民觉得这又方便又健康。虽然伦敦有出租车，但是游客都说，打车最贵了。

二、天气

伦敦一年有四季。夏天最热，冬天最冷，春、秋最舒服。虽然伦敦不常下雪，但是伦敦下雨不奇怪，以前还有"雾都"的名字。

三、旅游景点

伦敦是一座老城市，历史很长，有很多名胜古迹。那里有教堂、美术馆、博物馆。游客很喜欢参观伦敦的教堂，教堂的建筑很古老。

四、中国城

伦敦市内有很多不同民族的人，不少的更是华侨。如果你喜欢吃中餐的话，你可以到市中心的"中国城"。在中国城的附近有很多剧场，吃完饭后可以去看音乐剧。

词语 VOCABULARY

1	只	zhǐ	only
2	越来越……	yuè lái yuè……	more and more…
3	游客	yóu kè	tourist
4	欢迎	huān yíng	popular, welcoming; to welcome
5	一般	yì bān	usually
6	种	zhǒng	a measure word for kind(s)/type(s)
7	不常	bù cháng	not often
8	奇怪	qí guài	strange
9	座	zuò	a measure word for cities
10	老	lǎo	old
11	教堂	jiào táng	church
12	美术馆	měi shù guǎn	art gallery
13	建筑	jiàn zhù	architecture
14	古老	gǔ lǎo	old, historical
15	民族	mín zú	nationality
16	剧场	jù chǎng	theatre
17	华侨	huá qiáo	overseas Chinese
18	一样	yí yàng	same

补充词语 SUPPLEMENTARY VOCABULARY

| 中国城 | Zhōng guó chéng | Chinatown |

一、请用下列词组填空。

1 Fill in the gaps using the words provided below.

| 首都　介绍　方便　健康　贵　古老 |
| 奇怪　华侨　民族 |

1 游客不选择打车，因为很_____。
2 下雨天伦敦的人不会觉得_____。
3 北京跟伦敦一样，都是一个国家的_____。
4 在伦敦坐地铁最_____。

Unit C 15 The world around us: Holidays: Travel experiences

二、根据上面的短文，回答问题。

2 Based on the passage above, answer the following questions.

1. 伦敦的公共汽车和什么很方便？
2. 在伦敦哪里有很多人选择健康的交通工具？
3. 为什么游客不喜欢出租车？
4. 小王怕冷，哪一个季节他不应该去伦敦？
5. "雾都"指天气怎么样？
6. 为什么游客喜欢参观伦敦的教堂？
7. 在中国城可以做什么？
8. 要去看音乐剧的话，应该去哪儿？

句型
LANGUAGE

越来越…… (Becoming) more and more + Adjective

This expression is to describe something that becomes more and more so of an adjective over time.

The structure is:

Subject + 越来越 + Adjective

e.g.

a 伦敦的空气越来越好。 The air quality in London is getting better and better.

b 北京越来越受游客欢迎。 Beijing is getting more and more popular among tourists.

c 香港的房子越来越贵。 The property in Hong Kong is getting more and more expensive.

六 说话（二）
6 Speaking (2)

一、朗读以下短文。

1 Read aloud the following text. CD 01, Track 57

这个暑假，我和我的家人一起去了北京旅游。北京是中国的首都，有很多名胜古迹。我在那儿呆了一个星期，昨天才回到家。

我们参观了很多旅游景点。我们先去了天安门广场，然后去看了故宫。我最喜欢故宫，因为它在市中心，交通方便。我们还爬了长城，长城在山上，环境很美，空气新鲜。我们要回城里的时候迷路了，后来一位中国人给我们指路。我们越走越快，赶上了去北京的公交车。

北京的夏天很热，下午有时候下雨，我觉得伦敦的夏天比北京的凉快。

我们在一家中国餐馆吃饺子、面条。菜单上的中文字很深，很多字我都不明白，但是我很喜欢中国菜，我也很喜欢北京。

词语
VOCABULARY

1	才	cái	not… until (to express lateness)
2	天安门广场	Tiān ān mén guǎng chǎng	Tiananmen Square
3	爬	pá	to climb; 爬长城 to tour the Great Wall
4	城里	chéng lǐ	in the city
5	后来	hòu lái	afterwards
6	位	wèi	a measure word for persons in a respectful and courteous way
7	越……越……	yuè……yuè……	more and more/ less and less…
8	赶上	gǎn shàng	to keep up with, meet with, catch up with
9	深	shēn	difficult, hard

Cambridge IGCSE Mandarin as a Foreign Language

句型
LANGUAGE

越 …… 越 ……

Similar to 越来越……, 越……越…… is used to express 'more and more' or 'less and less'. The basic pattern is:

越 + Adjective/Verb + 越 + Adjective

e.g.
a 我们越走越快。We walked faster and faster.
b 游戏越多越好玩儿。The more games the more fun.

小贴士
TOP TIP

Many words in Chinese can have two or even more different meanings in English depending on the context, e.g. 深 means 'difficult' in the text above, but in 游泳池很深 it means the water is deep in the swimming pool.

二、请以"我的旅游经历"做一个不多于两分钟的短讲。你可以运用活动一的句型。

2 Make a presentation on 我的旅游经历 (*My Travel Experience*). Your presentation should not be more than two minutes. You may use the sentence structures in Activity 1.

小贴士
TOP TIP

Pay special attention to the use of 了 and 过. You can include time expressions such as 去年 and 两年前. If you have been to China, it would be great if you could talk about that experience.

七 阅读（三）
7 Reading (3)

阅读下面的短文，然后回答问题，选择唯一的正确的答案，在方格内打勾。

Read the text below, and then answer the questions by ticking one box for each question. **CD 01, Track 58**

到台湾生活 1

刚放暑假，妈妈就要王一心到台 2
湾生活一个月。爸爸不想王一心去，但 3
是他很宠自己的妻子，所以赞成了。王 4
一心的父母都是印尼的华侨，但是王 5
一心的中文不太好。他经常在家里看 6
电视，父母生气地跟他说："你一定要 7
在台湾学好中文。" 8

从印尼到台湾要坐五个半小时的 9
飞机。在学校，王一心学到了很多新东 10
西，也认识了很多好朋友。他两个好朋 11
友都是中国人，一个是桂林人，一个是 12
武汉人。他们上午上课，下午游览台湾 13
的名胜古迹。他们印象最深刻的是台 14
北动物园。他觉得学中文是很好玩儿 15
的，不过他有点儿累。 16

有一天，在去台湾山区的时候，他 17
遇上车祸了。事故发生后，王一心马上 18
给妈妈打了个电话，说刚才有事故，但 19
是他没事儿。王一心的朋友要住院，所 20
以他很伤心。他祝朋友身体健康，早日 21
出院。 22

词语
VOCABULARY

1	刚	gāng	only, just
2	印尼	Yìn ní	Indonesia
3	生气	shēng qì	to get angry

Unit C 15 The world around us: Holidays: Travel experiences

词语
VOCABULARY

4	一定	yí dìng	definitely
5	游览	yóu lǎn	to visit, to travel
6	印象	yìn xiàng	impression
7	深刻	shēn kè	deep (印象深刻 to make a deep impression)
8	桂林	Guì lín	Guilin
9	武汉	Wǔ hàn	Wuhan
10	动物园	dòng wù yuán	zoo
11	累	lèi	tired
12	山区	shān qū	mountainous area
13	车祸	chē huò	car accident
14	事故	shì gù	accident
15	马上	mǎ shàng	immediately
16	刚才	gāng cái	just now
17	伤心	shāng xīn	sad

补充词语
SUPPLEMENTARY VOCABULARY

1	宠	chǒng	to spoil
2	赞成	zàn chéng	to agree

1 为什么王一心的父母很生气?
   - A 他们都很喜欢台湾。☐
   - B 王一心的中文不好。☐
   - C 他常常看电影。☐

2 从印尼到台湾
   - A 不到六个小时。☐
   - B 五个小时。☐
   - C 五分钟三十秒。☐

3 王一心跟他的朋友们最有印象的是
   - A 台北动物园。☐
   - B 新东西。☐
   - C 很累的。☐

4 为什么王一心最后很伤心?
   - A 他的朋友身体健康。☐
   - B 去了台湾的山区。☐
   - C 他朋友在车祸中受伤了。☐

语言
LANGUAGE

Using 是 + adjective + 的:"学中文是很好玩儿的。"

1 In Chapter 1, we explained that in a declarative sentence you use 'subject + adjective' (e.g. 你很漂亮) and we do not need a verb like 是. However, if you want to emphasise the adjective, you should use this sentence structure:

   Subject + 是 + Adjective + 的

   e.g.

   a 做运动是健康的。 Exercising is really good for your health.

   b 香港是很好玩儿的。 Hong Kong is a really fun place.

2 The 是……的 structure can also be used to highlight the circumstances of past events, e.g. 他是去年去的 emphasises that he went last year.

八 写作
8 Writing

你跟家人一起去了一个<u>中国</u>城市玩儿了几天。请给<u>中国</u>笔友写一封信。信里说一说：

You and your family went to a Chinese city for a few days. Write a letter to your Chinese pen pal describing your trip. Your letter can include:

- 你去了哪个地方？
- 那个地方有什么旅游景点？
- 那里的天气怎么样？
- 城市有什么交通工具？

自我评估
Self-Assessment

- ☐ I have learnt more vocabulary about travelling in China
- ☐ I can read a diary and a narrative about travel experiences
- ☐ I can listen to a dialogue about someone's journey
- ☐ I can respond to questions and make a short presentation about one of my travel experiences
- ☐ I can write a letter about a trip taken in the past
- ☐ 了, 过 and other time expressions indicating past events
- ☐ Sentence structures 是……的, 越……越…… and 越来越……

Unit C 15 The world around us: Holidays: Travel experiences

lǚ yóu jì huà
旅游计划
16 Holidays: Planning a trip

Learning objectives

This unit will concentrate on travel planning when you go on a holiday. You will learn how to:

- Understand people's travel plans in both written and spoken forms
- Read a travel guide on how to plan a trip more efficiently
- Listen to a dialogue of booking a hotel room
- Reserve a hotel room in Chinese
- Talk about your travel plans

In addition, you will learn:

- Future (2): 会, 要, 打算
- Sentence structure: 比如……等等
- Time expressions about the future

学习目标

本单元你会：

- 看得明白、听得懂别人的旅游计划
- 阅读旅游指南
- 听得懂订酒店的对话
- 学习如何用中文订酒店
- 说一说你的旅游计划

另外，你会学到：

- 未来 (2)：会、要、打算
- 句型：比如……等等
- 与未来有关的时间词

Cambridge IGCSE Mandarin as a Foreign Language

一 温故知新
1 'Before starting' activities

一、张文在讲他寒假的旅游计划。请听对话，选择唯一正确的答案回答问题。

1 Zhang Wen is talking about his travel plans with his friend. Listen to the conversation and answer each question by choosing the correct picture.
CD 01, Track 59

词语
VOCABULARY

计划 jì huà plan

1 张文寒假要去哪里？
A 北京 ☐ 
B 上海 ☐ 
C 香港 ☐

2 张文想去哪里？
A 天安门广场 ☐ 
B 长城 ☐ 
C 故宫 ☐

3 他还会去看什么？
A ☐ 
B ☐ 
C ☐

4 回美国之前，他要去哪个城市？
A 北京 ☐ 
B 上海 ☐ 
C 香港 ☐

Unit C 16 The world around us: Holidays: Planning a trip

二、请看以下短文，选择"是"或"非"回答问题。

2 Read the passage below and choose 'true' or 'false' for each statement.

<u>李树</u>的旅游计划

我打算这个暑假去印尼。虽然印尼的大城市都很热闹，但是我会去那里的山区，因为树林的空气好，环境舒服。我还想去参观那里的动物园，看动物很有意思。我打算以后在家里养一只小猫。

	是	非
1 <u>李树</u>这个暑假要去<u>印度</u>。	☐	☐
2 <u>李树</u>会去那里的大城市和山区。	☐	☐
3 <u>李树</u>在那儿的动物园工作。	☐	☐
4 <u>李树</u>现在的家里有一只小猫。	☐	☐

词语 VOCABULARY

打算 dǎ suàn to plan

语法 GRAMMAR

Using 打算 and 会 to express a future meaning

1 When making plans, 打算 and 会 can be used, e.g.

 a 我打算这个暑假去<u>印尼</u>。 I plan to go to Indonesia this summer.

 b 我打算以后当老师。 I plan to become a teacher in the future.

2 会 can mean 'to be able to', but it can also be used to express the possibility of an action happening in the future, e.g. 我会去那里的山区 I will go to the hilly region there.

3 These two words are auxiliary verbs (see Chapter 19 for further explanation) and should be put before the main verb.

二 阅读（一）
2 Reading (1)

一、把以下的中文和英文词搭配起来。

1 Match the Chinese with the English meanings.

1 最近 (zuì jìn) — A next month
2 这个星期 (zhè ge xīng qī) — B next week
3 这个月 (zhè ge yuè) — C recently
4 下个月 (xià ge yuè) — D this month
5 下个星期 (xià ge xīng qī) — E this week

二、请阅读下面的文字，然后填表。

2 Read the passages below, and then fill in the table.
CD 01, Track 60

四个朋友谈论旅游计划

小英：

> 我最喜欢到<u>香港</u>度假。很多人都不知道，<u>香港</u>有很多大楼，但也有很多沙滩。我喜欢到那儿的海边，吹吹海风。这个星期我打算再去<u>香港</u>，我这一次会住在酒店，那儿有一个很大的游泳池，我会在那儿晒太阳。

Cambridge IGCSE Mandarin as a Foreign Language

小东：

> 最近，我去了拉萨。从那儿出发，我们去了附近的森林，空气非常好。下个星期，我们就会坐飞机去重庆。重庆在长江附近，那里也有很多很有特色的桥和庙。我们会参观那儿的农村，相当有意思。

小李：

> 我的朋友住在杭州。那里有很多古老的建筑。除了古迹以外，那里还有很多河和湖。我下个月放假的时候会去西湖，西湖是中国有名的湖，那儿的风景很有特色。

小明：

> 我这个月将要坐船游黄河。黄河在中国的北部，我没去过。我会去看看风景，希望会好玩儿！

	他/她要去哪儿？	什么时候去？	在那儿做什么？
小英	香港	(1)	(2)
小东	(3)	(4)	(5)
小李	(6)	下个月	(7)
小明	(8)	(9)	(10)

词语
VOCABULARY

1	度假	dù jià	to go on holiday/vacation
2	大楼	dà lóu	tall buildings
3	沙滩	shā tān	beach
4	酒店	jiǔ diàn	hotel
5	拉萨	Lā sà	Lhasa
6	森林	sēn lín	forest
7	重庆	Chóng qìng	Chongqing
8	长江	Cháng jiāng	Yangtze River
9	农村	nóng cūn	countryside
10	杭州	Háng zhōu	Hangzhou
11	相当	xiāng dāng	quite
12	桥	qiáo	bridge
13	庙	miào	temple
14	古迹	gǔ jī	historical site
15	河	hé	river
16	湖	hú	lake
17	放假	fàng jià	to have a holiday or vacation
18	西湖	Xī hú	the West Lake in Hangzhou
19	黄河	Huáng hé	Yellow River

补充词语
SUPPLEMENTARY VOCABULARY

1	晒太阳	shài tài yang	sunbathing
2	特色	tè sè	characteristic
3	壮观	zhuàng guān	(of scenery) magnificent

语法
GRAMMAR

Using time expressions to indicate future meaning

1 In Activity 1, five time expressions are introduced. Four of them can be used to express future meaning; they are 这个星期, 这个月, 下个月 and 下个星期. Depending on the context, 这个

> 星期 and 这个月 can be used to talk about something in the past, too.
> 2 Identify the sentences with future time expressions in the passages of Activity 2.
> 3 Discuss with your classmates what the word order should be when using a time expression in a sentence.

三 听力（一）
3 🔊 Listening (1)

五个朋友在谈论他们的旅游计划。听下面的录音，将字母填入方格内。

Five friends are talking about their travel plans. Listen to the recording and for each question choose the correct city.

CD 01, Track 61

A 新加坡	B 西安	C 香港	D 上海
E 北京			

1 小王	2 小刘	3 小张	4 小龙	5 小红

中国首都——北京

上海是中国的大城市。

很多游客都想去香港买东西。

四 听力（二）
4 🔊 Listening (2)

李大海要去西安。他给西安的酒店经理打电话，他想订酒店。

Li Dahai is going to Xi'an. He calls the hotel manager in Xi'an to make a reservation.

请听对话，用数字 / 中文 / 拼音回答问题。

Listen to the conversation. Fill in the reservation form below by writing your answers in numbers, Chinese characters or pinyin. **CD 01, Track 62**

星海饭店 订房表
1 李大海先生
2 从_____来。
3 出发的日期：_____月_____日。
4 呆_____天_____夜。
5 飞机降落的时间：_____：_____。
6 多少人：_____。

词语 VOCABULARY

1	订	dìng	to book, to reserve
2	呆	dāi	to stay
3	天	tiān	day
4	夜	yè	night
5	降落	jiàng luò	(of a flight) to land

补充词语 SUPPLEMENTARY VOCABULARY

1	订房表	dìng fáng biǎo	reservation form
2	单人房	dān rén fáng	single room
3	双人房	shuāng rén fáng	double room

Cambridge IGCSE Mandarin as a Foreign Language

五 说话（一）
5 Speaking (1)

两人一组，做角色扮演。

A 一位旅馆经理　　B 游客

情景1：你要去中国旅行。你给北京的一家旅馆的经理打电话。

A1: 您好！您什么时候来北京？
B1: _____。

A2: 您跟谁一起来北京？
B2: _____。

A3: 您要单人房还是双人房？
B3: _____。

A4: 您在北京呆多长时间？
B4: _____。

A5: 您打算要有空调的房间吗？
B5: _____。

词语 VOCABULARY

1 旅馆　lǚ guǎn　hotel
2 野餐　yě cān　picnic

A 一个中国朋友　　B 你自己

情景2：你要去香港旅游。你跟一个中国朋友说话。

A1: 你怎么去香港？
B1: _____。

A2: 你要在香港做什么？
B2: _____。

A3: 你打算去野餐吗？
B3: _____。

A4: 你去香港多久？
B4: _____。

A5: 你去完香港之后去哪儿？
B5: _____。

六 阅读（二）
6 Reading (2)

一、你和汉语班的朋友在看以下的博客。请阅读下面的短文，然后回答问题。

1 You and your friends are reading the following blog. Read the passage and answer the questions.
CD 01, Track 63

马明去旅游 (2016-10-01 08:33:05)

标签：马明　行走　摄影　坚持　分享　　分类：旅游

假期的时候，很多人都打算去旅游。旅游的时候要注意什么呢？

1. 出发旅游前，一定要准备自己的护照。拿中国护照的人，到很多国家都要签证。过海关时，如果没有签证的话，你是不能进这个国家的，所以不要忘记先去大使馆办签证。

2. 旅客要小心自己的东西。很多青年都喜欢背包旅游。到了宾馆之后，不要忘记自己的东西，比如电话、现钱等等。

3. 很多酒店严禁吸烟。吸烟会引起火灾，十分危险。

4. 很多人都喜欢参加旅游团。旅行社的导游会带你参观每个城市的名胜古迹，导游都知道哪里拍照最好，但是"自由行"要自己看地图。

5. 记得带药，感冒时也可以吃药。但是还觉得不舒服的话，要去看医生。

作者：马明　发表时间：2016-10-1　点击量：1989

词语
VOCABULARY

1	准备	zhǔn bèi	to prepare
2	护照	hù zhào	passport
3	签证	qiān zhèng	visa
4	办（签证）	bàn (qiān zhèng)	to get (a visa)
5	海关	hǎi guān	customs
6	忘记	wàng jì	to forget
7	大使馆	dà shǐ guǎn	embassy
8	旅客	lǚ kè	traveller, passenger
9	小心	xiǎo xīn	to be careful
10	青年	qīng nián	young people
11	背包	bèi bāo	backpack; 背包旅游 backpacking
12	宾馆	bīn guǎn	hotel
13	现钱	xiàn qián	cash
14	严禁	yán jìn	to strictly forbid, prohibit
15	危险	wēi xiǎn	dangerous
16	旅行社	lǚ xíng shè	travel agent
17	导游	dǎo yóu	tour guide
18	忘	wàng	to forget; same as 忘记

补充词语
SUPPLEMENTARY VOCABULARY

1	注意	zhù yì	to be careful; to notice; to pay attention
2	旅游团	lǚ yóu tuán	package tour; a group of travellers going to the same destination
3	引起	yǐn qǐ	to cause
4	火灾	huǒ zāi	fire hazard
5	作者	zuò zhě	writer/author
6	发表时间	fā biǎo shí jiān	time of publication
7	点击量	diǎn jí liàng	hits (of a blog/website)

1 过海关时，没有签证的话会怎么样？
  A 参观名胜古迹☐ B 没有护照☐
  C 要回去☐

2 要办签证的话，要做什么？
  A 准备自己的护照☐ B 到大使馆☐
  C 过海关☐

3 很多青年喜欢做什么？
  A 背包旅游☐ B 忘记自己的钱包☐
  C 在旅馆睡觉☐

4 为什么酒店严禁旅客吸烟？
  A 酒店有火灾☐ B 房间不好看☐
  C 很危险☐

5 有导游有什么好处？
  A 可以拍照☐
  B 自己不用看书、看地图☐
  C 便宜☐

6 旅游时觉得不舒服，应该怎么办？
  A 多吃感冒药☐ B 去医院☐
  C 看医生☐

二、请用下列词组填空。

2 Use the following phrases to fill in the gaps.

| 准备 护照 签证 大使馆 导游 |
| 严禁 青年 忘记 |

1 每到暑假，很多人都_____去旅游。
2 很多酒店都_____旅客在房间里吸烟。
3 我们参加了一个旅游团，_____告诉我们哪里拍照最好。
4 过海关时，因为我没有办_____，所以要回去。
5 我去买东西，但是_____带自己的钱包，所以要回去宾馆。

句型
LANGUAGE

比如……等等 (For example … etc.)

To exemplify, the sentence structure 比如……等等 is used in Chinese. A general statement is made first, then examples are given using the above structure. Remember to put a comma after the general statement, e.g.

a 不要忘记自己的东西 (general statement)，比如电话、钱包等等 (examples)。

b "自由行"要自己准备 (general statement)，比如看书、看地图等等 (examples)。

七 写作
7 Writing

一、试在这一课中找出三个意思是 'hotel' 的词语。

1 Find three words which mean 'hotel' in this chapter.

二、你的一个朋友小东给你发电子邮件。他打算去中国的一个城市旅游，请你说一说：

2 Your friend Xiaodong has sent you an email. He is planning to visit a Chinese city. In your reply to Xiaodong, talk about:

- 去哪一个城市最好？为什么？
- 那个城市天气怎么样？交通怎么样？
- 有什么旅游景点？
- 旅游时要带什么？
- 你以后想去这个城市吗？为什么？

词语 VOCABULARY

| 1 | 发 | fā | to send |
| 2 | 电子邮件 | diàn zǐ yóu jiàn | email |

八 说话（二）
8 Speaking (2)

请用写作的文章做一个口头报告。介绍一个中国的城市，说一说这个城市：

Make a presentation based on your reply to Xiaodong in the previous Writing activity. Introduce a Chinese city. Talk about:

- 那个城市的天气怎么样？交通怎么样？
- 有什么旅游景点？
- 旅游时要带什么？
- 你以后想去这个城市吗？为什么？

说一到两分钟。

Your talk should last one to two minutes.

九 说话（三）
9 Speaking (3)

口头回答以下的问题。

Answer the following questions.

- 你最想去中国的哪一个城市旅游？为什么？那儿的天气怎么样？
- 那儿有什么旅游景点？
- 你这个暑假打算去哪里度假？为什么选择那个地方？
- 度假的话，你喜欢去大城市还是郊区？为什么？

十 阅读（三）
10 Reading (3)

王田要去新加坡旅游，要订酒店。请阅读以下的酒店评论，然后回答问题。

Wang Tian is going to Singapore and he is booking a hotel room. Read the hotel reviews below, then answer the questions. **CD 01, Track 64**

Unit C 16 The world around us: Holidays: Planning a trip

1 美丽酒店 ★★★★☆ 评分: 3.8/5　📱 2016-07-08

早餐两百块一个人，没有香肠，也没有鸡蛋，早餐很难吃。这家酒店的设施齐备，包括有游泳池、健身房。酒店的服务员很友好。

2 好好宾馆 ★★★★☆ 评分: 4.0/5　📱 2016-08-10

好好宾馆虽然只有三星，但是早餐不用钱，东西也很好吃。宾馆不太干净，也没有游泳池、健身房，但是有图书馆。宾馆一晚很便宜，只要三百块一个人。

3 公园旅馆 ★★★★☆ 评分: 4.2/5　📱 2016-08-15

酒店没有游泳池，但是海滩离旅馆很近，走七、八分钟就到，可以去晒太阳。在附近的公园可以做运动，比如跑步、打羽毛球等等。一个人每晚六百块左右。酒店很干净，就是没什么好设施。

词语 VOCABULARY

| 健身房 | jiàn shēn fáng | gym; fitness centre |

补充词语 SUPPLEMENTARY VOCABULARY

| 1 | 酒店评论 | jiǔ diàn píng lùn | hotel reviews |
| 2 | 评分 | píng fēn | review score |

1 在美丽酒店，早餐一人多少钱？
2 美丽酒店的早餐没有什么？
3 美丽酒店的设施有什么？
4 好好宾馆的早餐多少钱？
5 好好宾馆有什么设施？
6 住在公园旅馆，但想做运动的话，可以怎么办？
7 在附近的公园可以做什么运动？
8 公园旅馆比好好宾馆贵多少？

延伸活动 AIM HIGHER

你是王田的话，你会选择哪一家酒店？为什么？跟同学说一说。

王田：

> 我打算在酒店吃早餐，也想在酒店做运动、游泳。酒店不能太贵，但是评分也不能太低。

自我评估 Self-Assessment

- ☐ I can understand people's travel plans in both written and spoken forms
- ☐ I can read a travel guide on how to plan a trip more efficiently
- ☐ I can listen to a dialogue of booking a hotel room
- ☐ I can reserve a hotel room in Chinese
- ☐ I can talk about my travel plans
- ☐ Use of 会，要，打算
- ☐ Sentence structure 比如……等等
- ☐ Use of time expressions such as 下个星期，下个月

Cambridge IGCSE Mandarin as a Foreign Language

gōng gòng fú wù yǔ hǎi guān

公共服务与海关
17 Public services and customs

Learning objectives

This unit will concentrate on learning vocabulary about public services and customs. You will:

- Read travel guidelines for travellers entering China
- Fill in an arrival card when entering China
- Respond to questions appropriately at customs and in a bank and post office
- Write a postcard to your friend about your travel experience

In addition, you are going to learn:

- Verbal aspect marker 着
- Measure words 本, 张, 封
- 把 construction (1)
- Sentence structures
  ……也……, ……都……, 除了……以外

学习目标

本单元你会：

- 阅读游客入境指南
- 用中文填写中国入境卡
- 用角色扮演的形式回答在海关、银行、邮局的问题
- 写一张明信片给朋友

你还会学到：

- "着"的用法
- 量词：本、张、封
- 句型："把"结构（1）
- 句型：……也……、……都……、除了……以外……

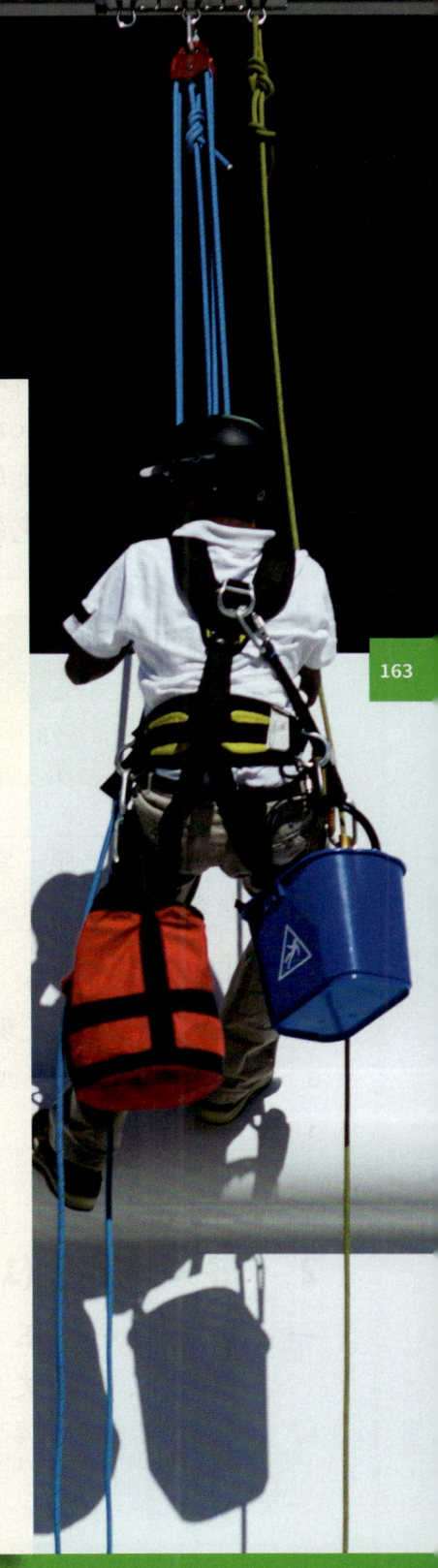

163

Unit C 17 The world around us: Public services and customs

一 温故知新
1 'Before starting' activity

请阅读下面王小明的日记，然后用下列词组填空。

Read this diary entry by Wang Xiaoming, then use the words provided to fill in the gaps.

六月五日　　　　星期五　　　　　晴

　　今天早上，我坐出租车去机场，1
准备去西安度假。过海关的时候，我2
发现我拿了妈妈的护照。我家离机场3
不远，所以可以回家拿。到了西安的4
宾馆后，职员跟我说，我订了六天五5
夜，但是我第五天的晚上就要坐飞机6
走，我多付了一晚的钱！7

词语 VOCABULARY

职员　zhí yuán　staff

度假　海关　护照　宾馆　飞机场　天
夜　准备

1 王小明到了机场，_____去西安。
2 他过_____时，发现没带自己的护照。
3 他在西安呆五___四___，不是六天。
4 王小明在西安住_____。

二 阅读（一）
2 Reading (1)

一、航空公司给王小明一份文件。请阅读以下的文字。

1 The airline gave Wang Xiaoming a document. Read the following text on the document. **CD 02, Track 02**

✈ 航空公司文件

1. 每个外国人到中国旅游都要旅游签证。　　　　　　　　　　1
　　　　　　　　　　　　　　　　　2
2. 签证应在出发前办好。申请签证　　3
时，除了要带文件、支票以外，　　4
还要填表。　　　　　　　　　　　5
3. 过海关前，准备好护照和机票。　　6
4. 过海关时，不可以带水，也不可　　7
以带可乐。过完海关后可以去商　　8
店买饮料，也可以在飞机上问航　　9
空服务员拿。　　　　　　　　　　10
5. 机场有兑换店，可以换钱。除了　　11
兑换店以外，机场也有"贵宾休　　12
息室"。里面有免费的饮料、食　　13
物，也可以在那儿洗澡。除了白　　14
酒一杯二十块以外，其他都是不　　15
用钱的。 每个到"贵宾休息室"　16
的乘客都要会员卡。　　　　　　　17
6. 机场有各式各样的商店和餐厅，　　18
游客都喜欢我们的机场。　　　　　19

请用下列词组填空。

Use the words provided to fill in the gaps.

旅游　支票　签证　饮料　商店　换钱
办　洗澡

1 王小明不是中国人，到中国旅游要_____。

2 在去中国之前，王小明已经去了中国大使馆_____签证。

3 想喝_____的话，要在过海关后去商店买。

4 王小明没有人民币，他应该在机场的兑换店_____。

5 游客喜欢这个机场，因为有很多不同的_____。

Cambridge IGCSE Mandarin as a Foreign Language

词语
VOCABULARY

1	航空公司	háng kōng gōng sī	airline
2	文件	wén jiàn	document
3	申请	shēn qǐng	to apply
4	填表	tián biǎo	to fill in a form; 填 to fill in; 表 table, form
5	航空服务员	háng kōng fú wù yuán	flight attendant
6	换钱	huàn qián	to change money into another currency; 换 to change
7	除了……以外	chú le… yǐ wài	apart from/besides (see Language box)

补充词语
SUPPLEMENTARY VOCABULARY

1	外国人	wài guó rén	foreigner
2	兑换店	duì huàn diàn	currency exchange
3	贵宾休息室	guì bīn xiū xí shì	VIP lounge; 贵宾 VIP; 休息室 lounge
4	其他	qí tā	other
5	会员卡	huì yuán kǎ	membership card

二、 请再阅读活动一的文章，选择唯一正确的答案，在方格里打勾。

2 Read the text in Activity 1 again. Tick the correct answer to each question below.

1 王小明要去中国旅游，要带_____
   A 护照☐   B 兑换店☐   C 支票☐

2 过海关前，要准备_____
   A 水和可乐☐   B 支票和护照☐
   C 护照和机票☐

3 不想在商店买饮料，可以在_____问服务员。
   A 出租车☐   B 飞机上☐
   C 大使馆☐

4 在"贵宾休息室"，一杯咖啡要多少钱？
   A 0☐   B 10☐   C 20☐

5 到"贵宾休息室"，要带_____
   A 会员卡☐   B 会员☐   C 签证☐

句型
LANGUAGE

"……也……" 和 "……都……"

1 也 is an adverb which means 'also' (see Chapter 2). It is inserted after the subject but before the verb or an adjective, e.g.
   a 我也想学中文。 I also want to learn Chinese.
   b 我们也是中国人。 We are Chinese too.

2 都 is also an adverb, but it is used to express 'all' or 'both' in Chinese, e.g.
   a 我爸爸妈妈都是中国人。 Both of my parents are Chinese.

   都 is commonly used after 每, which means 'every', e.g.
   b 每个学生都坐地铁上学。 Every student takes the underground to school/All students take the underground to school.

3 也 and 都 can be used together to emphasise similarities among a group or between two things. The basic pattern is:

   | Subject ＋ 也 ＋ 都 ＋ Verb/Adj. |

   e.g. 你是美国人吗？他们也都是美国人。 Are you American? All of them are Americans too.

练习：
把活动一中有"也"和"都"的句子找出来，并翻译成英文。
Find the sentences with 也 and 都 in Activity 1 and translate them into English.

句型
LANGUAGE

除了……以外

The sentence structure 除了……以外 is used to express 'except' or 'in addition'.

1 Expressing 'except':

> 除了 + Noun phrase (+ 以外) + Noun phrase + 都 + Verb/Verb phrase

e.g. 除了爸爸以外，我们都喜欢听音乐。 Except for father, we all like listening to music.

2 Expressing 'in addition':

> 除了 + Noun phrase (+ 以外) + Noun phrase + 也 + Verb/Verb phrase.

e.g. 除了茶以外，他也很喜欢可乐。 In addition to tea, he likes cola a lot.

练习：

在活动一的文章中找出三句"除了……以外"的句子，并指出他们是 1 (expressing 'except') 还是 2 (expressing 'in addition')。

In Activity 1, find three sentences using 除了……以外. Point out whether each is 1 (expressing 'except') or 2 (expressing 'in addition').

三 听力（一）
3 Listening (1)

在飞机上，服务员给了王小明一张卡。请看一看中华人民共和国的"外国人入境卡"。

补充词语
SUPPLEMENTARY VOCABULARY

| 1 | 中华人民共和国 | Zhōng huá rén mín gòng hé guó | People's Republic of China |
| 2 | 入境卡 | rù jìng kǎ | entry card/arrival card |

文化
CULTURE

外国人入境卡

每个国家都需要外国人填写"外国人入境卡"。虽然中国的入境卡是印有英文的，但是可以看看自己认识多少个中文字。

王小明跟服务员聊天儿。请听下面的对话，用中文或拼音回答问题。

Wang Xiaoming is talking to the flight attendant. Listen, and write your answers in Chinese characters or pinyin.

CD 02, Track 03

```
        姓 王   名 小明
          □ 男 □ 女
国籍 (1) ____ 护照号码 (2) ____
在华住址 (3) ____
入境事由 (4) □ 观光  □ 学习
              □ 探亲访友
```

词语
VOCABULARY

填写   tián xiě   to fill in

Cambridge IGCSE Mandarin as a Foreign Language

补充词语
SUPPLEMENTARY VOCABULARY

探亲访友　tàn qīn fǎng yǒu　visiting family and friends

四　说话（一）
4　Speaking (1)

王小明到了中国海关。
Wang Xiaoming has arrived at the Chinese border and is going through customs.

请回答以下问题。
Answer the following questions.

职员：您叫什么名字？

王小明：我叫王小明。

职员：您填写"外国人入境卡"了吗？

王小明：_____ 1 _____

职员：您是哪国人？

王小明：_____ 2 _____

职员：您为什么要来中国？

王小明：我要_____ 3 _____名胜古迹。

职员：您要看什么名胜古迹？

王小明：_____ 4 _____

职员：谢谢。

五　写作
5　Writing

请给张南写一张明信片，写一写：
Write Wang Xiaoming's postcard to his friend Zhang Nan. You can write about:

1 西安的天气怎么样？
2 西安有什么名胜古迹？
3 西安有什么交通工具？
4 你喜欢西安吗？为什么？
5 你以后打算再来西安吗？为什么？

写不少于 150 字。

词语
VOCABULARY

明信片　míng xìn piàn　postcard

Unit C　17　The world around us: Public services and customs

文化 / CULTURE

历史古都——西安

西安是一个很受游客欢迎的城市，因为它是一座历史古都，有很多名胜古迹，包括兵马俑、大雁塔(Dà yàn tǎ)等等。

六 阅读（二）
6 Reading (2)

王小明写好了明信片后，在宾馆看见一张公告。他觉得在中国发邮件非常简单。阅读公告，然后回答问题。

After Wang Xiaoming has written the postcard, he sees the following notice in the hotel. He thinks it's very simple to send mail in China. Read the notice, then answer the questions.
CD 02, Track 04

在中国发邮件

1. 寄信可以选择寄本地，也可以选择航空信。航空价钱会更贵，但是更快。如果你是游客的话，寄一张明信片比寄一封信便宜。
2. 写好信后，把信放在信封里，贴上邮票，放进信箱就可以了。
3. 在中国寄邮包，要先填表，注明里面是什么，比如一份文件、一些软件、一本厚厚的书等等。邮包需要过海关，所以要填表。

词语 / VOCABULARY

1	简单	jiǎn dān	simple
2	寄信	jì xìn	to send a letter (寄 to send; 信 letter)
3	航空信	háng kōng xìn	airmail
4	封	fēng	a measure word for letters and mail
5	信封	xìn fēng	envelope
6	邮票	yóu piào	stamp
7	信箱	xìn xiāng	post box
8	邮包	yóu bāo	parcel
9	软件	ruǎn jiàn	software
10	本	běn	a measure word for books
11	厚	hòu	thick

补充词语 / SUPPLEMENTARY VOCABULARY

1	公告	gōng gào	notice
2	邮件	yóu jiàn	mail
3	本地	běn dì	local
4	注明	zhù míng	to give clear indication of, to specify

1 哪一种信更贵？
2 如果你要更快的话，你会选择本地还是航空信？
3 游客不想寄信的话，可以选择寄什么？
4 以下哪一个是正确的寄信程序？在正确的方格里打勾。
   A 信箱→贴邮票→把信放在信封里 ☐
   B 贴邮票→把信放在信封里→信箱 ☐
   C 把信放在信封里→贴邮票→信箱 ☐
5 在寄邮包的表上要填什么？

CAMBRIDGE IGCSE Mandarin as a Foreign Language

语法
GRAMMAR

Measure words: 本, 张, 封

1. 本 is the measure word for books, e.g. 一本书，两本词典
2. 张 is the measure word for objects with flat surfaces, e.g. 一张纸，两张床，三张桌子
3. However, 封 is the measure word for letters, e.g. 一封信，两封电子邮件

句型
LANGUAGE

The 把 construction (1)

bǎ

把 is a useful structure for emphasising the result or influence of an action. The 把 structure focuses on what is done to the object. The action on the object (i.e. the verb) comes after the object, inverting the usual word order:

Subject ＋ Verb phrase ＋ Object → Subject ＋ 把 ＋ Object ＋ Verb phrase

e.g.

a 把信放在信封里
b 把书拿出来

七 说话（二）
7 Speaking (2)

一、王小明在邮局与邮局职员对话。请用下列词组填空。

1 Wang Xiaoming is in a post office talking to one of the staff. Use the words provided to fill in the gaps.

| 一共 | 马来西亚 | 明信片 | 里面 |
| 还要别的吗 | | | |

王小明：
您好，我要寄一张_____1_____。请问邮票一枚多少钱？

邮局职员：
您要寄到哪儿？

王小明：
我要寄到_____2_____去。

邮局职员：
要寄航空吗？

王小明：
是航空，谢谢。

邮局职员：
您要寄多少张？

王小明：
一张。

邮局职员：
_____3_____？

王小明：
我要把邮包寄给一个在印尼的朋友。

邮局职员：
___4___是什么？

Unit C 17 The world around us: Public services and customs

王小明：
是一本书。

邮局职员：
我要看看有多重。……一枚到马来西亚的邮票五块，一个到印尼的邮包三十五块。___5___ 四十块。

王小明：
谢谢。

词语 VOCABULARY

1 还要别的吗　hái yào bié de ma　anything else?
2 枚　méi　measure word for stamp, coin, medal, etc.

二、角色扮演：参考活动一，回答以下问题。

2 Role play: Use Activity 1 as an example to answer the following questions.

王小明：
您好，我要寄一封信。请问邮票一枚多少钱？

邮局职员：
您要寄到哪儿？

王小明：
_____

邮局职员：
要寄航空吗？

王小明：
_____

邮局职员：
您要寄多少封/张/个？

王小明：
_____

邮局职员：
还要别的吗？

王小明：
_____

邮局职员：
去完邮局后去哪里？

王小明：
_____

八　听力（二）
8　Listening (2)

李夏在邮局。你将听到几个中文句子，在唯一正确的方格内打勾回答问题。

Lisa is in the post office. You will hear some short sentences in Chinese. Answer each question by ticking one box only.

CD 02, Track 05

Cambridge IGCSE Mandarin as a Foreign Language

1 李夏要寄信到哪里？
   A 法国 □ B 印尼 □ C 马来西亚 □
2 李夏的邮包里没有什么？
   A 书 □ B 围巾 □ C 文件 □
3 李夏要了多少枚邮票？
   A 一 □ B 两 □ C 三 □
4 李夏之后要去什么地方？
   A 足球场 □ B 网球场 □ C 篮球场 □
5 李夏的朋友是做什么工作的？
   A 唱歌的 □ B 老师 □ C 工程师 □

九 说话（三）
9 Speaking (3)

一、李红在银行。两人一组，朗读以下对话。

1 Li Hong is at the bank. Work in pairs to read aloud the following dialogue.

李红：
您好。

银行职员：
您好。

李红：
我之前给你们写过一封申请信用卡的信。

银行职员：
谢谢您的来信，我们收到了。您要几张卡？

李红：
我要两张卡，一张给我爸，一张给自己。

银行职员：
明白。您把文件带来了吗？

李红：
这是你们要的文件。

银行职员：
好，谢谢，请等一下。……信用卡已经办好，您还要别的吗？

李红：
我要一本支票簿。

银行职员：
没问题，谢谢。

词语
VOCABULARY

1 来信   lái xìn   incoming letter
2 等一下 děng yí xià   please wait a moment; 等 to wait

补充词语
SUPPLEMENTARY VOCABULARY

支票簿 zhī piào bù   cheque book

Unit C 17 The world around us: Public services and customs

二、角色扮演：李红回家后，妈妈问了她几个问题，请回答。

2 Role play: After Li Hong went home, her mum asked her some questions. Insert the answers.

1. 你去了哪里？
   _____

2. 你去那儿做什么？
   _____

3. 你申请了几张信用卡？
   _____

4. 你要带什么去？
   _____

5. 除了信用卡以外，你还要了什么？
   _____

十　阅读（三）
10 Reading (3)

请阅读下面的博客，然后回答问题。
Read the blog entry below, and then answer the questions.

旅游在中国　　　　刘思天 Lucy Taylor

1　我刚到<u>北京</u>的第二天，就要去
2　警察局。
3　　我第一个景点是<u>故宫</u>。但是
4　<u>故宫</u>每个星期一都不开门，我只
5　好在外面拍照。这时候，一个
6　<u>中国</u>人来到我面前，用英语说
7　"你好，你是来旅游的吗？"。
8　他说自己叫<u>李明</u>，是本地人，可
9　以带我去一些好玩儿的地方。
10　<u>李明</u>说："除了<u>故宫</u>以外，
11　茶馆也是一个很有意思的地方。"
12　没想到，他虽然不是小偷，没偷
13　我的东西，但是他是"黑导游"，
14　骗取游客的钱财。他带我去东城
15　区一个茶馆，把一张字条交给老
16　板，然后跟我说茶对健康很好，
17　一定要买。我用了信用卡买，但
18　不知道花了多少钱。我们坐着喝
19　茶，坐了会儿，<u>李明</u>就说："对
20　不起，今天是我妹妹的生日，她
21　在等着我呢。"然后他就跑着
22　离开，连眼镜都丢在茶馆里。
23　　回到宾馆后，我给银行打了个
24　电话，职员告诉我，我今天在茶
25　馆花了六千五百多块。我知道自

Cambridge IGCSE Mandarin as a Foreign Language

己受骗后，马上报警。警察说， 26
"李明"这个名字是在"黑导游" 27
的名单上。我辛苦存下来的钱， 28
就给骗了。 29

1 刘思天第二天到了北京后，除了去故宫和茶馆，还去了哪里？
2 故宫哪一天不开门？
3 李明为什么觉得刘思天一定要去茶馆？
4 李明把什么交给茶馆老板？
5 刘思天给谁打了电话？
6 刘思天给骗了多少钱？
7 知道受骗后，她马上做了什么？

词语
VOCABULARY

1	开（门）	kāi mén	to open (a door)
2	茶馆	chá guǎn	tea house
3	小偷	xiǎo tōu	thief; 偷 to steal
4	字条	zì tiáo	brief note
5	丢	diū	to leave something behind
6	名单	míng dān	list of names
7	存钱	cún qián	to save money

补充词语
SUPPLEMENTARY VOCABULARY

1	黑导游	hēi dǎo yóu	unqualified tour guide who cheats tourists
2	骗取	piàn qǔ	to cheat somebody out of something; 取 to take (something)
3	受骗	shòu piàn	to be cheated
4	报警	bào jǐng	to report to the police

语法
GRAMMAR

着

1 着 is a verbal aspect that expresses an ongoing state, similar to the use of 在 / 正在. The basic pattern is:

Verb ＋ 着

e.g.
a 家里的灯还开着。The light is still on at home.
b 旅游时要带着护照。When you are travelling you always need to carry your passport.

2 Putting two verbs together and using 着 can express the same meaning as 一边……一边…….
The basic pattern is: Verb 1 ＋ 着 ＋ Verb 2

e.g.
a 我们坐着喝茶。We are sitting down while drinking tea.
b 王小明听着音乐跑步。Wang Xiaoming is listening to music while running.

自我评估
Self-Assessment

☐ I can read travel guidelines for travellers entering China
☐ I am able to fill in an arrival card
☐ I can respond to questions appropriately at customs and in a bank and post office
☐ I am able to write a postcard to a friend talking about my travel experience
☐ Verbal aspect marker 着
☐ Measure words 本，张，封
☐ 把 construction (1)
☐ Sentence structures ……也……, ……都……, 除了……以外

Unit C 17 The world around us: Public services and customs

考试练习题
Exam-style question

阅读
📖 Reading

请阅读下面的短文，然后回答问题。选择唯一正确的答案，在方格内打（✓）。

给第一次来伦敦的游客

家庭度假

想带您的孩子到伦敦玩吗？他们一定会很喜欢这个城市。伦敦有很多孩子都喜欢的博物馆，比如科学博物馆、历史博物馆。你们也可以到国家美术馆参观。

交通

伦敦有五个机场和火车，让您方便的去不同的国家和城市。有五十多个国家从伦敦出发只要飞行三小时。北京、广州、香港和上海都有飞机去伦敦。伦敦的地下铁非常方便，也有很长的历史。有的旅客会坐黑色的出租车，也有旅客选择桑坦德(Santander)自行车。

餐厅

伦敦有6000家餐厅，所以您不用担心没有地方用餐。中国城就有80家中国餐厅。除了有名的餐馆，这里也有很多便宜的选择。

公园

伦敦是一个"绿色"城市，很多地方都是公园。在市中心，大家都认识的是海德公园，有四千棵树木，一个大湖泊，一大片草地，里面还有很多鸭子。

改编自《初游伦敦》www.london.cn

1. 孩子在伦敦，可以去
   A 伦敦地下铁 □　B 历史美术馆 □
   C 科学博物馆 □

2. 在中国，有多少个城市可以坐飞机到伦敦？
   A 3 □　B 4 □　C 50 □

3. 又方便又有很长历史的交通工具是
   A 伦敦的地下铁 □　B 黑色的出租车 □
   C 自行车 □

4. 有旅客可能会担心
   A 中国城有 80 家餐厅 □
   B 伦敦有 6000 家便宜的饭馆 □
   C 伦敦没有吃饭的地方 □

5. 要去有树有水的地方，可以去
   A 市中心 □　B 海德公园 □
   C 绿色城市 □

Cambridge IGCSE Mandarin as a Foreign Language

D The world of work
gōng zuò yǔ zhí yè guī huà
工作与职业规划

gōng zuò jīng yàn

工作经验
18 Work experience

Learning objectives

This unit will concentrate on narrating someone's work experience. You will:

- Revise vocabulary related to occupations
- Read a diary entry on work experience
- Listen to a conversation about work duties
- Respond to questions about work experience
- Describe someone's work experience in writing

In addition, you are going to learn:

- Auxiliary verbs such as 应该
- Prepositions (2): 跟, 给
- Approximate numbers: e.g. 三、四

学习目标

本单元你会：

- 重温跟工作有关的词语
- 阅读一篇与工作经历有关的日记
- 聆听一段讲述工作内容的对话
- 回答有关工作经历的问题
- 叙述工作经历

你还会学到：

- 助动词，比如"应该"
- 介词 (2)：跟、给
- 约数，比如"三、四"

Cambridge IGCSE Mandarin as a Foreign Language

一 温故知新

1 'Before starting' activities

一、🔊 五个人在谈论自己的工作。请听录音，把 2-6 写在正确的空格里。

CD 02, Track 06

例：1 我的工作是开车，接学生上学。

A	司机	1
B	科学家	
C	老师	
D	护士	
E	运动员	
F	演员	
G	医生	

词语 VOCABULARY

1 司机　　sī jī　　　　　　driver
2 科学家　kē xué jiā　　　scientist
3 运动员　yùn dòng yuán　sportsperson
4 演员　　yǎn yuán　　　 actor/actress

二、看一看

三个学生在谈自己的工作经验

小红：
我在寒假的时候，去了妈妈的公司做秘书。我认识了很多新朋友。

小蓝：
寒假时，我去了滑雪场工作，教小朋友怎么滑雪。

小绿：
暑假时，我去了马来西亚的一个小学当老师。我教小学生讲英文。

1 哪个学生在寒假去当了老师？
2 哪个学生在公司上班？
3 哪个学生的工作跟运动有关？
4 哪个学生在学校工作？

词语 VOCABULARY

秘书　mì shū　　secretary

补充词语 SUPPLEMENTARY VOCABULARY

有关　yǒu guān　　to be relevant, related to

延伸活动 AIM HIGHER

你在暑/寒期时，会去工作吗？会选择什么工作？为什么？

e.g. 我想在暑假的时候去迪斯尼乐园 (dí sī ní lè yuán)（Disneyland）工作，因为我喜欢跟小朋友玩儿，也喜欢那里的环境。

二 阅读（一）

2 📖 Reading (1)

请阅读下面王天生的日记。选择唯一正确的答案，在方格中打勾。　CD 02, Track 07

Unit D 18 The world of work: Work experience

一月十三日　星期六　晴天

　　这一周的实习生活终于结束了。刚放寒假，爸爸就跟我说，他已经安排了我去他的公司帮忙一个星期，他说工作会对我的将来好。我本来打算在放假的时候玩电脑游戏，不用说，我有点儿不开心。我想跟爸爸说："工作是多么无聊的一件事情！"

　　上班前我先去理发，然后爸爸告诉了我上班的地点。他说上班必须准时。到了公司，我要向其中一位经理学习，他叫陈明。他说，现在很多年轻人他都不满意。

　　第一天我需要接电话，因为我是国际学校的学生，能说英文，也能说中文，所以客人都很喜欢我。第二天我用英文给公司写了一篇新闻，大家都觉得新闻写得很好，陈经理也很满意。星期五的时候他给我写了一个电邮，跟我说，现在的年轻人不一定很懒，我应该继续努力。

词语
VOCABULARY

1　年轻人　nián qīng rén　young people
2　不一定　bù yí dìng　not certain, not definite

1　实习是在什么时候做的?
　A　暑假☐　B　寒假☐　C　春节☐
2　为什么爸爸希望王天生在他的公司工作?
　A　多一点儿电脑游戏☐
　B　无聊☐
　C　对王天生的将来好☐
3　上班前王天生做了什么?
　A　理发☐　B　告诉爸爸上班地点☐
　C　准时上班☐
4　为什么王天生能说中、英文?
　A　他是接电话的人☐
　B　他是国际学校☐
　C　他在学校学英文，也学汉语☐
5　陈经理觉得王天生怎么样?
　A　很懒☐
　B　跟现在的年轻人不一样☐
　C　可以当经理☐

Cambridge IGCSE Mandarin as a Foreign Language

语法
GRAMMAR
Prepositions (2): 跟 and 给

1 跟 is a preposition which is very similar to 'with' in English. However, in Chinese the 'with' phrase comes before the verb.

e.g.

a 爸爸跟我说

b 陈经理跟我说

Subject + 跟 + Person + Verb (+ Object)

Other examples:

c 我昨天跟妈妈去超市了。 I went to the supermarket with my mum yesterday.

d 大卫喜欢跟他的朋友聊天。 David likes chatting with his friends.

2 Sometimes 跟 is used with the word 一起 (together).

e.g. 我跟你一起去公园。 I go with you (together) to the park.

3 给 is used to indicate who is targeted in an action.

e.g.

a 我给他打电话。 I give him a phone call.

b 星期五的时候他给我写了一封电邮。 He sent me an email on Friday.

词语
VOCABULARY

1	结束	jié shù	to end
2	安排	ān pái	to arrange
3	帮忙	bāng máng	to help
4	将来	jiāng lái	future
5	本来	běn lái	originally, at first
6	不用	bú yòng	need not
7	理发	lǐ fà	to get a haircut
8	必须	bì xū	must
9	经理	jīng lǐ	manager
10	满意	mǎn yì	satisfied
11	需要	xū yào	need

词语
VOCABULARY

12	能	néng	can
13	继续	jì xù	to continue
14	应该	yīng gāi	should

补充词语
SUPPLEMENTARY VOCABULARY

| 1 | 实习 | shí xí | internship |
| 2 | 终于 | zhōng yú | finally |

三 听力（一）
3 Listening (1)

王天生的朋友刘一红在放假时也做了实习。请听录音，在唯一正确的方格内打勾回答问题。 CD 02, Track 08

1 刘一红的工作地点是
A 公司☐ B 学校☐ C 百货商店☐

2 她实习是有什么工作？
A 打电话☐ B 教小朋友英文☐
C 玩电脑游戏☐

3 刘一红上班前做了什么？
A 看电视☐ B 打电话☐ C 理发☐

Unit D 18 The world of work: Work experience

4 刘一红本来想在假期做什么？
　A 玩电脑游戏 □　B 看电影 □　C 看书 □

5 她每天怎么上班？
　A 走路 □　B 坐地铁 □　C 坐船 □

四　阅读（二）
4　Reading (2)

王天生爸爸的公司有很多规则。请阅读下面的文字，选择"是"或"非"。

CD 02, Track 09

> 1 上班必须准时，要在九点十五分前回到公司。
> 2 回到公司后要打卡，没带卡的人必须跟经理说。
> 3 不准在上班时看杂志，也不能跟其他人聊天。
> 4 客人打电话来公司，说话人讲英文，必须用英文回答；对方讲汉语时，必须用汉语回答。
> 5 你愿意加班的话，公司会按照加班时间支付加班费。

　　　　　　　　　　　　　　　　　是　非
1 上班不可以迟到。　　　　　　　　□　□
2 打卡之后要去见经理。　　　　　　□　□
3 王天生上班时，可以看
　《年轻人杂志》。　　　　　　　　□　□
4 客人打电话来，用汉语讲话，
　王天生应该用中文跟他说话。　　　□　□
5 加班两个小时的钱比一个小
　时的多。　　　　　　　　　　　　□　□

词语
VOCABULARY

1	不准	bù zhǔn	to forbid; not allowed
2	说话人	shuō huà rén	speaker
3	愿意	yuàn yì	willing to
4	按照	àn zhào	according to

补充词语
SUPPLEMENTARY VOCABULARY

1	规则	guī zé	rules, regulations
2	打卡	dǎ kǎ	to clock in/clock out
3	支付	zhī fù	to pay
4	加班费	jiā bān fèi	charge for overtime

语法
GRAMMAR

Auxiliary verbs, e.g. 应该, 准

1. An auxiliary verb is a verb that adds functional or grammatical meaning to the main verb. Examples of auxiliary verbs in English are 'may', 'need', 'should', etc. As in English, there are auxiliary verbs in Chinese such as 应该 (should) and 准 (can, to be allowed) that help express the tone or mood of the verb. Try to identify the auxiliary verbs which appear in Readings (1) and (2).
2. To negate a sentence with an auxiliary verb, put 不 before the auxiliary, e.g. 不准; never use 没.
3. Auxiliary verbs cannot be reduplicated, and aspect markers such as 了, 着, 过 should not be used with them.

小贴士
TOP TIP

When you are answering a question where an auxiliary verb is used, you should use the auxiliary verb in your answer, not the main verb, e.g. 我可以去厕所吗？ 可以。

Cambridge IGCSE Mandarin as a Foreign Language

五 听力（二）
5 🔊 Listening (2)

<u>刘一红</u>在寒假时在一个学校实习，<u>马明</u>是《年轻人杂志》的记者。以下是他的采访。请听录音，用中文或拼音回答问题。

CD 02, Track 10

词语 VOCABULARY
记者　jì zhě　journalist

例：刘一红在寒假时去了哪里实习？

答案：学校

1 什么学生不能上学？
2 刘一红每天除了量体温以外，还有什么其他工作？
　a _____
　b _____
3 她为什么喜欢教英文？
　a _____
　b _____
4 她以后要做什么工作？

六 阅读（三）
6 📖 Reading (3)

<u>王天生</u>在周会上给同学们做了一次演讲。

CD 02, Track 11

校长、老师、同学们：
　你们好，我是中学五年级的<u>王天生</u>同学。这个寒假，我到了爸爸的公司工作，学到了很多东西。
　我敢说，在工作之前，我觉得上班是一件无聊的事情。你别这么想，我试过工作后，觉得上班很有意思。
　我爸爸公司的职员差不多全都是大学毕业生。他们在那儿工作了大概三、四年，他们觉得上班很有意思。当然，有时候他们很想放假，因为放假的时候可以去玩儿。
　在这一个星期的实习里，我要做接电话、写新闻等工作。经理都觉得我的工作很好，他们希望我毕业之后再回来工作。不过我现在还没有计划，我决定先好好的读书，未来再决定。我喜欢演戏，有机会成为一个演员呢！谢谢大家！

Unit D　18　The world of work: Work experience

延伸活动
AIM HIGHER

Find the auxiliary verbs used in this passage.

词语
VOCABULARY

1	敢	gǎn	dare
2	别	bié	do not
3	差不多	chà bu duō	almost
4	全	quán	all, whole
5	公司	gōng sī	company
6	毕业	bì yè	graduation
7	当然	dāng rán	of course, naturally
8	决定	jué dìng	to decide
9	读书	dú shū	to study

补充词语
SUPPLEMENTARY VOCABULARY

演讲	yǎn jiǎng	speech/to give a speech

小贴士
TOP TIP

希望 and 计划 are used to say something which you wish to happen in the future, e.g.

a 我希望以后可以当老师。I want to become a teacher in the future.

b 我正在计划下个星期去日本。I am planning to go to Japan next week.

一、请阅读上面的短文，然后回答问题。

1 王天生在上班后，觉得上班是一件怎么样的事情？
2 为什么爸爸公司的职员想放假？
3 王天生在实习时做了什么？
4 王天生希望以后做什么工作？为什么？

二、根据上面的短文，判断"对"或"错"。

	对	错
1 王天生今年五岁。	☐	☐
2 王天生爸爸公司的职员都是大学生。	☐	☐
3 那些职员都在爸爸的公司工作了三十四年了。	☐	☐
4 职员都觉得上班很有意思。	☐	☐
5 职员上班的时候可以去玩儿。	☐	☐
6 经理都希望王天生毕业后回去大学工作。	☐	☐
7 王天生很想回去爸爸的公司工作。	☐	☐

三、请用下列词组填空。

毕业 希望 计划 读书 差不多 别 试

1 王天生＿＿＿后可以回去爸爸的公司工作。
2 爸爸公司的职员在那儿做了＿＿＿四年了。
3 爸爸对王天生说："你＿＿＿以为工作很无聊。"
4 在未来，王天生还没有什么＿＿＿，他也想＿＿＿一＿＿＿当演员。

CAMBRIDGE IGCSE Mandarin as a Foreign Language

> **语法**
> **GRAMMAR**
>
> Expressing approximate numbers, e.g. 三、四
>
> To express an approximate number in Chinese, two consecutive numbers are used, e.g. in Reading (3), to say the staff there have been working for around 3 to 4 years, 三、四年 is used. To say there are around 5 or 6 people in a room, 五、六个人 is used, e.g. 房间里有五、六个人。

七 说话
7 Speaking

两人一组，做角色扮演。

A 王天生学校的老师
B 王天生

王天生在学校跟老师讲话。

A1 你今年几年级？
A2 你在哪里实习？
A3 你实习了多久了？
A4 你实习的时候做了什么工作？
A5 你以后想做什么？

八 写作
8 Writing

一、请写出五种工作。

二、《年轻人杂志》想知道现在年轻人工作的经历。你是<u>王天生</u>，请你说一说：

1 你什么时候实习的？为什么要实习？
2 你实习的时候做了什么？
3 你觉得你的工作怎么样？
4 你以后要回去你工作过的公司上班吗？为什么？

> **好词好句**
> **USEFUL EXPRESSIONS**
>
> · 我在寒假的时候，到爸爸的公司实习了一个星期。
> · 第一天我要接电话……第二天我用英文给公司写了一篇新闻。
> · 我很喜欢我的工作。我觉得一点儿都不无聊，很有意思。
> · 我现在还没有计划，我决定先好好的读书，未来再决定。

自我评估
Self-Assessment

☐ I have had a chance to revise vocabulary related to occupations
☐ I can read a diary about someone's work experience
☐ I am able to listen to a conversation about someone's duties at work
☐ I can talk about someone's work experience based on second-hand materials
☐ I am able to write about someone's work experience
☐ Auxiliary verbs in Chinese
☐ Prepositions 跟, 给
☐ Expressing approximate numbers

shēn qǐng gōng zuò
申请工作
19 Applying for a job

Learning objectives

This unit will concentrate on learning how to apply for a job in Chinese. You will:

- Read a job advertisement
- Understand questions in a job interview and be able to respond
- Fill in a job application form in Chinese
- Write a job application letter

In addition, you are going to learn:

- Ordinal numbers: 第……
- Sentence structure: 用……来……
- Sentence structure: 不但……而且……

学习目标

本单元你会：

- 学习如何以中文申请工作
- 阅读招聘广告
- 理解面试的问题，并作出回应
- 以中文填写工作申请表
- 书写求职信

你还会学到：

- 序数词：第……
- 句型：用……来……
- 句型：不但……而且……

Cambridge IGCSE Mandarin as a Foreign Language

一　温故知新
1　'Before starting' activity

请把左边的职业与右边的工作地点连起来。

1 老师　　　　A 服装店
2 医生　　　　B 饭店
3 服务员　　　C 理发店
4 理发师　　　D 医院
5 售货员　　　E 学校

二　听力（一）
2　🔊 Listening (1)

你将听到几个中文句子。请在括号内填上唯一正确的答案。　CD 02, Track 12

1 (　) A 学校 B 公园 C 餐厅 D 游泳池
2 (　) A 老师 B 学生 C 校长 D 家长
3 (　) A 理发师 B 护士 C 售货员 D 导游
4 (　) A 服务员 B 医生 C 电影明星
　　　 D 售货员
5 (　) A 公司 B 花园 C 图书馆 D 医院

三　阅读（一）
3　📖 Reading (1)

一、请把左边的词语与右边的英语解释连起来。

   dǒng
1 懂　　　　　　　A email
   hé shì
2 合适　　　　　　B to apply
   xiáng xì
3 详细　　　　　　C suitable
   diàn zǐ yóu jiàn
4 电子邮件　　　　D notice

   tōng zhī
5 通知　　　　　　E to speak
   shēn qǐng
6 申请　　　　　　F detailed
   shuō huà
7 说话　　　　　　G to understand

二、请阅读下面的广告，然后回答问题。　CD 02, Track 13

需要暑期工五个

我们的主题乐园现需要暑期工五个，扮演不同的卡通人物与客人合照，让客人开心。加入我们，不但可以学习服务别人的方法，而且可以获得工作经验。只要你是十六岁以上就可以申请。男女都可以。不需要经验。最好懂得用多国语言交谈。性格要友好，喜欢跟客人说话。

加入我们后：
1 主题公园免费入场
2 主题公园购物打折

  有兴趣者，请将求职信和详细履历寄给主题乐园黄经理，或发电子邮件到 jobapplication@themepark.com，或在网站申请。

  我们会用电邮通知合适的申请人参加第一阶段面试，成功后可以马上上班。

词语　VOCABULARY

只要……就…… zhǐ yào… jiù… as long as…

Unit D　19　The world of work: Applying for a job

补充词语
SUPPLEMENTARY VOCABULARY

1. 主题公园　zhǔ tí gōng yuán　theme park
2. 扮演　bàn yǎn　to act, to play a role
3. 卡通人物　kǎ tōng rén wù　cartoon character
4. 经验　jīng yàn　experience
5. 面试　miàn shì　interview
6. 求职信　qiú zhí xìn　application letter

1. 这个主题公园需要多少个暑期工？
2. 这个职位的主要工作是什么？
3. 这个职位可以学习什么技巧？
4. 多少岁可以申请这份工作？
5. 有性别要求吗？
6. 对性格有什么要求？
7. 这个主题公园有什么好处？
8. 有兴趣者可以怎样申请？
9. 谁会获得面试通知？
10. 面试成功后可以怎么样？

句型
LANGUAGE

1. 不但……而且……

   This is a very commonly used pattern that means 'not only … but also …'.

   When there is only one subject in a sentence containing 不但……而且……, the subject has to come at the beginning of the sentence, before both 不但 and 而且.

   Subject + 不但 + Adj/Verb, 而且 + Adj/Verb

   When there are two different subjects, however, you need to put one after 不但 and one after 而且.

   不但 + Subject 1 + Adj/Verb, 而且 + Subject 2 + Adj/Verb

   e.g.
   a 你不但可以学习服务别人的方法，而且可以获得工作经验。
   b 学习汉语不但可以跟中国人沟通，而且可以在中国工作。

2. ……用……来…… (use … to …)
   The sentence structure ……用……来…… expresses using an object to complete an action.

   Subject + 用 + Object + 来 + Verb

   e.g.
   a 我用德语来说再见。
   b 中国人喜欢用筷子来吃饭。
   c 我喜欢用汉语来跟中国朋友说话。
   d 你最好能用多国语言来交谈。

三、　请用下列词组填空。　CD 02, Track 14

教育　比赛　唯一　第一　业余

黄经理：谢谢你申请我们主题乐园的工作。请问你为什么想申请这工作？

申请人：我从小____1____的爱好是拍照。

黄经理：你为什么想在这里工作？

申请人：____2____，因为我很喜欢去你们的主题公园玩；第二，你们的主题公园里有的游戏可以____3____小孩子。

黄经理：你现在有什么____4____爱好？

申请人：我喜欢看不同的书，例如历史书。

黄经理：你每天看书一般看多少？

申请人：我每天都看一段。我也喜欢唱歌，有时我会参加唱歌____5____。

黄经理：谢谢你来参加面试。

词语
VOCABULARY

1	唯一	wéi yī	only, unique
2	第一	dì yī	the first
3	有的	yǒu de	some
4	教育	jiào yù	to educate
5	业余	yè yú	amateur
6	例如	lì rú	for example
7	段	duàn	section
8	参加	cān jiā	to participate

补充词语
SUPPLEMENTARY VOCABULARY

| 内容 | nèi róng | content |

句型
LANGUAGE

Ordinal numbers

Ordinal numbers such as 'first' and 'second' are commonly used. In Chinese, the same prefix is used for all ordinal numbers: 第. This character is simply placed in front of the number. For example: 第一 first, 第二 second, 第三 third, 第四 fourth, 第五 fifth, and so on.

Sentence structure: 第 + Number

e.g.

第一，因为你们的学校非常有名。

四 说话（一）
4 Speaking (1)

角色扮演

老师：黄经理

你：考生

你在主题公园的餐厅参加面试。

1 你申请什么工作？
2 你为什么要申请这份工作？
3 你有没有到别的国家接受过教育？
4 你以前做过暑期工吗？
5 你有另外的资料要告诉我吗？

词语
VOCABULARY

1	考生	kǎo sheng	candidate
2	另外（的）	lìng wài (de)	additional; 另 another
3	别的	bié de	other

五 阅读（二）
5 Reading (2)

请阅读下面的网站申请表，然后回答问题。 CD 02, Track 15

Unit D 19 The world of work: Applying for a job

网站申请表
申请工作：开心法国餐厅厨师
姓名：<u>马小明</u> 先生 / <s>太太</s> / <s>小姐</s>
性别：男 / <s>女</s>
生日：1986 年 6 月 21 日
年龄：30 岁
出生地点：<u>广州</u>
电话号码：(86) 13045679950
住址：<u>广州光明大道</u> 100 <u>号光明大厦</u> 3 楼 305 室
电子邮件：maimingshun@china.com
教育：
2004 <u>广州市</u> <u>第一中学高中</u> 毕业
2006 <u>上海厨师学校</u> 毕业
工作经验：
2006 - 2010 <u>美味</u> 法国餐厅 厨师
2010 - 2016 <u>巴黎</u> 法国餐厅 厨师
申请日期：2017 年 8 月 1 日

词语
VOCABULARY

1	先生	xiān sheng	Mr
2	太太	tài tai	Mrs
3	小姐	xiǎo jiě	Miss
4	性别	xìng bié	gender
5	电话号码	diàn huà hào mǎ	telephone number
6	住址	zhù zhǐ	address
7	日期	rì qī	date

1 这是申请什么工作的申请表？
2 申请者是谁？
3 申请者的出生日期是什么？
4 申请者的出生地点在哪里？
5 申请者的通讯地址是什么？
6 写出申请者的学习背景。

7 申请者要有多少年的工作经验？
8 他曾经在哪里工作？

六 听力（二）
6 🔊 Listening (2)

<u>李国华</u>也有兴趣申请开心法国餐厅的厨师工作，请帮他填好下面的表格。

请听录音，然后填空。 CD 02, Track 16

网站申请表
申请工作：开心<u>法国</u>餐厅厨师
姓名：___1___ ___2___ 先生 / 太太 / 小姐
性别：___3___ 男 / 女
生日：___4___ 年 11 月 13 日
年龄：___5___
出生地点：___6___
电话号码：(86) 13013000130
住址：___7___ 快乐大道 9 号爱心大厦 7 楼 703 室
电子邮件：___8___
教育：
___9___ 南京市第一中学毕业
2004 ___10___ 毕业
工作经验：
2004 - 2016 ___11___ 法国餐厅 厨师
申请日期：2017 年 8 月 3 日

七 说话（二）
7 💬 Speaking (2)

一、请朗读以下的自我介绍。

CD 02, Track 17

词语
VOCABULARY

年纪　　nián jì　　age

你为什么适合这份工作？

我希望可以在图书馆工作。我从小就对各种各样的图书爱不释手，什么语言的书都喜欢看，最喜欢看的是学习语言的书和小说。我的性格是做事认真，爱干净，家里的书都放得很整齐，方便自己。我刚刚从马来西亚大学毕业。虽然我年纪轻，还没有工作经验，但是我每年暑假都会到公共图书馆帮忙，安排图书的摆放位置。由于上面的原因，我觉得我很适合这份工作，谢谢。

! 小贴士
TOP TIP

年纪 and 年龄 both mean 'age', but 年纪 can refer to a general age group, while 年龄 always means a particular age in years.

补充词语
SUPPLEMENTARY VOCABULARY

爱不释手　　ài bù shì shǒu　　to fondle admiringly

二、小演讲
请完成以下的填空，说一说"为什么我适合这份工作"：

- 你的理想工作是什么？
- 你为什么适合这份工作？
- 你的性格怎么样？
- 你的学习背景怎么样？
- 你有什么工作经验？

　　我希望可以在＿＿1＿＿（工作地方）做＿＿2＿＿（工作）。我从小就对＿＿3＿＿有兴趣，最喜欢＿＿4＿＿（爱好）。我的性格＿＿5＿＿（性格的形容词），＿＿6＿＿（例子）。我刚刚从＿＿7＿＿（学校）毕业。虽然我年纪轻，还没有工作经验，但是我＿＿8＿＿（其他经验）。由于上面的原因，我觉得我很适合这份工作，谢谢。

八　写作
8　Writing

一、请写出五个在申请表格上可看到的资料。

二、你对网页上的工作有兴趣。写一封求职信，信里讲一讲：
- 那是什么工作？
- 你在哪里看到这份工作？
- 你为什么想申请？
- 你从哪所学校毕业？
- 你的联系方式。

用中文写 80-100 个字。

Unit D　19　The world of work: Applying for a job

三、请为自己写履历表。表里应包括：
- 你的个人资料
- 你的教育
- 课外活动
- 爱好
- 你的工作经验

履历表

姓名：_____1_____
出生日期：_____2_____
出生地点：_____3_____
电话：_____4_____
地址：_____5_____
电邮：_____6_____
教育：
____7____年_____8_____
____9____年_____10_____
课外活动：_____11_____
爱好：_____12_____
工作经验：_____13_____

自我评估
Self-Assessment

- [ ] I can read a job advertisement
- [ ] I can understand questions in a job interview and am able to respond
- [ ] I can fill in a job application form in Chinese
- [ ] I can write a job application letter
- [ ] Ordinal numbers 第……
- [ ] Sentence structure 用……来……
- [ ] Sentence structure 不但……而且……

Cambridge IGCSE Mandarin as a Foreign Language

未来学业和职业规划
20 Future education and career plans

wèi lái xué yè hé zhí yè guī huà

Learning objectives

This unit will concentrate on future education and career plans. You will:

- Read an interview article about an alumnus of a school
- Read a dialogue of two students talking about their future education plans
- Listen to conversations about dream jobs
- Ask and answer questions about future plans
- Write about your future plans

In addition, you are going to learn:

- Sentences with an adverbial phrase after the verb, e.g. 小孩子走得很慢
- Measure words: 家，所
- Tag questions: 好不好？是不是？

学习目标

本单元你会：

- 阅读一篇介绍校友的文章
- 阅读两个学生谈论未来学业规划的文章
- 聆听有关理想职业的对话
- 以角色扮演的方式回答未来职业规划的问题
- 写一写你未来的计划

你还会学到：

- 副词短语：小孩子走得很慢
- 量词：家、所
- 附加疑问句：好不好？是不是？

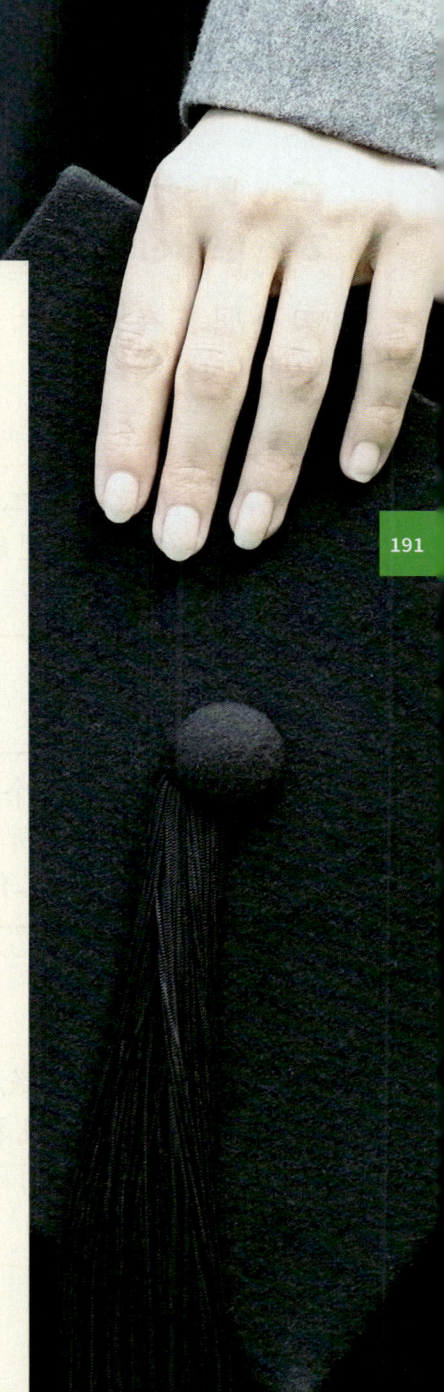

Unit D 20 The world of work: Future education and career plans

一　温故知新
1　'Before starting' activity

你将听到几个中文句子。请用中文或拼音回答问题。**CD 02, Track 18**

1　小明明年要学习什么？
2　姐姐在大学学习什么？
3　我要到哪个国家去学历史？
4　红红将来想做什么工作？
5　我的朋友喜欢踢足球和打篮球。他以后要做什么工作？

二　阅读（一）
2　Reading (1)

四个朋友在谈论未来的理想职业。
CD 02, Track 19

张年：

> 我以后想做一个工程师，在一家国际公司工作。我希望能在中国完成大学的课程。

吴海：

> 我未来希望做一个新闻记者，但是我不想写报纸上的新闻。做新闻记者挣的钱不多，但是工作很有意义。

王田：

> 我爸爸是一个农民。我以前在田里养了很多小动物。我喜欢宠物，所以我要当兽医。我要到国外念书，然后回国治疗动物。

李学林：

> 我爸爸是大学的教授，妈妈在一所中学教书。我喜欢艺术，喜欢画画儿，还喜欢写东西。他们都同意我以后当一个作家。

新闻记者　　农民
教授　　工程师

一、请用下列词组填空。

职业　国外　挣　念书　教书　作家

1　妈妈的理想＿＿＿是做老师，因为她很喜欢小朋友。
2　虽然老师＿＿＿的钱不多，但是工作很有意义。
3　李学林喜欢写东西，他想成为一个＿＿＿。
4　要到＿＿＿读书，一般都要办签证。

二、请选择"是"或"非"。

　　　　　　　　　　　　　　　是　非
1　张年想在中国读大学。　　　　□　□
2　吴海希望将来做一个报纸的新闻记者。　□　□
3　吴海想做记者，因为记者挣钱不多。　□　□
4　王田的爸爸是一个兽医。　　　□　□
5　李学林的妈妈是一个大学教授。　□　□

词语
VOCABULARY

1	职业	zhí yè	occupation
2	工程师	gōng chéng shī	engineer
3	工作	gōng zuò	job, occupation
4	完成	wán chéng	to finish
5	新闻记者	xīn wén jì zhě	news reporter
6	挣钱	zhèng qián	to earn money
7	农民	nóng mín	farmer, peasant
8	兽医	shòu yī	veterinarian
9	国外	guó wài	overseas, abroad
10	回国	huí guó	to return to one's homeland
11	治疗	zhì liáo	to cure
12	教授	jiào shòu	professor
13	教书	jiāo shū	to teach
14	同意	tóng yì	to agree
15	作家	zuò jiā	writer

补充词语
SUPPLEMENTARY VOCABULARY

1	理想	lǐ xiǎng	ideal
2	未来	wèi lái	future
3	念书	niàn shū	to study

语法
GRAMMAR

量词：家、所

1 家 is a measure word for companies, restaurants or shops, e.g. 一家公司, 两家饭馆, 三家商店.
2 所 is a measure word for small buildings/houses or universities, e.g. 一所房子, 两所学校, 三所大学.

三 听力（一）
3 🔊 Listening (1)

一、请把左边的中文词语与右边的英文意思搭配起来。

1 航空服务员 (háng kōng fú wù yuán) A businessperson
2 工人 (gōng rén) B accountant
3 画家 (huà jiā) C worker
4 会计师 (kuài jì shī) D painter
5 商人 (shāng rén) E flight attendant
6 邮递员 (yóu dì yuán) F postman
7 警察 (jǐng chá) G lawyer
8 律师 (lǜ shī) H police officer

二、同学们一起谈他们将来想做什么工作。请听录音，选择正确的答案，将字母填入方格内。

CD 02, Track 20

A 航空服务员	B 工人	C 画家
D 会计师	E 商人	F 邮递员
G 警察	H 律师	

1 张冰冰 ☐
2 刘红 ☐
3 吴小刚 ☐
4 马力 ☐
5 王晶晶 ☐

Unit D 20 The world of work: Future education and career plans

四 说话（一）
4 Speaking (1)

两人一组，做角色扮演。

A 一位中文老师　B 你自己

你在一所学校跟一位中文老师谈将来的职业。中文老师问你以下的问题：

1. 你今年多大了？
2. 你将来想做什么工作？
3. 为什么？
4. 你想在哪个国家读大学？
5. 那个国家气候怎么样？

小贴士 TOP TIP
Remember you can always use just the key words to answer the questions, e.g. 你将来想做什么工作？工程师。

五 阅读（二）
5 Reading (2)

林日山是中国实验国际学校的毕业生，学校的《实验杂志》采访了他。

请阅读下面的短文，然后回答问题。

CD 02, Track 21

林日山医生

1　林日山在2004年中学毕业后，
2　去了国外读医科。他目前是一位
3　"无国界医生"，在非洲工作。
4　他小时候已经跟爸爸妈妈说：
5　"我很想将来当医生"。根据他
6　以前的科学老师说，林日山念书
7　很用功，上课经常举手回答问
8　题，并且常常去图书馆看跟医科
9　有关的书。
10　读完中学之后，林日山决定到英国
11　读书。那时候，他要去香港办理到英国
12　的签证。虽然他觉得到国外读书很贵，
13　但是他可以比较两个地方的文化，可以
14　大开眼界，爸妈也点头同意了。到了
15　英国后，他成绩非常好，读完五年之后
16　就成为医生了。现在他在非洲工作，治
17　疗了不少的病人，所以他觉得工作很有
18　意义。林日山说，他希望以后能在大学
19　教书，当一位教授。
20　他太太是一个银行家，在一家国际
21　银行工作。他们两个人是在一次非洲拍
22　照时认识的。当时他太太是一个航空服
23　务员，刚好在非洲旅游。他们都很喜欢
24　野生动物和非洲的工艺。

1. 林日山是哪一年中学毕业的？
2. 他现在在哪个地方工作？
3. 林日山的科学老师觉得他读书怎么样？
4. 他要在哪里办理签证？
5. 为什么他觉得到英国可以大开眼界？
6. 为什么他觉得自己的工作很有意义？
7. 林日山打算以后继续做医生吗？他想做什么工作？
8. 林日山怎么认识他太太？

Cambridge IGCSE Mandarin as a Foreign Language

词语
VOCABULARY

1	目前	mù qián	currently
2	（根）据	(gēn) jù	according to
3	举	jǔ	to hold up, raise
4	并且	bìng qiě	and, also; same as 并
5	完	wán	to finish
6	办理	bàn lǐ	to handle; 办（理）签证 to apply for a visa
7	点头	diǎn tóu	to nod
8	比较	bǐ jiào	to compare
9	拍照	pāi zhào	to take photographs
10	野生动物	yě shēng dòng wù	wildlife
11	工艺	gōng yì	craft

补充词语
SUPPLEMENTARY VOCABULARY

1	大开眼界	dà kāi yǎn jiè	to broaden one's horizon
2	当时	dāng shí	at that time
3	文化	wén huà	culture

六 阅读（三）
6 Reading (3)

请阅读下面的对话，然后回答问题。选择唯一正确的答案，在方格中打勾。

CD 02, Track 22

黄雪：赵龙，我们明年就要上高考，我不知道应该选择什么科目。

赵龙：黄雪，选课应该根据自己的爱好。

黄雪：我最喜欢画画儿，也喜欢写小说。虽然我的艺术很好，但是爸爸妈妈不同意我明年学美术。

赵龙：为什么呢？

黄雪：因为他们希望我将来当医生，所以要我学化学和生物课。我爸爸学数学学得很好，他是一个会计师，在一个大公司工作。他说不做医生也可以，但是要当商人。

赵龙：可是念书的人是你，不是你爸爸！

黄雪：我知道，但是没有爸爸妈妈的同意，我们不能选课，对不对？

赵龙：你准备读大学吗？打算在大学里学习什么？

Unit D 20 The world of work: Future education and career plans

黄雪：

现在还不知道。我的成绩很一般，不一定能够上大学。如果可以选择的话，我希望在大学念美术。

赵龙：

你想在哪个国家念书呢？

黄雪：

我想去法国念书，因为我知道那里的美术课程很棒，而且我学法语学了三年了，我说得很好。如果我能够到那儿读书的话，我一定会认识很多都喜欢美术的朋友。

赵龙：

我知道张老师以前在美国住了八年。她以前住在纽约，在那儿上大学上了四年。我们去问问她。好不好？

黄雪：

好的，我们现在就去吧！

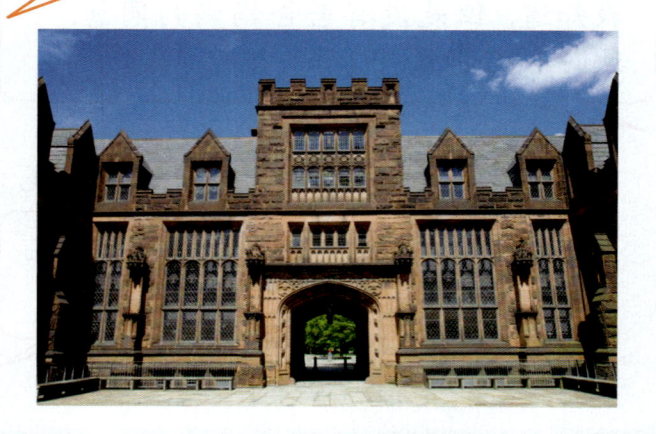

1 赵龙觉得，选课应该
 A 要看看自己喜欢什么。☐
 B 根据自己的画来选择。☐
 C 在高考时写小说。☐

2 黄雪为什么不一定明年学艺术？
 A 因为她要去法国念书。☐
 B 因为爸爸妈妈是医生。☐
 C 因为爸爸妈妈不准她读。☐

3 黄雪的爸爸觉得
 A 数学好就要做会计师。☐
 B 他以后要做医生。☐
 C 做医生跟商人一样的好。☐

4 为什么黄雪想去法国？
 A 因为她在法国住了三年了。☐
 B 因为她在那儿有很多喜欢美术的朋友。☐
 C 因为她的法语很不错。☐

5 为什么赵龙和黄雪去找张老师？
 A 张老师以前也在国外住过。☐
 B 张老师是美国人。☐
 C 张老师的爸爸妈妈不同意她学美术。☐

语法
GRAMMAR

Sentences with an adverbial phrase after the verb

In Chinese, an adverbial phrase can be put before or after a verb. It is put after a verb to describe time (duration), place (where) or manner (how).

1 To describe time, e.g.
 a 他住三天。 He is staying for three days.
 b 他住了三天。 He stayed for three days.
 c 他住了三天了。 He has stayed for three days.
 d 她学中文学了两年。 She learnt Chinese for two years.

2 To describe place, e.g. 她住在广州 She lives in Guangzhou.

3 To describe manner, the adverbial phrase is usually preceded by 得, e.g. 小孩子走得很慢。

Cambridge IGCSE Mandarin as a Foreign Language

七 说话（二）
7 🗨 Speaking (2)

在阅读（三）中，有几个很有意思的问题：

1 你明年要学习什么科目？为什么？
2 你准备上大学吗？为什么？
3 你爸爸妈妈同意你的选择吗？为什么？

你的答案是什么？跟老师/同学说一说。

好词好句
USEFUL EXPRESSIONS

- 我将来要到中国学中文，因为我觉得中文很有用，我很想学好中文。
- 我打算以后上大学。我要到英国的大学学习英国文学。我将来要成为一个作家。
- 我爸爸妈妈同意我的选择。他们都知道我喜欢旅行，所以同意我当航空服务员。
- 当航空服务员可以到世界各地旅行。我最想去非洲。

小贴士
TOP TIP

Try to expand each answer to 3–5 sentences. Include sentence structures or idioms where possible, e.g. 我将来要到美国当演员，因为我喜欢演戏，也喜欢电影。

八 听力（二）
8 🔊 Listening (2)

黄雪去找张老师。请先阅读以下问题。然后听采访，用中文或拼音回答问题。

CD 02, Track 23

1 为什么黄雪要找张老师？
2 张老师为什么去美国念书？
3 张老师觉得在国外念书有什么好处？
4 张老师觉得黄雪应该给爸爸妈妈看什么？
5 除了法国以外，黄雪也想去英国。为什么？

句型
LANGUAGE

Tag questions

A tag question serves the same purpose as the question word 吗. The basic pattern is:

| Verb + 不 + (same) Verb |

In Reading (3) and Listening (2), there are some tag questions such as 对不对 and 好不好. Here are some more examples:

a 我们是好朋友，对不对？（= 我们是好朋友吗？）
b 你现在去买票，好不好？（= 你可以现在去买票吗？）
c 你今年十一岁，是不是？（= 你今年十一岁吗？）

Unit D 20 The world of work: Future education and career plans

九　写作
9　Writing

你的老师想了解一下你将来的计划。请看一看下面的电邮，给老师回信。

From: Ms Zhang "zhang.ming@chineseschool.cn
To: Xiaoyun Li "xiaoyun.li@chineseschool.cn
Subject: 你将来的计划

李小云同学：

你好！我下个星期五会跟你爸爸妈妈见面。我要跟他们说一说你将来的计划。请给我写一封电邮，信里说说：

1　你明年要学习哪些科目？为什么？
2　你准备上大学吗？为什么？
3　你将来要做什么工作？为什么？

写不少于 150 个汉字。谢谢！

张老师 上

好词好句
USEFUL EXPRESSIONS

- 我打算以后上大学。我要到中国的大学学习中国文学，我将来要成为一个作家。
- 我很喜欢小动物，我想成为一个兽医，可以治疗生病的宠物。
- 英文很重要，因为在国外读书，英文一定要好，而且可以交到新朋友。

自我评估
Self-Assessment

☐ I can read an interview article about an alumnus of a school
☐ I can read a dialogue of two students talking about their future education plans
☐ I can listen to conversations about dream jobs
☐ I can ask and answer questions about future plans
☐ I can write about my future plans
☐ Use of an adverbial phrase after the verb
☐ Measure words: 家 and 所
☐ Tag questions such as 好不好? and 是不是?

考试练习题
Exam-style question

听力
Listening

对一个在中国的新闻记者陈一心的采访
An interview with a news reporter in China

请先阅读一下问题。
Read the questions first.

请听采访，用中文或拼音回答问题。
Listen to the interview, and answer the questions in Chinese. You may write your answers in Chinese characters or pinyin.
CD 02, Track 24

1　陈一心为什么想做记者？
　　_____

2　陈一心的爸妈觉得他应该找一份怎么样的工作？
　　_____

3　为什么陈一心以前来中国读书？
　　a _____
　　b _____

4　陈一心在中国有什么有趣的事情？

Cambridge IGCSE Mandarin as a Foreign Language

guó jì shì yě
国际视野
E International world

cǎi fǎng míng rén
采访名人
21 Interviewing Chinese celebrities

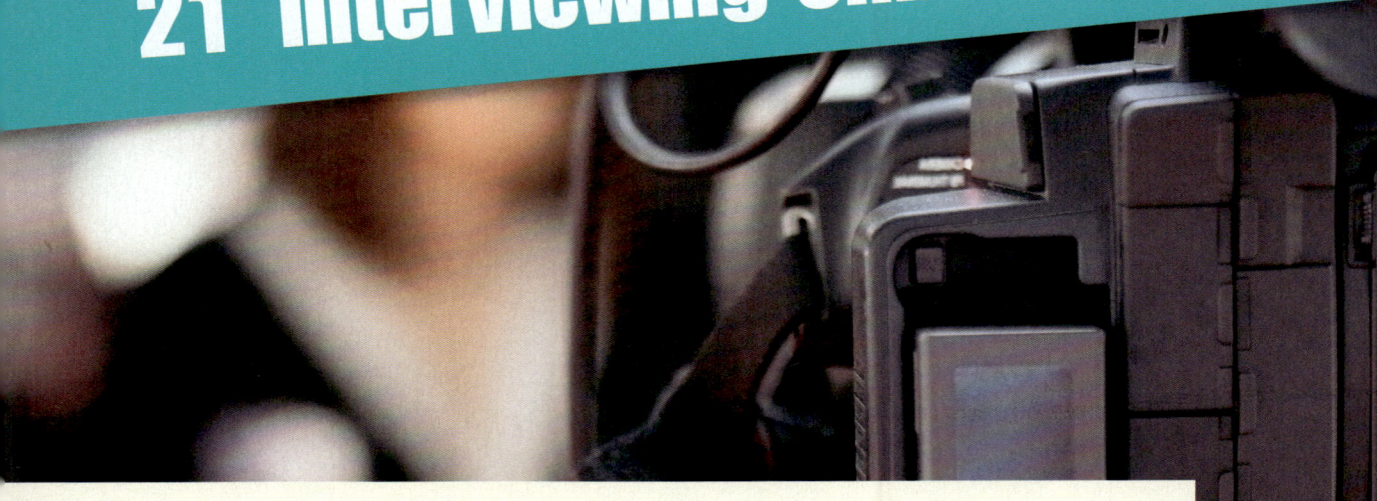

Learning objectives

This unit will concentrate on learning vocabulary for interviewing celebrities. You will:

- Listen to an interview about a celebrity and their hometown
- Read a dialogue about the healthy lifestyle of a celebrity
- Talk about the appearances of celebrities
- Write a letter to share an experience of meeting a celebrity

In addition, you are going to learn:

- Sentence structure: comparisons
  像……一样，跟……一样
- Sentence structure: the 被 construction

学习目标

本单元你会：

- 学习有关采访中国名人的词语
- 聆听名人的采访
- 阅读有关名人健康生活的对话
- 谈谈名人的外表
- 写信分享跟名人见面的经历

你还会学到：

- 句型：比较
  像……一样、跟……一样
- 句型："被"的用法

Cambridge IGCSE Mandarin as a Foreign Language

一　温故知新
1　'Before starting' activities

一、你知道以下图片中的人物是谁吗?

1
2
3

延伸活动
AIM HIGHER
你能说出一件跟每个人物有关的事吗?

二、两人一组,练习下面的对话。

词语
VOCABULARY

| 1 | 酷 | kù | cool |
| 2 | 成功 | chéng gōng | successful |

Q1 你最喜欢的名人是谁?

A1 我最喜欢的是运动员姚明。

Q2 他是哪国人?

A2 他是中国人。

Q3 你为什么欣赏他?

A3 因为他打篮球打得很好,非常酷。他应该是中国最成功的篮球运动员。

二　听力（一）
2　Listening (1)

你将听到几个中文句子。请在括号内填上唯一正确的答案。 CD 02, Track 25

1 ( ) A 工程师 B 老师 C 工人 D 航空服务员
2 ( ) A 演员 B 司机 C 记者 D 兽医
3 ( ) A 教授 B 明星 C 作家 D 画家
4 ( ) A 会计师 B 邮递员 C 秘书 D 医生
5 ( ) A 商人 B 护士 C 科学家 D 警察

词语
VOCABULARY

1	出版	chū bǎn	publishing
2	草药	cǎo yào	medicinal herbs
3	治疗	zhì liáo	to cure
4	中医	Zhōng yī	doctor of Chinese medicine
5	中药	Zhōng yào	Chinese medicine

Unit E 21 International world: Interviewing Chinese celebrities

文化 (一)
CULTURE (1)

孔子 Kǒng zǐ

孔子 (Confucius)（公元前 551–公元前 479 年）是中国著名的教育家。他的学生把他的话写成一本书，那本书叫《论语》(The Analects)。

三　阅读 (一)
3　Reading (1)

一、请阅读下面的短文，然后回答问题。 CD 02, Track 26

李安

1. 李安 (Ang Lee)，1954年在
2. 台湾出生，是著名的导演。
3. 他现在住在美国。他的太太
4. 不爱做饭，所以他常常自己做中国菜。
5. 他的太太在美国著名的大学工作，他们
6. 在1983年结婚。
7. 在1995年李安拍了第一部英语电影
8. 《理智与情感》(Sense and Sensibility)。
9. 1999年的《卧虎藏龙》(Crouching Tiger, Hidden Dragon) 拿了很多奥斯卡奖。在2013年他
10.
11. 的电影《少年派的奇幻漂流》(Life of Pi)
12. 拿了奥斯卡的导演奖。他是第一个拿
13. 到这个奖的亚洲导演。
14. 2009年李安被美国一本杂志选为
15. 《五十位最伟大的导演》之一，是华
16. 人导演中最高位。

文化

词语 VOCABULARY

| 1 | 结婚 | jié hūn | to marry |
| 2 | 位 | wèi | place, position |

补充词语 SUPPLEMENTARY VOCABULARY

1	奖	jiǎng	award
2	奥斯卡	Ào sī kǎ	Oscar
3	伟大	wěi dà	great

1. 李安在哪一年出生？
2. 李安在哪里出生？
3. 李安的职业是什么？
4. 李安现在住在哪里？
5. 李安的太太在哪里工作？
6. 李安在哪一年结婚？
7. 李安拍的第一部英语电影叫什么？
8. 李安是第几个拿到奥斯卡导演奖的亚洲导演？

句型 LANGUAGE

1. In passive sentences, the object of an action becomes the subject of the sentence, and the 'doer' of the action is demoted to lesser importance or omitted altogether.

   Subject + Verb + Object → Object + 被 + Subject + Verb

   e.g.
   a 李安被美国一本杂志选为《五十位最伟大的导演》之一。
   b 我的苹果汁被他喝了。
   c 他的电话被朋友拿走了。

2. 让 and 叫 are alternatives of the word 被, e.g.
   a 包子叫那只狗吃掉了。 The bun has been eaten by that dog.
   b 钱让他们拿走了。 The money was taken by them.

Cambridge IGCSE Mandarin as a Foreign Language

3 A negator (e.g. 没有) or modal verb (e.g. 应该) should be used before the word 被, e.g. 墙上的画儿没有被风吹走。 The painting on the wall has not been blown away by the wind.

词语 VOCABULARY

7	帅	shuài	handsome
8	着	zháo	睡着 to fall asleep
9	老虎	lǎo hǔ	tiger

二、请用下列词组填空。

| 一点儿 | 一会儿 | 空儿 | 紧张 |
| 认为 | 也许 | 印象 | |

《卧虎藏龙》(Crouching Tiger, Hidden Dragon)
影评★★★★
我非常喜欢看武打电影,我____1____这电影拍得真好,演员也很帅。有____2____你一定要去看。

《理智与情感》(Sense and Sensibility)
影评★★
这____3____是一部很好的电影,但我对爱情电影没有兴趣,我只是跟女朋友去看。我看了____4____后,觉得____5____意思都没有,所以我睡着了。

《少年派的奇幻漂流》(Life of Pi)
影评★★★★★
这是一个少年与老虎的故事,我对这电影的____6____非常深刻。我看的时候觉得很____7____,因为老虎有可能把少年吃了。我特别喜欢看这部电影也因为这是 3D 电影。

四 听力（二）
4 Listening (2)

节目主持人马运在电视台介绍国际著名的华人功夫演员李小龙。请听录音,选择正确的答案回答问题。 CD 02, Track 27

大家好!我是节目主持人马运,今天让 1 (A 自我介绍一下 /B 我来介绍一下) 这位国际著名的华人演员吧!1940 年他在美国出生,但在香港长大,所以他说香港才是他的家乡。他在香港的时候 2 (A 运气 /B 天气) 很好,得到很多可以拍电影的 3 (A 机器 /B 机会)。1959 年,18 岁的他到美国留学。留学时,他拍了很多美国的电视剧。

因为非常喜欢香港,所以在 1970 年他回到香港做演员,他在武术电影《唐山大兄》中的演出非常好,成为当时最受 4 (A 欢迎 /B 欢喜) 的演员。后来他被 5 (A 邀请 /B 请去) 拍更多武术的电影。他很喜欢吃中国菜,他最喜欢的中国菜是酱油炒肉。他不懂骑单车和游泳。他不喜欢参加宴会。你知道这位国际著名的华人演员是谁吗? 6 (A 这里是 /B 这位是) 李小龙。

词语 VOCABULARY

1	一点儿	yì diǎnr	a little
2	一会儿	yí huìr	a while
3	空儿	kòngr	free time
4	紧张	jǐn zhāng	tension
5	认为	rèn wéi	to think
6	也许	yě xǔ	perhaps, maybe

词语 VOCABULARY

1	欢迎	huān yíng	welcome
2	邀请	yāo qǐng	to invite
3	这位是……	zhè wèi shì…	this person is…

Unit E 21 International world: Interviewing Chinese celebrities

词语
VOCABULARY

4	我来介绍一下……	wǒ lái jiè shào yī xià…	let me introduce…
5	机会	jī huì	opportunity
6	运气	yùn qì	luck
7	家乡	jiā xiāng	home town
8	宴会	yàn huì	banquet

补充词语
SUPPLEMENTARY VOCABULARY

| 主持人 | zhǔ chí rén | host |

五 阅读（二）
5 Reading (2)

请阅读下面的信，然后回答问题，给每个问题选择唯一正确的答案。

CD 02, Track 28

康康表哥：
　　很久不见了！近况怎么样？你身体好吗？上个月有事儿，所以没有写信问好，对不起。我还是老样子，住在旧房子里。
　　我最近去了蜡像馆参观，这个蜡像馆很有名。我们从写着"欢迎光临"的门进去。里面有很多蜡像，包括演员、作家及运动员等。
　　当爸爸看到李小龙的蜡像时，他非常高兴，像一个小孩子一样，我们都没办法。他请妈妈帮他拍了很多照片后，还是不愿意走，妈妈还问我"怎么办呢？"，爸爸真可爱。妈妈喜欢罗琳的蜡像，因为她出版的《哈利波特》(Harry Potter) 是好书。妈妈想像她一样成功。
　　在参观时我认识了一位华侨，她性格很好，我们谈了很久，现在成了很熟的朋友。希望你会有机会跟她见面和对话。她说自己是性情中人，看到中国人她会很高兴。
　　你去过蜡像馆吗？如果没有，请你来看我吧，我会带你去。蜡像的大小跟明星是一样的。
　　下个月我会去旅行，你可以帮我照顾一下小猫吗？我等着你的回答。请代我向你的父母问好。
　　祝
好！
　　　　　　　　　　　明明表妹
　　　　　　　　　　　12月2日

词语
VOCABULARY

1	很久不见	hěn jiǔ bú jiàn	long time no see
2	近况	jìn kuàng	recent situation
3	你身体好吗？	nǐ shēn tǐ hǎo ma?	are you well?
4	样子	yàng zi	appearance
5	旧	jiù	old
6	有事儿	yǒu shì er	occupied
7	欢迎光临	huān yíng guāng lín	welcome
8	没办法	méi bàn fǎ	no way
9	怎么办呢？	zěn me bàn ne?	what to do?
10	性格	xìng gé	character
11	熟	shú	familiar
12	见面	jiàn miàn	to meet
13	对话	duì huà	dialogue

Cambridge IGCSE Mandarin as a Foreign Language

词语
VOCABULARY

14	照顾	zhào gù	to look after
15	性情	xìng qíng	disposition
16	大小	dà xiǎo	size
17	回答	huí dá	to answer
18	问好	wèn hǎo	to say hello

补充词语
SUPPLEMENTARY VOCABULARY

| 1 | 蜡像 | là xiàng | waxwork |
| 2 | 性情中人 | xìng qíng zhōng rén | sensitive person |

句型
LANGUAGE

Comparisons: 像……一样、跟……一样

This sentence structure is used for stating that two things are alike:

Noun 1 + 像 + Noun 2 + 一样

You can add an adjective after 一样:

Noun 1 + 像 + Noun 2 + 一样 + Adj.

This says that Noun 1 is as 'adjective' as Noun 2.

e.g.
a 妈妈想像她一样成功。
b 我想像爸爸一样高。
c 哥哥想像爷爷一样有名。

---

1 明明去了哪里参观?
 A 科学博物馆 B 图书馆 C 蜡像馆

2 明明跟谁去?
 A 朋友 B 父母 C 同学

3 爸爸非常高兴,是因为他看到了谁的蜡像?
 A 罗琳 B 李小龙 C 成龙

4 妈妈为什么喜欢罗琳的蜡像?
 A 因为她很漂亮 B 因为她是老师
 C 因为她出版了好书

5 明明下个月会去旅行,她希望康康可以帮她照顾什么动物?
 A 金鱼 B 小鸟 C 小猫

六 阅读(三)
6 📖 Reading (3)

请阅读下面的对话,然后用下列词组填空。 CD 02, Track 29

| 转告 | 请客 | 谈话 | 关系 | 接 |
| 名片 | 无所谓 | 迟 | | |

主持人:欢迎你来接受我的采访,今天我们会谈谈名人的健康生活。

演员:谢谢邀请我来_____1_____。

主持人:请你告诉大家你的生活习惯好吗?

演员:我每天早睡早起。晚上不会很_____2_____才吃饭。

主持人:晚饭大概几点吃呢?

演员:如果_____3_____到朋友的_____4_____会在七点吃。如果在家里就_____5_____,但一般在七点以前。

主持人:你喜欢喝什么?

演员:我喜欢喝汤,每天喝一碗。

主持人:在吃饭以前,还是以后喝呢?

演员:吃饭以前或以后都没有_____6_____。

主持人：如果生病，你会看中医还是西医？
演员：我不害怕喝那些中药，所以我会看中医，我觉得我的中医非常好。
主持人：我也想试一试你的中医，可以给我他的_____7_____吗？
演员：没问题，我还可以帮你_____8_____一下。
主持人：太感谢你了！
演员：不客气。

词语 VOCABULARY

1	转告	zhuǎn gào	to tell, to pass on a message
2	请客	qǐng kè	to invite for a meal
3	谈话	tán huà	to talk
4	关系	guān xì	relationship
5	接	jiē	to receive
6	名片	míng piàn	business card
7	无所谓	wú suǒ wèi	easy going; doesn't matter
8	迟	chí	late
9	请	qǐng	please
10	告诉	gào sù	to tell
11	那些	nà xiē	those

文化（二） CULTURE (2)

Huà tuó
华佗

华佗（公元 145 年－公元 208 年）是有名的中医，他会用中药治疗疾病。很多年轻人不喜欢喝中药，因为不好喝，有时候会觉得恶心。

词语 VOCABULARY

恶心　ě xīn　nausea; nauseous

七　说话
7　Speaking

一、角色扮演

老师：你的中国朋友
你：你自己

你在咖啡厅，跟朋友说你刚刚看见一个名人：
1 你刚刚看见谁？
2 他／她是哪国人？
3 他／她今年多大？
4 他／她在中国做什么？
5 你喜欢他／她吗？为什么？

二、小演讲

做一个两分钟的小演讲，说一说"我最喜欢的名人"：
- 你最喜欢的名人是谁？
- 他／她来自哪一个国家？
- 他／她的职业是什么？
- 他／她为什么有名？
- 你欣赏他／她的什么？

词语 VOCABULARY

自　zì　from

Cambridge IGCSE Mandarin as a Foreign Language

好词好句
USEFUL EXPRESSIONS

形容一个人的性格可以用"平易近人"、"和蔼可亲"和"温柔体贴"。

例句：周润发是一个平易近人(píng yì jìn rén)的大明星。(amiable and easy to approach)

形容一个人的外表可以用"一表人才"和"眉清目秀"。

例句：这女孩眉清目秀(méi qīng mù xiù)的，长得很好看。
(pretty with delicate features)

好词好句
USEFUL EXPRESSIONS

形容一个人的说话水平和态度可以分别用"出口成章"和"谦虚有礼"。

例句：
- 志明很喜欢看书，难怪他总是能出口成章(chū kǒu chéngzhāng)。(eloquent and articulate)
- 丽丽说话时非常谦虚有礼(qiān xū yǒu lǐ)，老师常常称赞她。(modest and polite)

形容一个人的打扮可以用"衣着得体"。

例句：
- 我的爸爸每天上班都衣着得体(yī zhuó dé tǐ)。
(dresses decently)

八 写作
8 Writing

一、请写出五个名人的名字。

二、请写一写你最喜欢的名人：

我最喜欢的名人是＿＿＿1＿＿＿，他／她是＿＿＿2＿＿＿（国家）人。他／她今年＿＿＿3＿＿＿岁。他／她的职业是＿＿＿4＿＿＿。我喜欢他／她因为＿＿＿5＿＿＿。我希望有一天我可以跟他／她一样＿＿＿6＿＿＿（形容词 adjective）。

三、明明今天看见了一位名人。请为明明回信给康康，信里讲一讲：

1 你今天看见了哪一位名人
2 你在哪里看见这位名人
3 你跟他／她说了什么
4 你跟他／她做了什么
5 你看到他／她后觉得怎么样

写 150 个字左右。

自我评估
Self-Assessment

- ☐ I can listen to an interview about a celebrity and their home town
- ☐ I can read a dialogue about the lifestyle of a celebrity
- ☐ I can talk about the appearances of celebrities
- ☐ I can write a letter to share an experience of meeting a celebrity
- ☐ Sentence structure: 像……一样，跟……一样
- ☐ Sentence structure: the 被 construction

kē jì yǔ shè jiāo méi tǐ
科技与社交媒体
22 Technology and social media

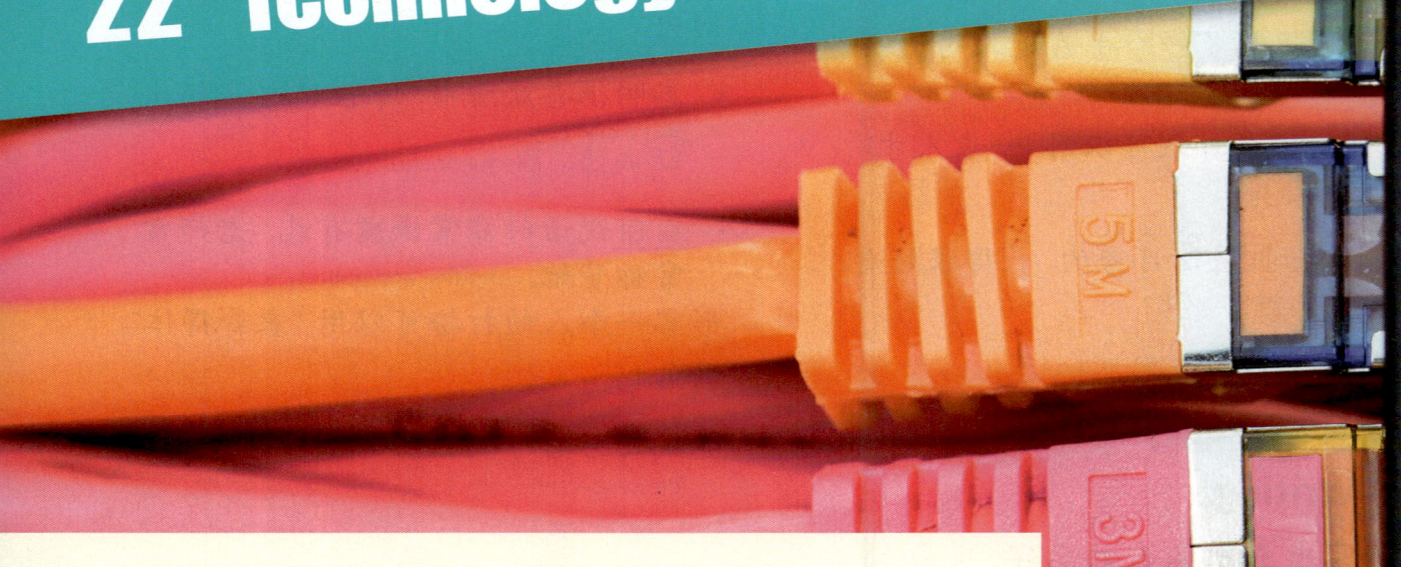

Learning objectives

学习目标

This unit will concentrate on vocabulary about the internet and technology. You will:

本单元你会：

- Listen to a dialogue about going to an internet café

- 聆听有关去网吧的对话

- Read an essay about social media

- 阅读有关社交媒体的文章

- Talk about the advantages and disadvantages of using the internet

- 谈谈上网的好处与坏处

- Write a diary and a letter to express your opinion on using the internet

- 写日记和信去表达使用互联网的意见

In addition, you are going to learn:

你还会学到：

- Modification of nouns using 的

- 名词修饰：的

- Sentence structure:
  尽管……还……

- 句型：尽管……还……

Cambridge IGCSE Mandarin as a Foreign Language

一 温故知新
1 'Before starting' activities

一、你们喜欢用电脑来做什么？

问一下你班上的同学，他们喜欢用电脑来做什么？

1 下载软件
2 听音乐
3 看故事片
4 做作业
5 买东西
6 看电视
7 看书
8 看纪录片
9 跟朋友聊天
10 玩电子游戏
11 看动画片
12 检查电子邮件

词语 VOCABULARY

1	下载	xià zài	to download
2	故事片	gù shì piàn	feature film
3	纪录片	jì lù piàn	documentary
4	电子游戏	diàn zǐ yóu xì	electronic games
5	动画片	dòng huà piàn	cartoon
6	检查	jiǎn chá	to check

延伸活动 AIM HIGHER

你班上的同学还喜欢用电脑来做什么呢？请说一说。

二、对以下有关互联网使用的句子，请选择"是"或"非"。

		是	非
1	现在大多数的手提电脑和电话都可以上网。	☐	☐
2	微信其中的一个特点是摇一摇就可以认识附近的朋友。	☐	☐
3	只有大人才可以用互联网。	☐	☐
4	现在的手机只能通话不能照相。	☐	☐
5	互联网里没有广告。	☐	☐

词语 VOCABULARY

1	手提电脑	shǒu tí diàn nǎo	laptop computer
2	特点	tè diǎn	feature
3	摇	yáo	to shake
4	大人	dà rén	adult
5	讲话	jiǎng huà	to speak
6	照相	zhào xiàng	to take a photo

文化 CULTURE

Internet 的中文是因特网，又可以叫做互联网。现在人们用电脑或电话都可以上网，有些餐厅还提供无线上网 (Wifi) 给客人使用。

词语 VOCABULARY

客人 kè rén guest

Unit E 22 International world: Technology and social media

二 听力（一）
2 🔊 Listening (1)

赵飞和朋友马俊通电话，相约到网吧见面。请听以下录音，选择正确的答案回答问题。 CD 02, Track 30

赵飞：喂！马俊，我约了两名网友到 1(**A** 酒吧 / **B** 网吧) 见面，你也一起来吧！

马俊：你们去网吧做什么呢？

赵飞：我们打算一起上网打游戏，只要到同一个网址的 2(**A** 网站 / **B** 车站) 就可以一起玩。

马俊：网上玩的人多吗？

赵飞：挺多的，一般有几十个 3(**A** 网民 / **B** 市民) 一起玩。

马俊：我现在不知道能不能来，我可不可以晚一点给你回 4(**A** 电话 / **B** 电脑)？

赵飞：没问题！电话留言或发 5(**A** 书信 / **B** 短信) 都可以。

词语 VOCABULARY

1	网友	wǎng yǒu	internet friend
2	网吧	wǎng bā	internet café
3	网址	wǎng zhǐ	web address
4	网站	wǎng zhàn	website
5	网民	wǎng mín	internet users
6	回电话	huí diàn huà	to call back
7	留言	liú yán	to leave a message
8	短信	duǎn xìn	SMS text message

三 阅读（一）
3 📖 Reading (1)

请阅读以下短文，然后回答问题。请选择唯一正确的答案，在方格里打勾。 CD 02, Track 31

社交网站

在香港、澳门和台湾，很多人喜欢使用社交网站脸书(Facebook)，特别是年轻人。只要登入一个网站就可以跟世界各地的朋友和家人联系与沟通。

脸书有很多功能，包括分享照片和短片，也可以跟朋友分享有趣的事。如果你喜欢朋友的照片或分享，可以点"赞"(like)让他知道。有空的时候又可以跟爱人和朋友聊天。使用脸书的好处是很容易就可以跟朋友交流，而且非常方便，只要有网络就行了。如果正确使用脸书，还可以用它来看新闻或学习新的知识。

但是现在很多青少年天天花过多时间在脸书和网络上，这是上网的坏处。有些人还在网上欺凌其他人，这是错误的，是一个严重的问题。所以我们要善用社交网站。

1 香港、澳门和台湾人喜欢使用哪一个社交网站？

A 变脸 ☐   **B** 看书 ☐
C 洗脸 ☐   **D** 脸书 ☐

2 哪些人特别喜欢用脸书？

A 老人 ☐   **B** 老师 ☐
C 年轻人 ☐   **D** 父母 ☐

3 以下哪一个不是脸书的功能？
  A 准备考试 ☐   B 分享照片 ☐
  C 跟朋友聊天 ☐ D 分享短片 ☐
4 如果正确使用脸书，还可以用它来做什么？
  A 购物 ☐   B 学习新的知识 ☐
  C 唱歌 ☐   D 玩游戏 ☐
5 现代的年轻人在使用网络时产生什么问题？
  A 健康有问题 ☐
  B 不出去跟朋友见面 ☐
  C 忘了关电脑 ☐
  D 花过多时间 ☐

脸书 (Facebook) 是现在最受欢迎的社交网站之一。从 2004 年 2 月 4 日开始被使用，到 2015 年用户数字已经超过十亿。主要的创始人是美国人马克扎克伯格 (Mark Zuckerberg)，他是哈佛大学的学生。脸书的网址是：
https://www.facebook.com/

词语 VOCABULARY

1	包括	bāo kuò	to include
2	有空儿	yǒu kòngr	free, have spare time
3	爱人	ài rén	sweetheart
4	正确	zhèng què	correct
5	知识	zhī shi	knowledge
6	现代	xiàn dài	modern
7	问题	wèn tí	problem

补充词语 SUPPLEMENTARY VOCABULARY

1	分享	fēn xiǎng	to share
2	网络	wǎng luò	network
3	产生	chǎn shēng	to produce
4	欺凌	qī líng	to bully
5	错误	cuò wù	wrong; mistake

词语 VOCABULARY

| 开始 | kāi shǐ | to begin |

补充词语 SUPPLEMENTARY VOCABULARY

1	创始人	chuàng shǐ rén	founder
2	用户	yòng hù	user
3	数字	shù zì	number
4	超过	chāo guò	to exceed

四 听力（二）
4 🔊 Listening (2)

小明的爸爸因小明使用网络的问题到学校和陈老师见面。请听录音，然后用下列词组填空。 **CD 02, Track 32**

Unit E 22 International world: Technology and social media

下降　技术　请进　要紧　上网

小明爸爸：请问陈老师在吗？

陈老师：在，____1____。

小明爸爸：陈老师，您好！我是黄小明的爸爸。

陈老师：你好！黄先生，请坐。

小明爸爸：老师，我想跟您谈谈小明____2____的问题。我发现他最近花很多时间来上网，没有时间做作业，所以成绩____3____。我的妻子很担心，她现在病了。

陈老师：一般小明在网上做什么？

小明爸爸：看电影、听音乐、打游戏。现在电脑坏了，我不想找____4____人员来修理。

陈老师：你可以跟小明谈谈这个问题，让他知道什么才是最重要的事。

小明爸爸：谢谢您的建议，我会跟小明谈一谈，让他明白学习才是最____5____的，不应该花太多时间来玩电脑，更不应该让妈妈担心。

词语
VOCABULARY

1	请进	qǐng jìn	please come in
2	请坐	qǐng zuò	please sit down
3	下降	xià jiàng	to decline
4	技术	jì shù	technology
5	修理	xiū lǐ	to repair
6	要紧	yào jǐn	critical

五　阅读（二）
5　Reading (2)

请阅读下面黄小明的博客，然后用中文回答问题。　CD 02, Track 33

黄小明 @huangxiaoming

1　今天老爸到学校来跟老师见面，
2　谁叫我的成绩下降那么多。回家后，
3　尽管爸爸很生气，他没有骂我，还
4　跟我谈了很久。我们谈到上网和安
5　排时间的问题，爸爸说的都是对的。
6　现在的科技日新月异，虽然上网有
7　很多好处，如可以玩电脑游戏、买
8　东西、看电视电影和听音乐，甚至
9　可以跟在外国学习的朋友们聊天。
10　但是我每天花三个小时上网，真的
11　太多了。我不但没有时间做功课，
12　而且也没有时间跟爸爸妈妈说话。
13　周末的时候我也在家里玩电脑游戏，
14　没有跟朋友见面，现在连朋友也没
15　有了，我很后悔。

16　　我决定从明天开始，每当我做作
17　业的时候，会把手机放在一个盒子
18　里，等到做完作业才拿出来。另外，
19　我要把作业做得整整齐齐的交给老
20　师，希望我的成绩会慢慢好起来。
21　我要加油！

#上网#朋友@上海
2016-10-12　20:04

1 和老师见面后爸爸跟小明做什么？
2 小明和爸爸说了什么？
3 人们可以在网上做什么？
4 小明为什么没时间做功课？
5 小明朋友不多的原因是什么？
6 这博客是在哪里写的？

词语
VOCABULARY

整齐　zhěng qí　neat

补充词语
SUPPLEMENTARY VOCABULARY

1 日新月异　rì xīn yuè yì　change rapidly
2 甚至　shèn zhì　even
3 后悔　hòu huǐ　regret

语法
GRAMMAR

Nominalising in noun phrases with 的

Sometimes you can use 的 to really add a kick to your responses, making them stronger, e.g.

a 爸爸说的都是对的。
b 他是写网页的。
c 他以前是卖报的，但是现在他全职写博客。

句型
LANGUAGE

尽管……还……

尽管 means 'although', and is a little stronger than 虽然, perhaps more like 'even though'.

尽管 A + 还 B

e.g.
a 尽管爸爸很生气，他没有骂我，还跟我谈了很久。
b 尽管他唱歌不好听，他还是要唱。

六　说话
6 Speaking

一、角色扮演

老师：你的中国朋友
你：你自己

你们在一家餐厅讨论使用手机的问题。

1 你觉得有需要用手机吗？为什么？
2 你一般上网做什么？
3 你有没有用社交网站？
4 你每天花多长时间上网？
5 不用手机一天可以吗？为什么？

二、小演讲

请准备一篇"上网的利与弊"，做一个两分钟的小演讲。说一说：

1 你上网做什么
2 上网有什么好处
3 上网有什么坏处
4 上网对你有什么影响

补充词语
SUPPLEMENTARY VOCABULARY

利与弊　lì yǔ bì　advantages and disadvantages

七　写作
7　Writing

一、写出五件你在网上做的事。

二、为黄小明写一篇日记，日记里说一说：

1. 最近发生了什么事
2. 知道爸爸跟老师见面后的心情
3. 之后打算做什么

用中文写80-100个字。

三、黄小明知道妈妈因为担心他而病了，心里不开心。现在想写信给表哥，信里讲一讲：

1. 自己的心情
2. 上网的好处与坏处
3. 以后有什么计划
4. 从这件事学到什么

写150个字左右。

自我评估
Self-Assessment

- ☐ I understand vocabulary relating to the internet and technology
- ☐ I can listen to a dialogue about going to an internet café
- ☐ I can read an essay about social media
- ☐ I can talk about the advantages and disadvantages of using the internet
- ☐ I can write a diary or a letter to express my opinion on using the internet
- ☐ Modification of nouns using 的
- ☐ Sentence structure: 尽管……还……

Zhōng guó jié rì

中国节日
23 Chinese festivals

Learning objectives

This unit will concentrate on learning vocabulary about the Chinese New Year and Mid-Autumn Festival. You will:

- Listen to a diary entry about celebrating the Chinese New Year in China

- Read a blog about celebrating the Mid-Autumn Festival with family

- Talk about your favourite Chinese festival

- Write an essay about Chinese festivals and food

In addition, you are going to learn:

- Sentence structure:
  也……也……

- Sentence structure: 因此……

- Sentence structure:
  the 把 construction (2)

学习目标

本单元你会：

- 学习有关春节与中秋节的词语

- 聆听在中国庆祝春节的日记

- 阅读与家人庆祝中秋节的博客

- 谈谈你最喜爱的中国节日

- 写有关中国节日和食物的文章

你还会学到：

- 句型：也……也……

- 句型：因此……

- 句型："把"结构 (2)

Unit E 23 International world: Chinese festivals

一 温故知新
1 'Before starting' activities

一、搭配：请把左边的节日与右边的应节食品连起来。

1	中秋节	A	汤圆 / 元宵
2	春节	B	粽子
3	元宵节	C	月饼
4	端午节	D	年糕

词语
VOCABULARY

1	春节	Chūn jié	Chinese New Year
2	端午节	Duān wǔ jié	Dragon Boat Festival
3	中秋节	Zhōng qiū jié	Mid-Autumn Festival

补充词语
SUPPLEMENTARY VOCABULARY

1	应节食品	yìng jié shí pǐn	festival food
2	元宵节	Yuán xiāo jié	Lantern Festival
3	汤圆 / 元宵	tāng yuán / yuán xiāo	round dumpling
4	粽子	zòng zi	rice dumpling
5	月饼	yuè bǐng	moon cake
6	年糕	nián gāo	new year cake

文化（一）
CULTURE (1)

元宵节，又称为中国情人节或花灯节，是在农历的正月十五。人们会在花灯晚会中看花灯和猜灯谜。元宵（南方叫汤圆）是元宵节的应节食品，一般是甜的。

补充词语
SUPPLEMENTARY VOCABULARY

猜灯谜　cāi dēng mí　to guess riddles

二、你认识中国节日的传统习俗吗？请选择"是"或"非"。

　　　　　　　　　　　　　　　　是 非
1 春节时小孩会给爸爸妈妈红包和送礼物。　　□ □
2 中国人会在除夕晚上一家人吃年夜饭。　　□ □
3 过中秋节时孩子们喜欢玩灯笼。　　□ □
4 中国人在庆祝新年时喜欢去酒吧。　　□ □
5 中国人喜欢在新年时说恭喜发财和新年快乐。　　□ □

词语
VOCABULARY

1	红包	hóng bāo	red packet
2	送礼物	sòng lǐ wù	to send a gift
3	除夕	Chú xì	Chinese New Year's Eve
4	过……	guò…	to celebrate (a festival)
5	庆祝	qìng zhù	to celebrate
6	新年	xīn nián	New Year
7	酒吧	jiǔ bā	bar, pub
8	新年快乐	xīn nián kuài lè	Happy New Year

Cambridge IGCSE Mandarin as a Foreign Language

二 听力（一）
2 🔊 Listening (1)

美美第一次从美国回来中国跟爷爷奶奶过春节。请听以下的日记，然后用下列词组填空。 **CD 02, Track 34**

| 生日快乐　婚礼　食品　圣诞节　儿童 |
| 饺子　重要 |

```
二月五日          晴

    今年是我第一次到中国过春节，              1
中国的春节跟西方的 ___1___ 差不多。            2
想起来上一次到中国是在三年前参                3
加表哥的 ___2___ 。这个春节假期我过           4
得很开心。在除夕晚上我和家人一起              5
吃年夜饭。他们特别为我准备了很多              6
 ___3___ ，例如桌子转盘上有北京最有           7
名的烤鸭。                                  8
    年初一我很早就起来，看到爷爷              9
奶奶时我跟他们说新年快乐，他们给              10
我红包，因为我是 ___4___ 。爷爷和奶          11
奶跟我说了很多中国节日的习俗。例              12
如新年前三天禁止洗头。我觉得知道              13
从前的人的想法是很 ___5___ 的，我慢          14
慢了解到更多中国的习俗。                     15
    明天我要回美国了，奶奶做了很              16
多 ___6___ 给我吃，我把饺子都吃完了。        17
经过这个假期我希望可以再来中国，              18
可能在爷爷生日的时候我会再来中                19
国跟他说 ___7___ 。                        20
```

词语
VOCABULARY

1	圣诞节	Shèng dàn jié	Christmas
2	婚礼	hūn lǐ	wedding
3	食品	shí pǐn	food
4	烤鸭	kǎo yā	roast duck
5	儿童	ér tong	child
6	禁止	jìn zhǐ	to ban
7	从前	cóng qián	in the past
8	了解	liǎo jiě	to understand
9	重要	zhòng yào	important
10	饺子	jiǎo zi	dumpling
11	经过	jīng guò	to pass, go through
12	生日快乐	shēng rì kuài lè	happy birthday

补充词语
SUPPLEMENTARY VOCABULARY

1	年夜饭	nián yè fàn	reunion dinner of a whole family on Chinese New Year's Eve
2	转盘	zhuàn pán	swivel plate
3	年初一	nián chū yī	first day of the year in the lunar calendar

语法
GRAMMAR

结果补语

In Chinese, a result complement is used after a verb to indicate the result. Result complements form verbal compounds and are usually verbs or adjectives, e.g.

Verb	Result complement	Result compound	Explanation
吃	完	吃完	To finish eating. In the text it says 吃完了 which means 'finished eating'.
写	错	写错	To write something incorrectly

Unit E 23 International world: Chinese festivals

To express negation, the result compound is usually associated with 没（有）, e.g. 没吃完, 没写错. To express that 'something will not happen in the future', 不会 can be used, e.g. 不会吃完, 不会写错.

句型
LANGUAGE

The 把 construction (2)

If a modal verb or a negator is used, it should come before 把, e.g.

a 虽然春节奶奶做了很多饺子，但是我没有把它们吃光。

b 春节前几天，我们就应该把垃圾扔掉。

文化（二）
CULTURE (2)

在过春节时有些事情是禁止做和说的，这些不可以做和说的事情人们叫做禁忌。以下是一些例子：

1 如果不小心打碎东西，要说"岁岁（碎碎）平安"。 *suì suì*

2 禁止洗头。

补充词语
SUPPLEMENTARY VOCABULARY

1 禁忌　jìn jì　taboo
2 碎　suì　broken

三 阅读（一）
3 📖 Reading (1)

请阅读下面的博客，然后回答问题。
CD 02, Track 35

陈大明 @Chendaming

　　中国的传统节日有很多：中秋节、重阳节、端午节……其中我最喜欢中秋节，因为中秋节是一家团圆的日子。 [1][2][3]

　　中秋节是每年农历的八月十五，今年的中秋节刚好是爷爷的七十岁生日。晚上，我们一家五口，包括爸爸、奶奶、爷爷、妈妈和我，在饭店吃饭，点了广东菜和四川菜的名菜，因为奶奶喜欢广东的春卷和馒头，但爷爷喜欢四川的麻婆豆腐。爸爸点了海鲜汤，但是我不喜欢喝汤，因此点了可口可乐。我们都吃得很高兴，虽然账单很贵，但是爸爸还是给了服务员很多小费。爸爸真是一个好人！ [4][5][6][7][8][9][10][11][12][13][14]

　　吃完饭后我们到一家茶馆外的花园一边喝茶，一边吃月饼。我最后吃了三个月饼，非常开心。今年我跟家人过了一个难忘的中秋节，希望以后每年的中秋节都过得这样开心。 [15][16][17][18][19]

#中秋节#八月十五#月饼 [20]
2016-09-15 23:09
西安

CAMBRIDGE IGCSE Mandarin as a Foreign Language

词语
VOCABULARY

1	广东菜	Guǎng dōng cài	Cantonese cuisine
2	四川菜	Sì chuān cài	Sichuan cuisine
3	名菜	míng cài	famous dish
4	春卷	chūn juǎn	spring roll
5	馒头	mán tou	steamed bun
6	豆腐	dòu fu	tofu
7	海鲜	hǎi xiān	seafood
8	可口可乐	Kě kǒu kě lè	Coca Cola
9	小费	xiǎo fèi	tip
10	每年	měi nián	every year

补充词语
SUPPLEMENTARY VOCABULARY

1	团圆	tuán yuán	to reunite
2	麻婆豆腐	má pó dòu fu	spicy tofu
3	账单	zhàng dān	bill

1 作者为什么喜欢中秋节?
2 为什么今天对爷爷来说很特别?
3 他们点了什么名菜?
4 为什么作者点了可口可乐?
5 爸爸为什么是一个好人?
6 吃完饭后,他们去了哪里?
7 他们在花园里做什么?

句型
LANGUAGE

因此 is a conjunction meaning 'therefore':

Cause + 因此 + Effect

e.g.
a 我不喜欢喝汤,因此点了可口可乐。
b 我吃了很多蛋糕,因此吃不了巧克力。
c 我每天都复习,因此考到好成绩。

四 听力(二)
4 Listening (2)

一、请把中文词语与英文答案搭配起来。

1	虫 chóng	A	sheep
2	大象 dà xiàng	B	panda
3	动物 dòng wù	C	fish
4	猴子 hóu zi	D	snake
5	老虎 lǎo hǔ	E	mouse
6	老鼠 lǎo shǔ	F	duck
7	牛 niú	G	tiger
8	蛇 shé	H	monkey
9	熊猫 xióng māo	I	cow
10	鸭 yā	J	animal
11	羊 yáng	K	pig
12	鱼 yú	L	elephant
13	猪 zhū	M	insect
14	龙 lóng	N	dragon

Unit E 23 International world: Chinese festivals

二、请听录音，选择"是"或"非"。
CD 02, Track 36

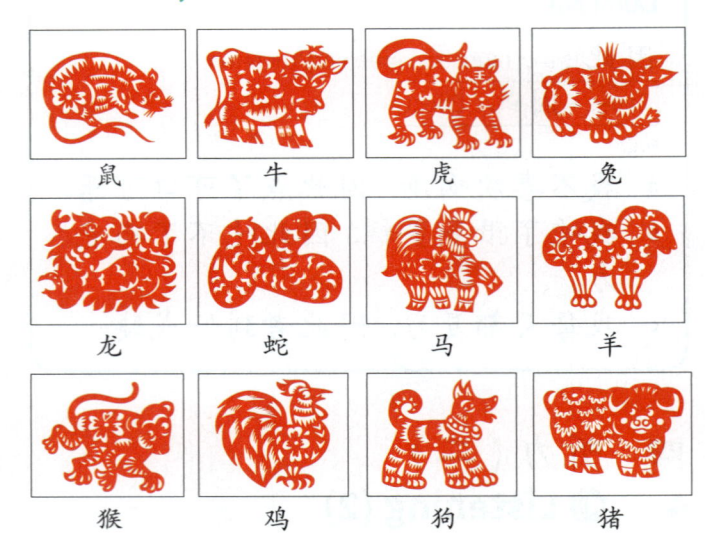

鼠	牛	虎	兔
龙	蛇	马	羊
猴	鸡	狗	猪

	是	非
1 蛇因为天气冷要在家里睡觉。	☐	☐
2 鱼和鸭忘了那天刚好也有游泳比赛。	☐	☐
3 老虎看不见其他动物所以走了。	☐	☐
4 大象和猴子还在家里做作业。	☐	☐
5 熊猫觉得饿，要回家拿香蕉。	☐	☐

词语
VOCABULARY

1 故事　gù shì　story
2 关于　guān yú　related to
3 举行　jǔ xíng　to hold; to organise
4 进行　jìn xíng　to carry out
5 饿　è　hungry

补充词语
SUPPLEMENTARY VOCABULARY

1 生肖　shēng xiào　zodiac
2 保留　bǎo liú　to retain

文化（三）
CULTURE (3)

十二生肖：鼠、牛、虎、兔、龙、蛇、马、羊、猴、鸡、狗、猪。每个人都以出生年的动物作为生肖。

五 听力（三）
5 🔊 Listening (3)

请听以下的对话，然后用下列词组填空。 **CD 02, Track 37**

| 咖啡　饺子　勺　特别　宴会 |

在咖啡馆，你听到：

马天：珊珊，昨晚在＿＿1＿＿里我吃了美味的饺子。中国的饺子真的很好吃。

珊珊：是的，中国人＿＿2＿＿爱吃饺子。

马天：中国人吃饺子时喜欢加醋，但是我比较喜欢在＿＿3＿＿里加酱油。有时候我会加一点点盐。

珊珊：有些中国人还会加点儿姜。

马天：你会做＿＿4＿＿吗？

珊珊：当然了！

马天：太好了！我请你喝＿＿5＿＿吧！

珊珊：谢谢你。

马天：不谢！服务员，请给我账单。

Cambridge IGCSE Mandarin as a Foreign Language

词语
VOCABULARY

1	咖啡馆	kā fēi guǎn	coffee shop
2	醋	cù	vinegar
3	酱油	jiàng yóu	soy sauce
4	盐	yán	salt
5	勺	sháo	spoon
6	请给我……	qǐng gěi wǒ……	please give me…

补充词语
SUPPLEMENTARY VOCABULARY

姜　jiāng　ginger

六　阅读（二）
6 Reading (2)

请阅读下面的短文，然后回答问题。
CD 02, Track 38

"年"的故事

　　中国古代有一种怪兽叫"年"，每到除夕"年"会出来伤害人，为了躲开它，老人小孩上山，大人也上山，动物也上山。

　　这年除夕，从村外来了个老人，大家都很忙，没有人关心这老人。只有一位老婆婆给了他一些食物，老人说："如果你让我留在你的家，我会把'年'赶走。"于是婆婆让他留了下来。晚上，"年"看见很多门上都有红纸。快到门口时，突然有"砰砰啪啪"的声音。"年"最怕红色和声音。这时，老人打开婆婆的家门看见"年"非常害怕地逃走了。第二天是正月初一，人们回来看见婆婆家门上贴着红纸，门外有爆竹。这件事大家很快就知道了。

　　从此以后，家家户户都贴红纸、放爆竹。年初一一大早，还要向亲朋好友问好。慢慢地这个风俗成了中国最重要的传统节日。

词语
VOCABULARY

打开　dǎ kāi　to open

补充词语
SUPPLEMENTARY VOCABULARY

1	古代	gǔ dài	ancient
2	怪兽	guài shòu	monster
3	伤害	shāng hài	to hurt
4	躲开	duǒ kāi	to escape from
5	关心	guan xīn	concern
6	老婆婆	lǎo pó po	old woman
7	赶走	gǎn zǒu	to drive away
8	突然	tū rán	suddenly
9	砰砰啪啪	pēng pēng pā pā	sound made by firecrackers
10	逃走	táo zǒu	to escape
11	贴着	tiē zhe	to post; to paste
12	爆竹	bào zhú	firecracker
13	风俗	fēng sú	custom

1 "年"是什么？
2 "年"在什么时候出现？
3 "年"出来做什么？
4 婆婆给了老人什么东西？
5 "年"最怕什么？

Unit E 23 International world: Chinese festivals

> ## 句型
> **LANGUAGE**
>
> Sentence structure 也……也……
>
> 也 (yě) is an adverb. It is inserted after the subject and before the verb or adjective.
>
> Subject + 也 + Verb/Adj.
>
> e.g.
> a 老人小孩上山，大人也上山，动物也上山。
> b 春节的时侯，她也来，她弟弟也来。
> c 学校运动会那天，爸爸也来了，爷爷也来了。

七 说话
7 Speaking

一、角色扮演

你：你自己
老师：你的中国同学

你在中国同学的家中过春节。同学问你：

1 你是哪国人？
2 你来了中国多久？
3 这是你第几次在中国过春节？
4 你喜欢吃什么春节食品？
5 你喜欢哪一个春节的庆祝活动？

二、小演讲

做一个两分钟的小演讲，说一说"我最喜欢的中国节日"：

- 你最喜欢哪一个中国节日？
- 你为什么喜欢这个节日？
- 你会跟谁庆祝这个节日？
- 你们会如何庆祝这个节日？
- 你们会吃什么应节食品？
- 你们会说什么？

八 写作
8 Writing

一、请写出跟春节有关的五个词语。

二、请介绍一个你曾经庆祝的中国节日：

1 那是什么节日
2 你在哪里庆祝这个节日
3 你跟谁一起庆祝
4 你们如何庆祝
5 你明年想再庆祝这个节日吗？

用中文写 80-100 个字。

三、《中学生杂志》想请你写一篇有关中国节日与食品的文章，文章里说说：

1 中国有哪些节日
2 各个节日有什么应节食品
3 这些食品健康吗
4 你最喜欢哪一种食品？为什么？

写 150 个字左右。

> **好词好句**
> **USEFUL EXPRESSION**
>
> 中秋节时家家户户都挂了灯笼，看起来喜气洋洋 (xǐ qì yáng yáng)。(full of joy)

CAMBRIDGE IGCSE Mandarin as a Foreign Language

自我评估
Self-Assessment

- [ ] I can listen to a diary entry about celebrating the Chinese New Year in China
- [ ] I can read a blog about celebrating the Mid-Autumn Festival with family
- [ ] I can talk about my favourite Chinese festival
- [ ] I can write an essay about Chinese festivals and food
- [ ] Sentence structure: 也……也……
- [ ] Sentence structure: 因此……
- [ ] Sentence structure: the 把 construction (2)

xué Zhōng wén

24 学中文
Learning Chinese as a foreign language

Learning objectives

This unit will concentrate on the phenomenon that more and more people are learning Chinese as a foreign language. You will:

- Read an online entry about the experience of learning Chinese and a magazine article about how popular Chinese currently is

- Listen to some conversations about how to learn Chinese through activities

- Talk about your own experience of learning Chinese in both written and spoken forms

In addition, you are going to learn:

- Potential complements: 得，不

- Topic–comment construction

- Sentence structure: 要是……，就…….

学习目标

本单元你会：

- 阅读讲述"汉语热"的不同短文，如博客、杂志文章等

- 聆听跟学中文有关的对话

- 说一说、写一写你学习中文的经历

你还会学到：

- 补语词：得、不

- 主谓结构

- 句型：要是……，就……

Cambridge IGCSE Mandarin as a Foreign Language

一 温故知新
1 'Before starting' activity

你用过以下的方法学中文吗?
1 听流行音乐☐
2 看电视剧☐
3 看中国电影☐
4 多做听写☐
5 多查词典☐
6 做练习☐
7 参加中文比赛☐
8 到中国旅游☐
9 上网跟中国朋友聊天☐
10 其他☐

词语 VOCABULARY

1 听写 tīng xiě dictation
2 练习 liàn xí exercise; to practise

延伸活动 AIM HIGHER
你班上的同学还有什么好的学习方法？请说一说。

二 阅读（一）
2 Reading (1)

一、黄冰学中文时，写了一张字条，告诉自己怎么学好中文，请看一看： CD 02, Track 39

老师说，学中文时：
1 写字时要按笔顺来写，笔画要正确。
2 遇上不明白的汉字，查词典是一个好方法。
3 汉语声调不容易。写拼音时，要写声调。
4 做听写的时候，一个方格只写一个汉字。

请把 1-4 跟以下图片搭配起来。

A ☐
B hàn yǔ 汉语 ☐
C 学 中 文 ☐
D ☐

词语 VOCABULARY

1 写字 xiě zì to write words
2 笔画 bǐ huà strokes (in writing Chinese characters)
3 笔顺 bǐ shùn stroke order
4 查词典 chá cí diǎn 查 to look up (a word); 词典 dictionary
5 方法 fāng fǎ method
6 拼音 pīn yīn pinyin
7 声调 shēng diào tone
8 方格 fāng gé square/box

二、想一想：你觉得这些方法有用吗？请说一说。

Unit E 24 International world: Learning Chinese as a foreign language

三 听力（一）
3 🔊 Listening (1)

丽丽是马来西亚华侨，她到了北京学中文。她跟好朋友小天一起安排学汉语的活动。请看以下的词语。

词语
VOCABULARY

| 胡同 | hú tòng | alleys in Beijing, also known as 'Hutong' |

听对话，在四个正确的方格内打勾，表明同学们的学汉语活动。 **CD 02, Track 40**

A 书法 ☐
B 画画 ☐
C 打羽毛球 ☐
D 参观名胜古迹 ☐
E 到餐厅吃饭 ☐
F 打功夫 ☐
G 做饺子 ☐
H 打羽毛球 ☐
I 跟中国朋友聊天 ☐

学中国书法，学中文笔顺

学做饺子

打功夫

四 阅读（二）
4 📖 Reading (2)

一、请阅读短文，然后用中文回答问题。 **CD 02, Track 41**

张天明 Timothy Jack

刚到台湾的时候，我听不懂国语，1
连"你好"也不会说。我是一个留学 2
生，所以一定要努力学中文，用中文 3
跟台湾人交流。我一开始使用拼音学 4
句子。我的音乐很好，唱歌唱得很好 5
听，不过在学外语方面就很笨，中文 6
总是学不好。 7
　　有一天，我在宿舍吃东西，别人跟 8
我用中文聊天。我说我中文不好，他 9
们马上就唱起一首叫《对不起，我的 10
中文不好》的歌来。我想，虽然我学 11
中文不聪明，但是唱歌是我的兴趣， 12
我找到了我的方法。慢慢地我喜欢唱 13
中文歌了，又跟朋友们一起去看戏， 14
学到了很多很有用的词语。后来，我 15
的朋友跟我参加了一个在台北举行的 16
歌唱比赛，竟然赢了。所以我觉得， 17
要学好中文，真的离不开生活与兴趣。 18

Cambridge IGCSE Mandarin as a Foreign Language

五年前 23/02/2011 上午8:00

第一次来到台湾！（我朋友帮我翻译的，我不会讲国语）

👍😂 10

👍点赞 10 💬留言 10

1 刚到台湾的时候，张天明不会说什么语言？
2 他希望到了台湾之后，跟台湾人做什么？
3 张天明一开始先学汉字，还是拼音？
4 张天明在什么地方很聪明？
5 在宿舍里，别人听见他说自己中文不好，唱起什么歌来？
6 后来张天明是用什么方法学中文的？
7 他跟谁参加了一个歌唱比赛？
8 怎么样才可以学好中文？

词语
VOCABULARY

1	国语	guó yǔ	the official name of Mandarin in Taiwan, it literally means 'the national language'
2	努力	nǔ lì	hardworking
3	交流	jiāo liú	to exchange
4	笨	bèn	stupid
5	宿舍	sù shè	dormitory
6	别人	bié rén	other people
7	聪明	cōng míng	smart, clever
8	兴趣	xìng qù	interest
9	看戏	kàn xì	to go to the theatre
10	词语	cí yǔ	words, phrases
11	赢	yíng	to win
12	离开	lí kāi	to leave

二、请用下列词组填空

| 笨 留学生 赢 句子 有一天 别人 聪明 离开 |

1 学中文＿＿＿了生活，学生就没兴趣了。
2 张天明觉得自己学中文不＿＿＿，因为总是学不会。
3 ＿＿＿，别人在张天明的宿舍内唱歌。
4 学了中文的张天明，在一个比赛中＿＿＿了。
5 张天明是美国人，他到了台湾做＿＿＿。

语法
GRAMMAR

Potential complements (补语) 得 or 不

A potential complement indicates the possibility of achieving an expected result. It describes someone's ability to achieve something in an affirmative form, or their inability to manage something in a negative form. There is no similar structure in English; the closest meaning is 'can/cannot'.

Verb + 得 / 不 + Complement (+ Object)

e.g.

	Verb	得/不	Complement	Object
中文总是	学	不	好。	

I always cannot learn Chinese well.

他	听	得	懂	我的话。

He can understand my words.

他	看	不	见	太阳。

He cannot see the sun.

练习：Rearrange the order of the words to make sentences:

1 盘 / 他们 / 完 / 吃 / 一 / 不 / 水饺 / 这 /。
2 老师 / 看 / 小雷 / 见 / 那个 / 不 /。

227

Unit E 24 International world: Learning Chinese as a foreign language

句型
LANGUAGE

……离不开…… cannot ... without ...

In the text of Reading (2), 要学好中文，真的离不开生活与兴趣 means 'one cannot improve their Chinese without using the language in real life and interesting contexts'. The pattern is:

Subject + 离不开 + Object 1 (+ 与 Object 2)

e.g.

a 意大利人喜欢喝咖啡，他们的生活离不开它。 Italians love coffee; they cannot live without it.

b 中国人的饮食离不开米饭和茶。 Chinese culinary culture cannot be without rice and tea.

五 听力（二）
5 🔊 Listening (2)

请听对印度在华留学生白心然 (Simran Balani) 的采访，回答问题。 CD 02, Track 42

1 记者在写一篇什么样的文章？
2 白心然从什么时候开始学中文？
3 白心然在科学学院学什么？
4 她在武汉多长时间了？
5 哪一个国家的学费更便宜？
6 写出两个白心然觉得可以学中文的方法。

词语
VOCABULARY

1	幼儿园	yòu ér yuán	nursery school, kindergarten
2	学院	xué yuàn	college, faculty
3	专业	zhuān yè	specialist field of study; 专 specific

六 阅读（三）
6 📖 Reading (3)

请阅读下面的文章，然后回答问题。
CD 02, Track 43

汉语热

现在，世界上学习汉语的人越来越多。在韩国，学习汉语的人已经比学英文的人多。很多人以为"韩语"就是"汉语"，因为他们的声调不对。发音不对，意思就不一样了。现在很多韩国学生都来华做留学生。

日本学生学中文特别容易有收获。日语汉字和中文汉字很像，一些字的笔画、笔顺差不多是一样的，所以他们在写字、生词方面比较好。他们最想提高的，是口语能力。我的日本学生山田一龙告诉我，他觉得自己的写作、语法都好，不过说话有口音，普通话讲不好。

法国学习中文的人比英国的多，欧洲很多国家的汉语学生如果要参加"汉语水平考试"（HSK），都必须来法国。在英国，不少中学已经有他们的中文课程、课本。里面教的除了拼音、句子之外，还有听力活动等等。刘英在德国教中文，她说："对学生来说，听写和查词典都很重要，而且教学中要是只做练习、看答案，中文是学不好的。"她也觉得学生应该多借书还书，提高水平。

1 在韩国，学习哪一种的语言更多？
2 为什么日本学生在写汉字方面比较好？
3 山田一龙觉得自己中文有什么问题？
4 在欧洲，有些学生要去法国做什么？
5 刘英觉得什么方法学中文很重要？

Cambridge IGCSE Mandarin as a Foreign Language

词语 VOCABULARY

1	收获	shōu huò	results, gains; literally means 'harvest'
2	生词	shēng cí	vocabulary
3	口语	kǒu yǔ	speaking skills
4	写作	xiě zuò	writing
5	语法	yǔ fǎ	grammar
6	口音	kǒu yīn	accent
7	普通话	Pǔ tōng huà	Putonghua, Mandarin
8	课本	kè běn	textbook
9	听力	tīng lì	listening
10	而且	ér qiě	and what is more
11	教学	jiào xué	teaching
12	答案	dá àn	answer
13	借	jiè	to borrow
14	还	huán	to return
15	要是	yào shì	if

句型 LANGUAGE

要是……，就……

This is a similar sentence structure to 如果……，就…….

要是 + Statement + 就 + Result

e.g.

a 要是只做练习、看答案，中文是学不好的。 If you only do exercises and look at the answers, you can never learn Chinese well.

b 要是你不上学，老师就会给你爸爸妈妈打电话。 If you do not come to school, your teacher will give your parents a call.

c 要是黄冰不来，我们就走吧。 If Huang Bing is not coming, then we will just go.

七 说话（一）
7 Speaking (1)

角色扮演

你：你自己

老师：一个中国朋友

你跟一个中国朋友谈学中文。

You are talking to a Chinese friend about learning Chinese.

你汉语学了几年了？

_____ 1

你在哪儿学习中文？

_____ 2

学习汉语对你有什么好处？

_____ 3

你想去中国哪个地方留学？

_____ 4

除了汉语以外，你最喜欢哪门课？

_____ 5

Unit E 24 International world: Learning Chinese as a foreign language

八 阅读（四）
8 Reading (4)

请阅读下面的文章，然后选择"是"或"非"。 CD 02, Track 44

汉语考试难在哪儿？

有很多学中文的外国人正在为参加汉语水平考试做准备。听力、语法，留学生都觉得很难。

中文学院的教师说，学生觉得听力考试很难。学生在考试碰见没见过的生词时，便会紧张，所以觉得考试很难。另外一个难点是中文的声调。同一个音加上不同的声调会变成不同的字，音调不同，意思就不一样。要提高听力能力，除了多复习以外，还要多听多练，多听广播、演讲、电视等。

汉语的语法也跟英语不一样，比如"很高兴服务为您"是用了英语的语法，所以汉语老师刘冰要求学生学好汉语语法。

改编自谢丹《汉语考试难在哪儿？》

		是	非
1	很多中国人在准备外国的考试。	☐	☐
2	听力比语法难。	☐	☐
3	汉语的声调对很多学生来说很难。	☐	☐
4	多听广播可以学中文。	☐	☐
5	"很高兴服务为您"在中文中是不对的。	☐	☐

词语 VOCABULARY

1	碰见	pèng jiàn	to meet unexpectedly
2	另外一个	lìng wài yí gè	another
3	复习	fù xí	revision
4	要求	yāo qiú	demand, expectation (from a teacher/boss); to require, to demand

补充词语 SUPPLEMENTARY VOCABULARY

难点　nán diǎn　difficulty

语法 GRAMMAR

Topic–comment structure

In Chinese, to emphasise a topic, you can put the topic at the beginning of the sentence, followed by a comment on the topic, e.g.

a 听力、语法，留学生都觉得很难。
b 新加坡的气候，我听说每天都很热。
c 这个手机，功能很多。

九 阅读（五）
9 Reading (5)

以下是一个中学五年级学生海天的演讲。请阅读以下短文，选择唯一正确的答案，在方格里打勾。 CD 02, Track 45

老师您好。今天我要说一说"学普通话的经验"。我在中学二年级的时候开始学汉语，我的老师<u>李</u>老师是<u>韩国</u>人，她以前在<u>中国</u>住过三年多，她很喜欢<u>中国</u>文化。

我们一开始学的是"你好"、"早"这些简单的词，后来我们学了怎么在<u>中国</u>餐馆点菜、怎么问路。说话时声调很重要，口语有点儿难。不过我觉得学中文很有用，最有用的是"行"这个字，我在<u>中国</u>城时常常听见<u>中国</u>人说这个字。

学中文最难的不是语法，而是写字。汉字有笔画、笔顺的要求。中文里很多字看起来都很像。我将来想到<u>中国</u>学中文，因为我可以在中国学习书法和参观名胜古迹。

词语 VOCABULARY

1	词	cí	word, phrase
2	行	xíng	okay

补充词语 SUPPLEMENTARY VOCABULARY

不是……，而是…… bú shì... ér shì... not... but... (e.g. 他不是她的哥哥，而是父亲。)

1 <u>海天</u>学了中文几年了？
　A 两年☐　B 三年☐　C 四年☐

2 <u>海天</u>的老师在哪里住过？
　A <u>马来西亚</u>☐　B <u>中国</u>☐　C 三年☐

3 <u>海天</u>在中文课上学过什么？
　A 在饭店点菜☐　B 声调☐　C 方向☐

4 <u>海天</u>觉得学中文最难的是
　A 语法☐　B 声调☐　C 汉字☐

十 说话（二）
10 Speaking (2)

一、请再读阅读（五）的文章，然后扮演<u>海天</u>，口头回答以下问题：

1 你什么时候开始学汉语？
2 你的中文老师是怎么样的？
3 你在中文课学了什么？
4 学中文最难的什么？
5 你打算以后去<u>中国</u>学中文吗？为什么？

二、请写一篇演讲稿，然后做小演讲。

　　老师您好。今天我要说一说"学普通话的经验"。我在_____的时候开始学汉语，我的老师_____老师是_____国人，_____，他/她很喜欢/不喜欢<u>中国</u>文化。

　　我们一开始学的是_____，后来我们学了_____，说话时_____，不过我觉得学中文_____。

　　学中文最难的不是____，而是____。_____。我将来想/不想到<u>中国</u>学中文，因为_____。

十一 写作
11 Writing

学汉语真的很难吗？《中学生杂志》要了解一下学生的看法。请给这家杂志写一篇文章，说说：

1 你什么时候开始学汉语？
2 你的中文老师是怎么样的？
3 你在中文课学了什么？
4 学中文最难的什么？
5 你打算以后去<u>中国</u>学中文吗？为什么？

Unit E　24　International world: Learning Chinese as a foreign language

> **小贴士**
> TOP TIP
>
> 这篇文章基本上跟"说话（二）"是一样的，不过这是一篇杂志文章，所以要加上一个标题 biāo tí (title)，比如"学汉语的经历"。

十二 说话（三）
12 Speaking (3)

口头回答以下问题：

1 你觉得学中文最难的是什么？
2 怎么样学中文最有意思？
3 你将来想去中国学中文吗？为什么？
4 你从什么时候开始学中文？

好词好句
USEFUL EXPRESSIONS

- 学中文最难的不是语法，而是写字。汉字有笔画、笔顺的要求。中文里很多文字看起来都很像。
- 我觉得唱歌学中文很有用。我最喜欢听中国的流行音乐，我听歌曲的时候可以学到新的词语。
- 我将来想到北京学中文，因为北京有很多名胜古迹，比如故宫、颐和园等等。
- 我从中学一年级开始学中文，老师是一个英国人，他的中文说得很好。

文化
CULTURE

学中文？不难！

1 汉语桥 (Chinese Bridge)
汉语桥是由孔子学院举办的中文比赛，世界大学生、世界中学生和在华留学生都可以参加。"汉语桥"已经是很多国家大学生学习汉语、了解中国的一个很好的方法。比赛有汉语的语言能力比赛、文化知识比赛等等。赢出的学生都是学中文成功的例子。

2 汉语水平考试
汉语水平考试 (HSK) 的测试对象是外国人、华侨和中国少数民族考生，是一个国际汉语能力考试，一共分六级，考试有听、说、读、写四个部分。
www.hanban.edu.cn

自我评估
Self-Assessment

☐ I can read online entries and magazine articles about people's experiences learning Chinese
☐ I can listen to conversations about how to learn Chinese through activities
☐ I can suggest some methods to learn Chinese in a more interesting and fun way
☐ I can write about my own experience of learning Chinese
☐ Potential complements 得 and 不
☐ Topic-comment construction in Chinese
☐ Sentence structure 要是……，就……

25 救救地球
Saving the planet

Learning objectives

This unit will concentrate on learning vocabulary about protecting our environment. You will:

- Listen to a conversation about recycling
- Talk about how we can protect the environment
- Read about different ways to avoid wasting food
- Write a speech to your school to explain the importance of environmental protection

In addition, you are going to learn:

- Sentence structure:
  不是……就是……

- Sentence structures:
  除非……才……，只有……才……，只要……就……

- Sentence structure:
  ……或者……

学习目标

本单元你会：

- 聆听有关回收的会话
- 谈谈你可以如何保护环境
- 阅读节约食物的方法
- 写一篇演讲稿向同学解释环保的重要性

你还会学到：

- 句型：不是……就是……
- 句型：除非……才……、只有……才……、只要……就……
- 句型：……或者……

Unit E 25 International world: Saving the planet

一 温故知新
1 'Before starting' activities

一、请写出三种可回收的东西。

补充词语
SUPPLEMENTARY VOCABULARY

回收　huí shōu　to recycle

延伸活动
AIM HIGHER
你还能说出多少种可回收的东西？

二、请先读以下的对话。

Q1: 你住在哪一个城市？

A1: 我住在香港。

Q2: 香港有环境污染吗？

A2: 有，香港的光污染很严重的，原因是有很多灯。你住在哪个城市呢？

Q3: 我住在北京，北京的空气污染很严重，我们要想办法解决。你去过北京吗？

A3: 我从来没去过。

词语
VOCABULARY

1　原因　yuán yīn　reason
2　解决　jiě jué　to solve
3　从来　cóng lái　always; all the time

补充词语
SUPPLEMENTARY VOCABULARY

污染　wū rǎn　pollution

请跟同学两人一组，练习以下对话。

Q1: 你住在哪一个城市？

A1: 我住在_____。

Q2: _____有环境污染吗？

A2: _____。你住在哪个城市呢？

Q3: 我住在_____。你去过_____吗？

A3: _____

二 听力（一）
2 🔊 Listening (1)

张明在街上跟朋友黄芬谈污染的问题。请听录音，选择正确的答案。在方格内打勾（✓）。　CD 02, Track 46

1 黄芬刚刚去了哪儿？

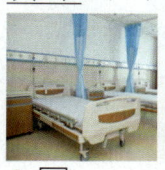

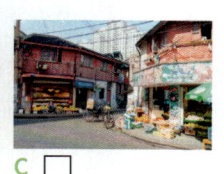

A ☐　　B ☐　　C ☐

2 为什么会有空气污染？

A ☐　　B ☐　　C ☐

3 张明想去哪里？

A ☐　　B ☐　　C ☐

4 张明要买什么？

A ☐　　B ☐　　C ☐

5 买东西后张明和黄芬一起去吃什么？

A ☐　　B ☐　　C ☐

词语 VOCABULARY

1 由于　yóu yú　because of, due to, since
2 意见　yì jiàn　opinion

三 听力（二）
3 🔊 Listening (2)

你正在跟家人讨论去哪里旅行。请听下面录音，选择正确的答案填入适当的空格内。　CD 02, Track 47

| A 夏城 | B 冬城 | C 秋城 | D 春城 |

地点	原因
1	空气污染
2	水污染
3	光污染
4	没有污染

词语 VOCABULARY

1 讨厌　tǎo yàn　to dislike
2 脏　zāng　dirty
3 植物　zhí wù　plant

补充词语 SUPPLEMENTARY VOCABULARY

风光如画　fēng guāng rú huà　picturesque landscape

Unit E　25　International world: Saving the planet

四 阅读（一）
4 Reading (1)

请阅读下面的采访，然后用中文回答问题。 CD 02, Track 48

访问环境保护官员林先生

主持人：大家好，今天很欢迎负责环境保护的官员林先生来接受我们的采访。林先生，香港的空气污染情况越来越严重，不是因为有很多森林被破坏，就是因为有很多汽车。请问环保局在这方面用什么方法来改善环境？

林先生：谢谢你采访我。第一，前年开始政府要求汽车司机把车子停下来后，要在三分钟内完全把它关上，这样有助改善空气污染。

主持人：此外，还有别的方法吗？

林先生：另外，政府会教育市民少用纸张，因为纸张是用树木来做的。最后，在香港买东西时如果你想要一个袋子，包括纸袋或塑料袋，你要付五毛钱，目的是为了改善环境。

主持人：只要每一位市民都帮助保护环境，污染情况就可以很顺利地改善。最后，再次谢谢林先生。

词语 VOCABULARY

1	负责	fù zé	responsible
2	官员	guān yuán	official
3	方面	fāng miàn	aspect
4	破坏	pò huài	to destroy
5	前年	qián nián	the year before last year
6	关上	guān shàng	to turn off/switch off
7	目的	mù dì	objective, goal
8	情况	qíng kuàng	situation
9	救	jiù	to save
10	顺利	shùn lì	smoothly

补充词语 SUPPLEMENTARY VOCABULARY

1	改善	gǎi shàn	to improve
2	此外	cǐ wài	in addition, besides
3	关掉	guān diào	to switch off

1 节目主持人邀请了谁来做访问？
2 香港有什么污染问题？
3 环保局用哪两个方法去改善环境？
4 车辆完全关掉有什么作用？
5 在买东西时如果想要袋子，要付多少钱？
6 怎样可以顺利地改善污染的情况？

句型
LANGUAGE

1 不是……就是…… if it's not ..., then it's ...

To describe a situation as being one of only two possibilities, you can use the alternative relation sentence structure 不是……就是……. This is like saying 'if it's not A, then it's B' in English. A and B can be verbs, adjectives or nouns.

不是 A (verb, adjective or noun) + 就是 B (verb, adjective or noun)

e.g.
a 不是因为有很多森林被破坏，就是因为有很多汽车。
b 不是口渴，就是肚子饿。
c 不是小明做的，就是大明做的。

2 只要……就…… as long as/only if
(or 只有……才……, 除非……才……)

只要……就…… is a conditional relation sentence structure. Use this structure to express that as long as something happens, then something else will happen. In logic, this is referred to as a sufficient condition, meaning that it may not be the only way to bring about these specific consequences, but it is one way.

只要 + Condition + 就 + Result

e.g.
a 只要每一位市民都愿意负责，香港的污染情况就可以大大改善。
b 只要你用功学，就可以考到好成绩。
c 只要你多练习，就可以成功。
d 只要下雨，他就会不开心。

文化
CULTURE

北京的环保措施之一

中国的首都北京人多车多，在二零零八年奥运会前为了让空气清新，北京市实行了汽车单双号限行计划，安排不同的车号在不同的日子上路。目的是让街上的车辆越来越少，改善空气污染。

五 听力（三）
5 Listening (3)

彤彤刚搬到一个新社区，她正跟邻居陈太太谈社区内回收的情况。请看图片。

请听下面的对话，在五个正确的方格内打勾（✓），指出新社区的回收箱可以回收哪些物品。 CD 02, Track 49

Unit E 25 International world: Saving the planet

浪费粮食

　　有些国家因为食物不够，很多人饿死，有部分是小孩，使人十分难过，因此越来越多人学会不浪费食物。有些超市会把卖不去的食物送给慈善机构，避免浪费。有餐厅会鼓励客人把吃不完的食物带回家，他们还会给客人一些进口的可循环再用的饭盒。

　　有些餐厅的食物会有不同的分量，客人可以选择大中小的分量。有些喜欢跟朋友分享食物的人，可以点一个餐两个人分享，或者点两个餐三个人分享。

　　在我们学校，餐厅的米饭吃完后是可以再取的，所以工作人员每次只会给半碗饭，如果不够可以再去拿，这样浪费米饭就不会发生。

　　有些客人在餐厅吃饭总是想点很多菜，但又怕到最后吃不完，心里很矛盾，觉得很可惜。有的餐厅想到一个好办法，就是吃不完的食物要额外付钱。

词语
VOCABULARY

1 变化　　biàn huà　　change
2 志愿者　zhì yuàn zhě　volunteers
3 说明　　shuō míng　　to interpret; to explain
4 靠近　　kào jìn　　close

补充词语
SUPPLEMENTARY VOCABULARY

可信　kě xìn　trustworthy

六　阅读（二）
6 Reading (2)

请阅读下面的短文，然后回答问题。

词语
VOCABULARY

1 死　　sǐ　　to die
2 部分　bù fèn　part
3 难过　nán guò　sad
4 进口　jìn kǒu　to import
5 或者　huò zhě　or
6 人员　rén yuán　staff
7 发生　fā shēng　to happen

Cambridge IGCSE Mandarin as a Foreign Language

词语
VOCABULARY

| 8 | 矛盾 | máo dùn | contradiction, conflict |
| 9 | 可惜 | kě xī | regrettable |

补充词语
SUPPLEMENTARY VOCABULARY

1	慈善机构	cí shàn jī gòu	charity
2	避免	bì miǎn	to avoid
3	鼓励	gǔ lì	to encourage
4	分量	fèn liàng	component, portion
5	分享	fēn xiǎng	to share
6	额外	é wài	extra

句型
LANGUAGE

…… 或者 …… (… or …)

或者 is used to connect words when offering/considering options. The options can be verbs, adjectives or nouns. 或者 indicates that 'it must be one or the other'. It is usually used in statements.

Option 1 + 或者 + Option 2

e.g.

a 可以选择点一个餐两个人分享，或者点两个餐三个人分享。

b 你可以选择去<u>美国</u>或者<u>英国</u>学习。

1 为什么有些国家因为粮食不足会让人难过？
2 越来越多的人学会了什么？
3 有些餐厅会鼓励客人做什么？
4 他们甚至会给客人提供什么饭盒？
5 客人可以选择哪三种分量？
6 喜欢跟朋友分享食物的人可以怎样做？
7 在学校的餐厅吃饭，如果米饭不够可以怎样做？
8 为什么在餐厅吃饭有时候会让人心里很矛盾？
9 有的餐厅想到什么好办法？

七 说话
7 Speaking

一、角色扮演

老师：你的<u>中国</u>朋友
你：你自己

你们在<u>上海</u>的一家餐厅吃饭。
1 你喜欢吃什么菜？
2 吃不完的食物你会怎样做？
3 你的城市有回收箱吗？
4 你的城市会回收什么东西？
5 你是怎样支持环保的？

二、小演讲

请准备一篇"保护环境，人人有责"的文章，做一个两分钟的小演讲。说一说：

1 你住在哪里？
2 那里的环境怎么样？有什么污染问题？
3 市民可以怎样保护环境？
4 你会怎样支持环保？
5 你为什么要支持环保？

Unit E 25 International world: Saving the planet

好词好句
USEFUL EXPRESSIONS

- 国庆节那天，天安门广场上人山人海。(many people)
  _{rén shān rén hǎi}
- 地铁线路四通八达。(extend in all directions)
  _{sì tōng bā dá}

八　写作
8　Writing

一、写出五个可回收物品的名字。

二、请写一篇环保指引 (guidelines) 告诉同学们在学校里可以怎样支持环保。

用中文写 80-100 个字。

三、请写一篇演讲稿 (speech)，跟同学们谈谈保护环境的重要性：

1. 我们的环境正在面对什么问题？
2. 学校可以做什么？
3. 学生可以做什么？
4. 为什么要保护环境？
5. 不保护环境会有什么后果？

写 150 个字左右。

小贴士
TOP TIP

演讲稿格式 (format)

各位老师、各位同学：

　　今天我想跟大家谈谈……………
………………………………………。
………………………………………
………………………………………
　　　　谢谢大家！

自我评估
Self-Assessment

☐ I can listen to a conversation about recycling
☐ I can talk about how we can protect the environment
☐ I can read about different ways to avoid wasting food
☐ I can write a speech to explain to my school the importance of environmental protection
☐ Sentence structure 不是……就是……
☐ Sentence structure 只要……就……
　(or 只有……才……，除非……才……)
☐ Sentence structure ……或者……

考试练习题
Exam-style question

写作
Writing

一、请介绍一个你认识的中国科技名人：

- 他是谁？
- 他为什么是名人？
- 他在科技方面做了什么？
- 他在环保方面做了什么？

用中文写 80-100 个字。

二、《中学生杂志》想请你写一篇介绍中国的文章，文章里说说：

- 在中国的生活
- 中国的节日
- 学习汉语
- 中国的环保措施

写 150 个字左右。

Cambridge IGCSE Mandarin as a Foreign Language